Network Security

FOR

DUMMIES®

Network Security

FOR

DUMMIES®

by Chey Cobb, CISSP

Wiley Publishing, Inc.

Network Security For Dummies®

Published by
Wiley Publishing, Inc.
909 Third Avenue
New York, NY 10022
www.wiley.com

Copyright © 2003 by Wiley Publishing, Inc., Indianapolis, Indiana

Published by Wiley Publishing, Inc., Indianapolis, Indiana

Published simultaneously in Canada

For general information on our other products and services or to obtain technical support, please contact our Customer Care Department within the U.S. at 800-762-2974, outside the U.S. at 317-572-3993, or fax 317-572-4002.

Wiley also publishes its books in a variety of electronic formats. Some content that appears in print may not be available in electronic books.

Library of Congress Control Number: 2002110283

ISBN: 0-7645-1679-5

Manufactured in the United States of America

10 9 8 7 6 5 4 3 2 1

1O/SS/RQ/QS/IN

ⓌWiley Publishing, Inc. is a trademark of Wiley Publishing, Inc.

About the Author

Chey Cobb began her career in information security while at the National Computer Security Association (now known as TruSecure/ICSA Labs). During her tenure as the NCSA award-winning Webmaster, she discovered that Web servers often created security holes in networks and became an outspoken advocate of systems security.

Later, while developing secure networks for the Air Force in Florida, her work captured the attention of the U.S. intelligence agencies. Chey moved to Virginia and began working for the National Reconnaissance Office (NRO) as the Senior Technical Security Advisor on highly classified projects. Ultimately, she went on to manage the security program at an overseas site.

Chey is now semi-retired and has moved back to her native Florida. She writes books and articles on computer security and is a frequent speaker at security conferences. Her e-mail address is chey@patriot.net.

Dedication

Dedicated to Claire Deserable Ewertz, who would have been so proud.

Author's Acknowledgments

Many thanks to Melody, Andrea, Kevin, and all the other people who work behind the scenes and never get a pat on the back. Thanks for all your hard work to make me look so good in print! I hope we can all work together again soon.

Thanks to David Fugate, my agent, for helping me to decide to do this book. I look forward to a long relationship!

Last, but not least, thanks to my husband, Stephen, and our daughter, Erin who make it all worthwhile — even though I can be a nasty ogre when I'm writing!

Publisher's Acknowledgments

We're proud of this book; please send us your comments through our online registration form located at www.dummies.com/register/.

Some of the people who helped bring this book to market include the following:

Acquisitions, Editorial, and Media Development

Project Editor: Andrea C. Boucher

Acquisitions Editor: Melody Layne

Technical Editor: Kevin Beaver, CISSP

Editorial Manager: Carol Sheehan

Permissions Editor: Carmen Krikorian

Media Development Manager: Laura VanWinkle

Media Development Supervisor: Richard Graves

Editorial Assistant: Amanda Foxworth

Cartoons: Rich Tennant, www.the5thwave.com

Production

Project Coordinator: Nancee Reeves

Layout and Graphics: Amanda Carter, LeAndra Johnson, Jackie Nicholas, Jeremey Unger

Proofreader: TECHBOOKS Production Services

Indexer: TECHBOOKS Production Services

Publishing and Editorial for Technology Dummies

Richard Swadley, Vice President and Executive Group Publisher

Andy Cummings, Vice President and Publisher

Mary C. Corder, Editorial Director

Publishing for Consumer Dummies

Diane Graves Steele, Vice President and Publisher

Joyce Pepple, Acquisitions Director

Composition Services

Gerry Fahey, Vice President of Production Services

Debbie Stailey, Director of Composition Services

Contents at a Glance

Table of Contents

Introduction

· ·

Welcome to *Network Security For Dummies* where the often confusing and complex world of security is finally explained in a way that makes sense. This book has been written to help you, the Average Person, to not only understand basic security measures and mechanisms, but to actually incorporate them into your network. It doesn't matter if your system consists of just one computer at home or gazillions of servers and workstations located in a dozen offices — the basics are still the same and apply the world over.

You've probably picked up this book because you've heard the horror stories about hacks and viruses and you don't know what to do. On the other hand, maybe you just need to check that the security measures you've already implemented are enough. Whatever the case, this book is for you!

Yes, network security can be expensive and difficult, but it doesn't have to be. The topics covered in this book are, for the most part, fairly easy to incorporate and you don't have to rob a bank to be able to afford them. Many of the measures consist of simple changes you can make to your computers. There are no complex formulas or programs to learn and, when you've finished this book, you'll wonder why everyone hasn't secured their systems.

We've all had to plow through technical manuals that are about as much fun as changing tires in the rain. I hope you'll find the writing simple without being simplistic and I'll try to give you a few grins with stories from the trenches.

About This Book

This book is meant to be more of a reference book than a set of step-by-step instructions. However, if you go through the book in sequence, you'll find that the subject matter gets more complex the deeper you get. The subjects covered are based on the unwritten code of "Computer Security Best Practices." These are a set of rules that every network administrator or security manager agrees should be done, but are hardly ever consistently done.

How to Use This Book

You don't have to read this book from beginning to end to be able to begin securing your network. Simply peruse the table of contents and jump right in where the mood strikes you. There is no right or wrong way to use this book. Each chapter stands on its own, although you may find that certain phrases or concepts were explained in an earlier chapter. Where appropriate, I've made mention of the other chapters that relate to the same subject matter.

What You Don't Need to Read

You don't have to read every single word in the book to get the gist of the subject. Certain technical terms and miscellaneous information is included in shaded sidebars and are marked with icons such as Technical Stuff, Remember, and Tip. I would urge you to read the cautions that are marked with the Warning icon.

Foolish Assumptions

In order to keep this book from becoming a 1,500-page tome, I made a few assumptions about you, the reader. I'm assuming the following:

1. You own a computer and know about operating systems and applications.

2. Your computer or computers are connected to the Internet.

3. You know a little bit about networking and are familiar with many of the networking concepts and terms.

4. You've read or heard stories about viruses and hackers.

5. You've decided not to rely upon the software vendors to do the protection for you.

How This Book Is Organized

As soon as you look at the Table of Contents, you'll notice that this book is divided into five parts with a varying number of chapters for each part. In some chapters, you'll find checklists to help you determine what needs to be done to your system and to make decisions. Hopping about from one part to another won't hurt, so jump in and get your feet wet!

Part 1: The Path to Network Security

The chapters in this part take you through the questions you need to ask to ensure that you are looking in the right places for possible security holes and are implementing the right kind of security to meet your needs. You're given up-to-date information on vulnerabilities and the basic rules for securing systems.

Security means more than just securing against hackers and viruses, so the physical aspects of security are covered as well as hazards you should be aware of.

Part 11: Your Network 1s Your Business

Before you can develop a total security stance, you need to assess your risks and be aware of some of the new legislation that may affect you. Medical offices in particular are subject to news laws to protect patient privacy and a secure system will go a long way in protecting yourself as well as your clients.

Figuring out the costs of securing your network are covered as well as how to develop risk assessments and security plans. If you don't have security rules for employees to follow, how will you know when the rules have been broken? This part will help you get the jump on all those questions.

Part 111: The All-Important Security Mechanisms

Time to get out those screwdrivers and flashlights! This is the down and dirty part where all the specifics of security measures and mechanisms are spelled out: anti-virus, firewalls, special configurations, intrusion detection, and more. Getting to know what's in these chapters will help you join the ranks of uber-geeks and is a definite plus on your resume!

Part 1V: Special Needs Networking

Some network architectures require special considerations when it comes to security. This includes e-commerce and business-to-business networks. In addition, there are complex technologies to use for encryption of data. Some networks also require stronger authentication of identification because the data they store is ultra-sensitive. I'll cover these considerations and discuss the situations in which you may require more security than normal.

Part V: Dealing with the Unthinkable

Even the best networks occasionally run into problems — some of them are man-made events and others are the works of nature. Learning how to deal with problems is an important part of network security. Advance preparation for disasters and problems can make a difference between being able to recover and having to close your doors for good.

Sometimes you can't do it all yourself and you need to call in reinforcements. This is especially true if your building has been hit by a tornado or all your data has been stolen by a hacker. Both of these are real-world problems. In this part I detail all the jobs that need to be done so you can decide what needs to be accomplished and whether or not you can handle it yourself.

Part VI: The Part of Tens

This is the part that all Dummies books are known for — the cool lists of things in the back of the book. I've included other lists of do's and don'ts and tons of excellent Websites to visit. There's also the Ten Commandments of Network Security and a list of questions to ask computer security consultants. Enjoy!

Note: For even more information that you can use in your network security practices, go to this book's Web site at www.dummies.com/extras, where I've included the following lists and forms, all in Word format for ease of use:

- ✔ Access control checklist
- ✔ Anti-virus policy
- ✔ Dangerous services
- ✔ Employee agreement
- ✔ Hardware checklist
- ✔ Software checklist
- ✔ Internet use policy
- ✔ URL list for security-related Web sites

Icons Used in This Book

Technical Stuff is there purely if you feel the need to know. Concepts and technologies are explained; using jargon only where necessary. If you feel like joining the ranks of alpha geeks, this is one place to start. Geeks love learning and sharing trivia about their jobs. In reality, they are no smarter than you are; they just know the jargon.

 Danger, danger, Will Robinson! When you see this icon, be sure to read it and take care. Changing configurations on a computer and installing software can have unexpected results. It's very easy to do something incorrectly and sometimes very hard to reverse.

Sometimes you need to be reminded of something that was covered earlier in the book. These items don't *have* to be committed to memory — but it certainly wouldn't hurt, either.

Trivia and little-known tricks are shown with the Tip icon. Sometimes a little background is included to help clarify a concept.

Where to Go from Here

You can tear out the Cheat Sheet from the front of the book and frame it. You can leave the book on your desk to impress your boss. You can use the book as a paperweight to hold down all those projects you haven't completed yet. You can send the book to me with return postage and I'll sign it for you. Or, you can jump in and just start reading and learn more than you ever imagined. There is no wrong or right at this point — except when it comes to securing your network.

Part I
The Path to
Network Security

The 5th Wave   By Rich Tennant

"We take network security very seriously here."

In this part . . .

You've just watched another report on CNN about a vicious new virus attacking the world's computer networks and causing vast amounts of damage. You've finished reading the FBI report on computer crime that was featured in the Business Section of your newspaper. On the radio you hear that someone has hacked into a popular Web site and stolen thousands of credit card numbers — and you've visited that site!

By now you are shaking in your boots and paralyzed with fear about the state of your company's own network. What if you get hacked and lose everything? How will you know? What will you do?

It's time to relax and take a deep breath. The stories about doom and gloom are true, but there are things you can do to protect yourself and your network from harm. The chapters in this part will get you pointed in the right direction towards network security. If you don't know what causes the most common security problems, then this is the place to start!

Chapter 1

Starting Down the Road to Network Security

As you travel along the road to network security, the journey doesn't have to be a long and arduous one. Although many experts in the industry would like you to believe that network security is complicated, expensive, and best left to their capable hands, the truth is that anyone with a medium level of experience with networks and computers can undertake many basic network security measures. FBI studies show that more than 80 percent of network security attacks could have been avoided if only the most basic steps had been taken. Unfortunately, ignorance of what needs to be done is the reason for this sad statistic. This book is your tool to educating both yourself and others on what you need to do to keep your network safe and secure.

A question that people frequently ask me is, "I'm just a small business, a nobody. Would a hacker really be interested in me?" The short answer to that question is "Yes!" All computers on a network, and the Internet is a network, are just a number — not unlike a telephone number. A hacker can't tell by the number whether you're a large network or a small one. As far as the hacker knows, you're just another target; hackers will probe anything that looks interesting. If hackers don't find anything of interest in your network, they can possibly use your network to attack others. But you can prevent hackers from attacking your network — or, at least, you can make it much more difficult for them to attack.

In this chapter, I start you down the network security highway by stressing that everyone is vulnerable and helping you to identify the important network security issues. Next, you find out how to become intimately familiar with your network. (If you don't know what's there in the first place, how can you know when something's amiss?)

Identifying the Important Network Security Issues

Although networks vary in their architecture, uses, and complexity, they are amazingly similar when it comes to the basic security requirements. All networks are accessed with passwords and all networks are vulnerable to virus infections to some degree, for example. In order to effectively plan and implement security for your network, you'll need to run through all these issues and decide whether or not you need protection and what sort of protection you'll use.

The method of protection, the strength of your protection, and your philosophy of protection will determine your *security posture*. If your protections are minimal and you don't really see the need for security, then your security posture is said to be weak or passive. On the other hand, if you implement strong protection measures, have a thorough training and education program, and monitor your security levels regularly, your posture can be considered strong.

In the following section I'll cover the vast and varied areas of network security issues, along with some general information. These areas of interest are covered in more detail in subsequent chapters.

Passwords

Passwords are the keys to any network — and the easiest thing to find. Just one insecure password could enable anyone to successfully log on to your computer — and access your network. I'm not just talking about hackers, either. Many disgruntled employees would love to ruin your day by messing with your network. Bad passwords are just as bad as no passwords at all. Despite this fact, many companies don't enforce password rules because they consider the rules an inconvenience. That shortsighted view has been the downfall of quite a few highly regarded corporate and government networks!

Getting passwords off the network can be very easy, even if you aren't logged on to a particular system. Passwords traverse networks on an almost constant basis, and all it takes is a well-placed eavesdropping program (called a *password sniffer*) to gather hundreds and thousands of passwords in a matter of hours.

Ah, you say, but these passwords are encrypted! That's true some of the time, but the encryption method used is usually very weak. *Password crackers* — programs that use a combination of logic and dictionary words to crack encrypted password files — are freely available on the Internet and can usually unjumble the passwords in short order.

Using strong, hard-to-crack passwords is an easy line of defense against a breach of security. See the section "Use strong passwords," later in this chapter, where I give you the criteria for solid passwords.

Viruses, e-mail, and executable files

E-mail is a wonderful tool for increasing work productivity. Unfortunately, e-mail is now also one of the most common avenues for viruses and malicious programs that can wreak havoc and damage data. Only six years ago, I was advising people that they could never get a virus by simply opening an e-mail message. Today, e-mail is one of the most prevalent methods of transmission. Most e-mail viruses are more a nuisance than a danger, but you still need to spend precious man-hours to rid your system of the nasty little buggers. Anti-virus programs are the best protection here. (See the later section "Always use anti-virus software.")

Viruses aren't the only problem with e-mail programs. Do you allow attachments to come in with e-mail? What about executable programs, such as screen savers and games? Many malicious programs enter a system via this avenue. These programs, called *Trojans*, can do direct harm (such as erasing a hard drive) or indirect harm (such as installing sniffers to gather logons and passwords).

l0pht crack + 15 seconds = 670 security breaches

I once did a demonstration of a popular cracker program called *l0pht crack* (that's the letter l-zero-p-h-t). I ran the included sniffer at 8:00 a.m. when most of the employees were logging on for the day. By 9:00 a.m., I had over 1,400 encrypted passwords and user logins. I then ran the decryption program and broke 47 percent of the passwords in 15 SECONDS! How many passwords does it take to get into a network? Only one; l0pht crack had given me nearly 670! Among these passwords were the company president's password and many of the network administrators' passwords.

Two weeks later I ran the same program after everyone in the company had been taught how to create strong passwords and they had all changed their passwords. The result was that the stronger passwords were incredibly hard to decipher. The cracking program ran for 72 hours straight before I had any usable passwords.

Take some precautions that prevent executables from indiscriminately entering your network. Configuring content filters and anti-virus software can help with this problem; see Chapter 8 for the details.

Software

All operating systems and software applications have security holes. Some are more problematic than others, but all have the potential to give an unauthorized person access to your network. The holes are inadvertently created by the software developers, limited beta testing, and an overall lack of quality control. Programs contain millions upon millions of lines of text, called *code*, and determining which sections of code will leave security holes is extremely difficult and labor intensive. Most software companies say they can't justify the increase cost securing their code would entail. However, the dedicated, sophisticated hacker will examine code and program functionality for these flaws and then write programs that exploit the holes. The sophisticated hacker will often release his exploitation software for free on the Internet so that anyone can use it.

Software companies are aware that security holes exist in the thousands and are fairly responsible in releasing fixes in a timely manner. These fixes are known as *bug fixes*, *hot fixes*, *patches*, and sometimes *updates*. For the most part, fixes are easy to download and install, but the installation on many computers can take hours. Sometimes the fixes will cause problems with other software if the fixes haven't been properly tested prior to their release. Firewalls can block some of the security holes in software, but to be properly prepared, I recommend that you install fixes as they become available. I cover this information in more depth in Chapters 12, 13, and 14.

A number of Web sites and mail lists notify users when holes are found in a particular program and a fix is either upcoming or currently available. The issuance of such alerts, however, has been the catalyst for much debate. The situation is a double-edged sword: On one hand, notifying users of holes is a valuable service to network administrators; on the other hand, the alerts make hackers aware of the problems, too. Usually an alert isn't sent out until a fix is available, but hackers rely on the fact that most network administrators won't get around to installing the fix right away. The hackers will troll the Internet for computers that haven't yet been fixed and target them for attack.

Sometimes software applications are a security problem because they allow for the casual transference of files. Web servers top my list because they allow people to anonymously connect to your network. If you don't have your Web server properly configured, an unauthorized user can use your Web server to connect to computers inside your network. Some Web servers are better than others in thwarting attacks, a topic that I address in depth in Chapter 15.

Social engineering

Although hackers and other malicious folks have figured out many methods of attacking your network, one of the most commonly overlooked is what I call the Human Element. Yes, unfortunately, the people in your organization can be one of the biggest weaknesses in your network security. People are trusting souls and are particularly vulnerable to *social engineering*. In simple terms, social engineering is just another phrase for a scam. People are scammed into giving away passwords and valuable data every day.

Here's an example: The phone rings, and Jenny answers it,

> *"Hello, this is Jenny."*
>
> *"Hi, Jenny. This is Eric in network administration. We've had trouble with the way the computers have been storing passwords, and we're having users reset them today. Can you help?"*
>
> *"Sure, Eric, what do you want me to do?"*
>
> *"I want you to change your password to the word 'password99' and leave it like that for a few days."*
>
> *"No problem, Eric. But, would you mind taking me through the steps to change it? I don't do it very often, and I forget."*
>
> *"Sure thing. Here's what you do. . . ."*

Social engineering is that simple. Jenny didn't verify that the call was coming from inside or outside the building, and she probably doesn't know the names of the network administrators. She just wants to be helpful. The call could have been from a legitimate person, or it could have been a hacker who just gained entry into your network with a valid username and password.

A lesson in social engineering

A friend of mine once tested a company's security (with the permission of the higher ups, of course!) through social engineering. Dressed up in his best suit, my friend walked into the office carrying a briefcase and a clipboard. He told the receptionist that he was an auditor and asked her where the file room was. She directed him to it and asked if he wanted some coffee. She didn't ask for identification even as he began rifling through the cabinets and pulling out files. He even managed to hide in the office and remained there after the office closed and all personnel had gone for the night.

The next day my friend discussed his findings with the company's president. It didn't take much persuading to get the president to agree to make immediate changes in the way the company handled visitors!

No amount of firewalling or software patching can stop this type of threat. Employee education and awareness is the only security mechanism that will work in this case. Not only do you have to be able to stop intruders at the network level, you also have to be able to stop them at the physical level in order to have an effective security program.

Getting to Know Your Network

All network security rules apply to you, whether you have one connected computer or hundreds. However, in order to set an appropriate security posture, you have to know what you have before you can decide what needs to be done. In this section, I discuss components of the network, explaining which are potential problem areas. There is more specific information on how to fix the problems in Chapter 2.

Connections

Connections are the devices that allow computers to communicate with one another. You may have a single connection consisting of a modem that you use to dial in to an *ISP* (Internet Service Provider) such as AOL or Earthlink, or you can have hundreds of computers with network cards that connect to central servers in your building. Since connections imply trust between computers, it's important not only to know how you are connected, but who you are connecting to.

Dial-up modems

Modems are dial-up devices that connect your computer to the Internet via your telephone line. They are usually very small boxes that hook up your computer to the phone line with a regular phone cable. The word modem stands for *Modulator/Demodulator* and it changes the digital data created by your computer into electronic pulses that can be carried by the phone line, and vice versa.

If you're connecting to the Internet via modem, chances are that your vulnerability to hack attacks is quite small. A computer that's connected by modem isn't on the network all the time and doesn't have a set address — a static *IP address*. Each time you connect, your ISP gives you a changing address — a *dynamic IP address* — that's taken from a table of available addresses that the ISP has on its network. Because a number that changes constantly can't be found easily, hackers generally don't bother with these connections. That's not to say that modem connections aren't completely without danger. You're still vulnerable to e-mail viruses and Trojans. (See the previous section "Viruses, e-mail, and executable files.")

Modems can be a danger to companies, however. Some employees have brought in modems from home, hooked them up to their work computers, and set the modem's software to answer incoming calls. Frequently this is done without the company's knowledge or permission. The employees see this as a convenience because it allows them to dial up their work computers from their home computers and access the data on the work computer. Even if the company has allowed this practice for telecommuting, if it's not done properly, unauthorized persons may also be able to access that computer.

Hackers employ a device or a software program called a *demon dialer* or *war dialer*. The dialer dials phone numbers within a range (say, every number between 555-0000 and 555-9999) in rapid succession. If any phone number that is dialed responds with a modem's *handshake* signal, then the dialing stops and the hacker can try to connect to the computer that answered. The modem handshake signal is that somewhat annoying series of beeps, boops, and buzzing sounds that you hear when the modem is trying to complete a connection. If a hacker has dialed the phone number of the work computer and that computer's modem answers, he may be able to connect to the work computer. In addition, you may never know that a hacker has gained access to the computer and stolen important information.

Cable modems

Many homes and some businesses now connect to the Internet with a *cable modem*, which uses the same technology as your subscriber cable TV and uses a coaxial cable instead of a telephone line for connection. Typically, the TV and computer services are split and don't run on the same channel. The modem itself is a very simple *router*. A router is like a border crossing. All traffic coming to the border must declare its onward destination. The router checks its listings and then tells the traffic where to go and where to stop next. Routers can keep some traffic out, but you have to be explicit. I explain routers and how you can configure them in Chapter 10.

Because a cable modem is always on — that is, always connected to — the Internet, the risk to your security increases. You'll probably have a static IP address, which can make it much easier for the outside world to see your computers. In addition, many cable modems run services on them, such as Web servers and telnet, so that you can configure the modem remotely. If an intruder can find the IP address of your cable modem, he will try to access it using telnet or http. If he can guess the password — or if there is no password — the intruder can possibly alter the configuration of the cable modem so he has access whenever he wants it. That means he can get to your computer, steal, change, or delete data, and can install hacking programs or viruses.

DSL

Another method of connecting to the Internet is *DSL* or Digital Subscriber Line. These connections are made through your regular telephone line, but the traffic is split so that you can simultaneously use your phone for incoming and outgoing calls. The connection from your computer involves a DSL modem or router. This router is a bit more sophisticated than a cable modem (see the preceding section), but it still gives you the convenience of your connection being always on.

The dangers of DSL routers are similar to the dangers of cable modems:

- ✔ You're always connected.
- ✔ You have a static IP address.
- ✔ You can remotely access the routers to configure the box.

One of the best security measures for all types of modems is to use long passwords that cannot be easily guessed and include numbers and both upper- and lowercase letters. Personal firewalls are a great way to protect small systems from intrusions if you are using DSL connections. Personal firewalls are discussed in Chapter 9.

Wireless

A wireless connection is one of the newest connection methods to hit the streets. (I use this type in my home. After dinner, my husband and I sit in the living room, laptops on laps, and engage in dueling Web surfing.) Wireless at home involves having some sort of land line connection to the Internet (such as a cable modem or DSL) and special wireless network cards (type 802.11). Although extremely convenient (how else could I enjoy Web surfing in the comfort of my living room?), wireless connections are fraught with danger.

If incorrectly configured, a wireless access point will allow *anyone* who has a wireless card in his or her computer to connect to the network! Many companies have forgotten or chosen not to turn on the encryption of their wireless signals. This means that any computer within range can receive the broadcast and "see" the network. Some of the broadcasts reach quite far — many floors and thousands of feet away from the station. In addition, if the company has not set stringent access controls for their wireless network, not only can an unauthorized person see the network, he can log on and gain access with little or no problem.

Recently, an infamous ex-hacker drove around the streets of San Francisco, logging on to dozens of company networks from the comfort of his car! Being able to successfully log on to a network — with no one the wiser — is a hacker's dream come true.

You have many ways of securing a wireless network from spurious logons: strong passwords, well-defined users' access lists, and various levels of encryption are some of the basic protection measures available.

T1s, T3s, and more

The ultimate Internet connection is a *T1* or *fractional T1 service* direct from the backbone of the Internet. These connections allow vast amounts of data to be transferred at lightning fast speeds. Direct connections of this sort are extremely expensive and are beyond the reach of home users and many small businesses.

However, you'll find that most large corporations, the government, and the military all use T1, T3, and OC-3 connections, which require heavy-duty routers able to support thousands of connections at once. Needless to say, these are the types of networks that serious hackers look for and are the ones that make the news when the hackers are successful. Firewalls, intrusion detection systems, anti-virus software, and other extensive security measures are required to protect these networks.

Remote connections

Do you allow remote connections to your network? If so, you can add remote connectivity to your list of security issues. Remote connections via modems are a big a concern because you are trusting someone outside the physical confines of your building to use your network. The computer being used to connect remotely should be as secure as your internal network otherwise you create additional problems for yourself.

Take a laptop, for instance. Many employees use their company laptops while they are on the road to connect to the company's network from their hotel rooms. Since the laptop is used frequently in this manner, the employee will also allow their computer to store their logon name and password to make the connection faster and easier. However, if the laptop is stolen and there is nothing preventing the thief from using it, he can also quickly and easily connect to your network. That is because all of the logon information has been stored on the laptop and is ready for use. What's almost worse is that you won't see the connection as unauthorized because the thief had used an appropriate logon and password. No alarms will ring!

All computers used for remote connections should be protected from unauthorized use such as enabling the BIOS password to be set. If a BIOS password is used, the computer won't boot up without it. In addition, you may want to consider encrypting the data on laptops because most thieves won't go to the time and trouble of trying to decrypt the data. They'll just reformat the drive and sell the computer.

Some remote computer connections use PCAnywhere or similar programs to allow the two computers to exchange data. These remote connection programs have their own security problems, and you should check with the vendors for any security fixes that have been released.

Telnet and FTP are two remote connections that folks tend to frequently overlook as having security issues. Telnet is a remote connection program that allows you to act as if you are sitting directly in front of the computer. It's frequently used by system administrators who have to make important changes to computers that are physically located in another office or another building. Being able to use telnet saves them the time and bother of walking to the other computer. But, because telnet allows authorized persons to access a computer located elsewhere, they can possibly allow malicious intruders to enter your system, too. If the password for telnet can be guessed or cracked, the intruder can telnet into your system, change configurations, or install unauthorized programs.

FTP programs have a list of problems that have been big on the exploitation lists of late. FTP stands for *file transfer protocol* and is used to move, copy, or delete files. Like telnet, it's a program that is used to connect to a computer that is physically located somewhere else. The problems associated with FTP are much discussed in mail lists such as Bugtraq and SecurityFocus. There are security patches and configuration advice available online and proper user accounts and permissions are needed to secure these services. As always, strong passwords are a must!

Workstations and servers

Computer workstations are common in both home environments and large corporate networks. Workstations need to be protected with well-defined user accounts and permissions. For example, not everyone in a corporate environment should have permission to install programs on their workstations. That responsibility is best left to system administrators.

A network often employs the use of computers called *servers*. As the name implies, servers serve the individual workstations with files that can be shared and moved around. It's important that you understand the security issues involved with your server's operating system because some OSs pose more of a security problem than others. Microsoft Windows NT, for example, was touted as secure upon its release when, in fact, it was only secure when the computer wasn't connected to the network! Make it your business to know how secure your OS is. More on OS security can be found in Chapters 12, 13, and 14.

Servers often contain application programs to accomplish special tasks. These may include, but aren't limited to: Web servers, database servers, FTP servers, mail servers, firewalls, and intrusion detection systems. All of these programs have their own security problems that I cover in detail later in this book. However, the danger increases when services are combined on one server.

One of the biggest mistakes that you can make is to combine a Web server and a database on the same computer. Web servers are notoriously easy to breach; getting into the database is much easier if the files are physically located on the same computer as the Web server. If you place a firewall between a Web server and a database server, you make it much harder for a malicious intruder to destroy your entire system.

One of the best things that you can do to protect your workstations and servers is to install anti-virus software. Viruses, worms, and Trojans cost businesses tens of billions of dollars a year in damage and lost revenue. Contrary to popular belief, firewalls don't protect your systems against viruses; you need anti-virus software for that, which I cover later in this chapter (in the section "Always use anti-virus software") and in Chapter 9.

Your network users

You may find it funny that I'm including network users as a network component, but what good is a network if you don't have users using it? Knowing your users and how they use and react with your system can help you identify possible weaknesses in your system. Following is a list of questions that you should ask yourself about your users, along with my commentary explaining why you'd want the answers to these particular questions:

- ✓ **Does each user have an individual logon ID and a strong password?** Everyone should have a unique logon ID and a strong, ungues sable password associated with each logon ID. This is so that any action on the network can be attributed to an individual. If you do not have individual logon IDs, then you won't be able to keep track of who is doing what on your network. Of course, each person should have a strong password in order to keep unauthorized users from guessing their password and accessing the network in their name.

- ✓ **Are you keeping a log of all logon attempts?** Your operating system has the ability to write all logon attempts to a text file called a *log*. You have to tell your system whether to log all successful or unsuccessful logons. It's important to have your system log the unsuccessful attempts at logging on because this can tell you that someone is trying to guess a password and is probably not authorized to use your system. This may be the first indication that someone is trying to hack into your system. It goes without saying, then, that all these logs should be reviewed regularly!

- ✓ **Are users locked out after a small number of incorrect logons?** If someone is trying to guess a password to gain unauthorized access, he will probably keep guessing until he gets in. This is called a *brute force* attack and is like someone hammering on a door until it eventually caves in. An effective method of disabling repeated guesses is to *lock out* the user ID after a certain number of failed attempts — say three to five tries. When the account is locked out, then the real user has to call the administrators to unlock the account. This may be an inconvenience, but it is a cheap and easy way to ensure that hackers or other unauthorized personnel cannot get into your system simply by repeatedly trying to guess a password. Of course, a log of these attempts should be kept and reviewed, too.

✔ **Do you allow group accounts?** Frequently, the network administrators use group accounts as a convenience. That way, when a shift changes, the users don't have to log out — the new users just use the existing open accounts. *This is an absolute no-no.* For one thing, if everyone is logged in under the same user ID, you have no way of knowing who did what on the system. You'd be surprised how resistant some people are to getting rid of group accounts.

✔ **Do you have any inactive accounts?** Any time a person goes on leave or will not be using the system for an extended period, you should make that person's account inactive by disabling it from use. If the user is going to be gone for longer than a month or is an infrequent user of the system, then you should delete those accounts. For your safety, creating new accounts is better and safer — although maybe less convenient — than leaving inactive accounts that a hacker can take advantage of. When an employee terminates employment, the account should be deleted before that person leaves the building.

Tools and Procedures

Of course, to do any job well, you need to have the proper tools and know the correct way to proceed with the job. Network security is no different. Some of the tools are quite common while others are specific to networking. The procedures are a methodical step-by-step process to discovering your weaknesses and then implementing security measures to protect yourself against them. In any case, it's not too difficult, but it is time consuming and well worth the effort.

Paper and pencil

Yes, one of the most effective tools you need is paper and pencil! Sounds archaic and old-fashioned, but lists and documentation are key to effective network security. You need to have a record of what you've done and *why* you've done it. In the unlikely scenario that you're unable to come to work for an extended period of time, documentation can help others to continue your good work.

You should make lists of everything you have, including as much detail as possible. Your list should include

✔ **Organization chart:** You need to know who everyone is and what their level of authority is in order to define their roles for access and security.

✔ **Hardware lists:** You need to have a list of all your equipment, the makes and models, and who the support vendors are. Make this list as you would for insurance purposes.

✔ **Software lists:** This is important to not only know what you have, but to ensure that you possess all the legal licenses for the software. You should list the maker, program, and version of the software as well as the number of copies you are using. If the software is something you have developed, it is an important asset that needs protection.

✔ **Network map:** Draw a map of your network and indicate the trusted connections inside and outside of the internal network. If your network connects to another company's network, this is an example of a trusted connection outside your domain. Show all the major computing resources and any protection mechanisms you already have in place — such as firewalls or filtering routers.

✔ **Building plan:** You need to indicate where your computers are located and any special purpose areas such as server rooms. The fire escapes, sprinkler systems, doors, stairways, windows, and all physical features should be included in the plans. This will give you an indication of what physical security measures need to be implemented to protect your treasures.

If you don't want to type and print this documentation, write everything down; a written journal is better than nothing written at all. Later on, this journal will go a long way when you get ready to write your security plan and security policies.

Administrative accounts

For many of the implementations that I mention in this book, you'll need an administrative level account. If you don't have such an account, make arrangements to get one or have a network administrator assigned to help you. Be sure that the administrator is trusted and has the skills needed to make changes to the network.

Port scanners

For *network discovery*, that is, mapping all your computers, software, and services that run on your network, you'll probably need a *port scanner*. Port scanners send queries across the network, enabling you to see what protocols and ports are open on all the connected computers. You'll often find services running that aren't required. Many port scanners are free on the Internet and others you'll have to purchase. Also, many port scanners are UNIX-based programs, so be sure that the port scanner you get will run on your operating system.

Port scanners are very powerful programs. If you're not careful, you can do serious damage to programs running on your network. Because a port scanner floods the network with queries, running too many queries at once can bring a healthy network to a screeching halt. Be sure to read all the directions for your port scanner before you unleash it on your network.

Network mappers

An invaluable tool, a *network mapper* is a program that works by querying the network, looking for computers and their addresses. The cleverly named network mapper then uses this information to make a physical map of your network. The map enables you to see all your connections in a graphical format. In addition, network maps can give you a listing of all the operating systems and applications installed on the network. One word of warning, though — these programs aren't easy to operate and some of them can be very expensive. A list of where to acquire these and other tools is available in Chapter 24.

Vulnerability assessment

A *vulnerability assessment tool* tests applications, computers, and network devices, such as routers and firewalls, for known flaws and weaknesses that can leave your systems susceptible to malicious attacks. It uses a database of vulnerabilities that compares those vulnerabilities against the particular operating systems and applications installed on your network. These vulnerabilities can include such things as missing security patches, the running of vulnerable services, and improper operating system configurations.

Although vulnerability assessment tools are not 100 percent accurate and may give you many false positives, they are an extremely useful discovery tool that can provide tangible evidence of known weaknesses and exposures before they are exploited. Some vulnerability assessment tools are easier to use than others, and some only scan for vulnerabilities on the Windows or UNIX platforms exclusively. Before purchasing one of these tools, be sure to confirm that it can scan for vulnerabilities in most, if not all, of the different applications and operating systems that you have running on your network. Because no one that's serious about network security should be without one of these tools, I've included some in the list of tools in Chapter 24.

Upper-management support

You should not start work on network security in a vacuum. You need important feedback from all users, and, more importantly, you need permission and support from the higher-ups. Begin with upper management: Tell them what you propose to do, why you need to do it, and how you're going to proceed. Set a schedule so that, at regular intervals, you're giving them your progress reports, and they're giving you their feedback. The more you include both upper management and general users during your initial phase, the more likely they are to work with you — rather than against you.

The first step may be to convince upper management that network security is serious work that must be done. If they need heavy-duty convincing, you can use the next section, "Knowing Your Enemy," in which I describe many attacks and methods used by hackers and virus writers. Unfortunately, many companies wait until after they've experienced serious problems before deciding to secure their networks.

The Federal Computer Incident Response Center (FedCIRC; www.fedcirc.gov/index.html) and the Government Accounting Office (GAO; www.gao.gov) have informative reports with some very interesting statistics on the types and prevalence of computer crimes and intrusions. The GOA site has a text search of reports available. If you search under Information Management, you'll find dozens of critical reports on computer security successes and failures from 1997 to the present.

An assessment team

Before you actually start the securing of your network, you need to form an *assessment team*: Each member of the team should have a good working knowledge of computing and networks and understand the value of a good computer security program. Divide the duties among the team members. I suggest a minimum of three team members:

- **Team Manager:** Responsible for determining the scope and direction of the security effort; acts as the main liaison between other members of the team and upper management; must understand basic risk assessment.

- **Head Geek:** Responsible for all hands-on work with the computers; must understand basic vulnerability assessment; must have an in-depth knowledge of computing and networks; must be able to communicate well with other team members.

- **Documenter:** Responsible for all reports and documentation; must be detail-oriented; must have a working knowledge of computing and networks.

The team will work together to identify the assets that need to be protected and will research and prepare the initial security plan. The plan will describe what needs to be protected, how they should be protected, and the security roles and responsibilities of everyone in the company.

Don't despair if you're the sole member of the assessment team. Many companies will not accept the cost of a three person team. One person can do the work, but you must give yourself adequate time in which to accomplish the tasks. The trick is to prioritize the jobs to be done. You must realize right now that setting up network security, especially for the first time, can be a full-time job. Much depends on how large your network is and how many vulnerabilities apply to your system. If you have only a few workstations and a few applications, the job will be much easier than if you have hundreds of servers and different applications on each one.

All in all, I recommend going slowly and documenting as you go. If you rush through setting up network security and forget much of what you've done, no one will be able to follow up after you. In addition, when the time comes to apply patches and updates, much of the effort will go to finding out what needs patching instead of to actually doing the work.

Knowing Your Enemy

It's an overused cliché, I know, but you really do need to know your enemy in the world of network security. If you can think as deviously as your enemies can, you may be able to head them off at the path they're taking into your network. Many people have underestimated hackers, virus writers, and even their own employees — to the detriment of the security of the network. Don't let this happen to you. You can begin to safeguard your network by simply arming yourself with knowledge of who your enemy is.

Hackers

Hackers are computer terrorists; they keep you on edge because you don't know when or where they're going to strike. You do know that they won't go away, so you have to do your best to keep them out of your network. Hackers are also extremely organized: Unfortunately, they share their exploits, tools, and findings with other hackers, which only exacerbates the threat.

That hackers are unkempt and unsociable misfits is a myth. Hackers are the bag boys at your grocery store, the girl at the department store counter, your polite and quiet neighbor, or even the guy nearing retirement in the production department. You can't tell a hacker by looks.

Accurately profiling a hacker is difficult because so many types are out there, all motivated by different factors. However, I categorize hackers into three categories: the uber-hacker, the common hacker, and the script kiddie. In the following sections, I profile each type.

Where the hackers meet: DefCon

The first DefCon hacker conference (www.defcon.org) took place in 1992. About 150 people attended. In 2001, the estimated attendance grew to more than 5,000 people — and the event wasn't even advertised!

Hackers, wannabes, security experts, and a myriad of characters attend DefCon to participate in seminars that detail the security problems with applications, network architectures, and security devices and mechanisms. There are also sales of hardware, software, and books and quite a few hands-on classes such as on lock picking. Much of the important information is behind the scenes and is shared amongst groups of friends in hotel rooms and in bars. It's quite the place for networking and to be seen — or not, as the case may be.

Hackers aren't the only attendees at DefCon; a fair number of agents from the FBI, DEA, DOJ, and CIA are also on hand. This has become such a popular intelligence gathering spot for government agencies that the hackers have created a contest called *Spot The Fed:* Hackers are encouraged to "out" those they think are spooks or cops.

Uber-hacker

An uber-hacker hacks for the money or personal gain, not the glory. Typically, uber-hackers live and breathe computer protocols and are able to write sophisticated programs in their sleep.

The typical targets for this type of hacker are financial institutions, military and government sites, software companies, and universities with close ties to intelligence agencies. No one knows how many uber-hackers are out there because so few have been caught. Many in the security business think that hostile foreign governments employ these hackers to gather intelligence or to use *information warfare* against an enemy. Information warfare campaigns look to disable a country's infrastructure in many ways: data networks, telecommunications, energy, transportation, banking and finance, emergency services, and government operations. It's a type of terrorism. While there have not been any attributable attacks of this type, many believe it is the battle place of the future.

If you're a small business, this doesn't mean that you don't need to fear the uber-hacker. If the uber-hacker can use your network as an attack base against other networks, he will. It's important to protect your network against all intruders — regardless of their motives.

Common hacker

Typically, the common hacker — who usually has a system administration level of expertise and knows a lot about operating systems and applications — is holding a grudge or has something to prove. Common hackers are able to write common attack programs and have an in-depth knowledge of how networks communicate. Because common hackers know a lot about your system, they're quite likely to steal your organization's proprietary information.

To gain acceptance from other hackers and to be held in high regard, common hackers often release their hacking programs on the Internet for others to use. Common hackers are a real threat: they know how to hack and will enter your network — almost any network — if you leave openings.

Common hackers are also looking for the easy hacks — the known vulnerabilities that system administrators haven't patched. Most often, the common hacker will burrow in through Web sites to get to the back-end servers or databases and then steal the data contained in them.

The common hacker is also often involved in *hactivism*, which relates to geopolitical conflicts and issues. Hactivists will often attack networks that they think are supporting their political opponents. Web site defacements are popular with this group.

Script kiddie

Script kiddies are the vandals and graffiti artists of the Internet. They have little or no actual programming skill and can only hack with tools available on the Internet; script kiddies can't create their own tools. Script kiddies visit IRC (Internet Relay Chat) rooms to share their "conquests" and will write messages in juvenile script kiddie code, which consists of numbers exchanged for certain letters and intentional misspellings. One example that you'll often see is the word 31337 for eleet [sic] — meaning, of course, the greatest. They're in it purely for the bragging rights. You'll often see their messages sprawled across hacked Web site pages.

Script kiddies can and will do real damage to your network if they find it and gain access to it. The damage they do is indiscriminate — they don't care if you're a large or small network. If an automated program on the Internet attracts their interests, script kiddies will use it, not knowing or caring about the outcome.

Virus writers

Virus writers aren't hackers. A friend of mine, named Sarah Gordon, is a recognized profiler of virus writers. Amazingly, in her years of associating with and sometimes living with virus writers, she has discovered that no common thread runs among them. You would expect them to meet the stereotype of the hacker — surly, unkempt, in trouble with authority, and unable to maintain relationships. But my friend has found that virus writers range in age from 10 to 60 and that many have loving relationships with their families.

That begs the question, "If virus writers are well adjusted, why do they write viruses?" I think that they all want to write a program that does something that's never been done before. Virus writers appear to have nothing to lose and don't seem to be in it for personal gain. Because of this, they constitute a large danger to networks. I don't think I've ever heard of a virus writer who released a virus, realized the damage it causes, and then offered to write an antidote as an apology.

One small point in your favor is that virus writers seem to focus on Microsoft systems and applications because of their widespread use, the ease of interoperability between programs, and the numerous security flaws. Therefore, if you don't use Microsoft products, you'll be immune to many viruses. Not using Microsoft products isn't feasible for much of the networking world, however, so anti-virus products are a must.

Employees — former and current

People in an organization can and do pose a real security threat to your system, although this point is one of the most commonly overlooked components of network security. Do your employees take company files with them when they leave? What keeps them from doing it? You should seriously consider these questions, and then answer yourself honestly. You can't hope to ensure the security of your company's physical perimeter unless you also have secured all access to your company's information systems. During times of economic downturn, employees and contractors can have a hard time turning away from temptation; they may steal proprietary data, trade secrets, or even engage in network sabotage.

Employees who feel they have been dealt with improperly or unethically by your company may leave and harbor a grudge. These employees may try to access your network to either do damage or to steal important data. If the employee is not able to gain access to your system, he or she may try to acquire an accomplice within the company to help with nefarious activities. For this reason you should always immediately disable all accounts for terminated personnel — especially if the parting wasn't amicable.

In June of 2002, a former employee of Prudential stole the private data of more than 60,000 Prudential employees and then tried to sell that information on the Internet to create false identities. This former employee felt he had been dealt with unjustly when he worked for Prudential. Using the knowledge he obtained while a database administrator for the company, he broke into their system and stole the personnel data from the database.

The following is a list of precautions a company can take to safeguard network security in the event of employee termination:

- **Recovery of keys and identification:** Many, but not all, companies have employees turn in keys and identification upon their termination, a practice that guarantees former employees can't later physically enter the premises.

- **Property search:** Some companies conduct a physical search of any file boxes that employees have with them on their last day. Companies search boxes to recover hardcopies of files and sensitive reports. But what about all the stuff that employees may carry out in briefcases or pockets prior to the actual termination date? You may want to consider random searches of boxes, bags, briefcases, and so on that the employee is using to move belongings before the actual termination date.

- **Physical bodily search:** Often, a company that conducts a property search will forget to look for floppy disks that may be on the person's body. A physical bodily search may be humiliating to the employee — and it may sound like an extreme scenario to you — but sometimes such action is a necessary precaution if you plan to keep your network totally secure.

- **Disabled network access:** When an employee is set for departure, you should disable their e-mail and network access immediately. If administrators need access to any files from the user's home directory, the system administrators have commands and tools that will give them access to that data. Make sure there is nothing left that the old employee can use to gain entry to the system.

- **Exit interviews:** If your company conducts exit interviews upon employee termination, keep a record of the entire exit interview process. If the employee makes threats against the company, even veiled threats, you then have a record of what was said and to whom.

Back up and store e-mail files for a number of years. You never know when you may need this information. There have been cases where old e-mail files saved employers from costly law suits.

The competition

Don't underestimate your competition. I can't stress that point enough. I'm not saying that companies would actively recruit a hacker to infiltrate your site, but I wouldn't be surprised if some companies allowed employees to try. Executives of a famous company once told me that they were safe from their competition entering their e-commerce site to gather sensitive information. I boldly asked the executives which one of them was willing to bet his job on that fact. All faces paled while no one leapt to the challenge. They did, however, agree to a survey of their site. I found holes in their e-commerce site's Web servers and databases that would have allowed sensitive company data to reach the hands of their competitors.

Many companies have made errors in what they put up on their Web sites. Seemingly innocuous information can become dangerous and potentially damaging in the wrong hands. For example, a company listed the names, addresses, and home phone numbers of their company executives. A man who worked for the competition called one of the executives at home one night and pretended to be on the production team of the executive's company. He made up some excuse about problems with the production schedule and engaged the executive in a long conversation about how a change in production would hurt them economically. The executive never questioned the imposter because he assumed anyone who had his home phone number would be a member of his company. The result was that his competition now had his production schedule and they used that information to their advantage.

I'm not saying you shouldn't list names, but be careful of your reasons for including more personal information such as addresses and phone numbers. Don't give the public more detail about your company on your Web site than they really need.

The competition frequently employs social engineering to gather sensitive data as mentioned previously. For example, an employee of one of your competitors, posing as an employee on a business trip, can call and ask the receptionist to look up data for him or to ask how he can get access to the files. This is made easier if he has knowledge of the chain of command from information he got on the Web site. Be sure your staff knows the identity of persons asking for information over the phone and have them refer unusual requests to human resources or your security officer.

The Basic Rules of Network Security

Network security can be as simple as adhering to a set of rules; technology alone can't thwart hack attacks and other security breaches. All network system administrators and security officers agree on the basic security rules, but hardly anyone follows all of them. Why not? The biggest roadblock seems to be a lack of time and money to see that all the rules are implemented. Correctly configuring all the computers on the network and documenting the changes and following up when necessary are all time-consuming tasks. Because upper management wants to see the return on an investment, it has a hard time accepting that security costs money and isn't a profit-making arm of the organization.

Users are also at fault because they want everything to be easy. They don't want to have to create hard passwords and then change them every 60 days. If users can circumvent a security mechanism they see as inconvenient, they'll do it without a second thought.

Here, then, are the rules, the Eight Commandments of network security:

- ✔ Use strong passwords
- ✔ Always use anti-virus software
- ✔ Always change default configurations
- ✔ Don't run services that you don't need
- ✔ Immediately install security updates
- ✔ Back-up early and often
- ✔ Protect against surges and losses
- ✔ Know who you trust

They seem simple and most are relatively easy to implement. I highlight each in painstaking detail in the following sections, urging you to take these Eight Commandments seriously. I guarantee that if everyone followed these rules, network attacks would soon be a rare occurrence.

Use strong passwords

Passwords are often the only protection used on a system. A user ID is only a name and doesn't verify an identification, but the password associated with the user ID works as an identifier. Therefore, passwords are the keys to your network, and you should protect them as such. Firewalls and intrusion detection systems mean nothing if your passwords are compromised.

So just what do I mean by a *strong* password? In general terms, a strong password is one that you can't find in any dictionary — English or foreign. It also means a password that isn't easily guessed. Longer passwords are harder to guess or crack than short passwords are.

Following is a list that you can use to set (and help your users set) strong passwords:

- ✔ **Use a nonsensical combination of letters:** The best passwords appear to be sheer nonsense. For example, if you take the phrase, "Nighty, night and don't let the bed bugs bite," and use just the first letter of each word, your password would appear to be nnadltbbb. That's a good one (and easy for the user to remember), but see the next bullet to make it even more difficult.

✔ **Include a mix of upper- and lowercase letters:** You should include an uppercase letter somewhere other than at the beginning and also include a number. Because the letter *l* looks like the number one, you could use a one instead of that letter; your password then becomes: `nnAd1tbbb`. A password cracker could conceivably still crack this word with a *brute force attack* (letter by letter), but that process takes many hours. Believe me, a hacker doesn't want to waste that much time.

✔ **Longer passwords are better:** Your password should be at least 8 characters in length.

✔ **Change your passwords regularly:** Even the best of passwords should be changed regularly (every 60 days or so) to prevent its being used long-term if it's cracked. Many operating systems enable you to set this rule for each user. The user will most likely find this practice inconvenient, but it's smart security.

✔ **Set *new* passwords instead of reusing the same ones over and over:** Your users should not be using the same password again within the same year or even 18 months.

✔ **Don't use a set of characters straight off the keyboard:** You should never use something like qwerty, 12345678, or asdfghj for passwords. Even though they look nonsensical, they follow a distinct pattern of consecutive keys on the keyboard and password crackers will break them in seconds.

✔ **Treat your passwords as top-secret information:** All passwords should be protected and not shared! This is the biggest security no-no there is. Many users write their passwords on sticky notes attached to their computers or put them under their keyboards. That's not fooling anyone! I used to check people's computers and desks at night, and if I found passwords in plain sight, I'd purposefully lock those users out so that they'd have to call me.

Root and administrative level passwords are the keys to the kingdom for an intruder. System administrators with *root* privileges — that is, with no access restrictions and the ability to make any sort of changes — should therefore have the hardest passwords and the most stringent rules about changing and reusing them. Follow these guidelines:

✔ **Write down all root passwords and store them in a safe:** Then, if an administrator is incapacitated for a time or leaves the job suddenly, the password isn't lost forever. Password recovery programs are available, but you don't really want to rely on them in an emergency.

✔ **Change ALL user passwords if you suspect a root password has been compromised:** You can't guarantee that the all the passwords haven't been stolen if an unknown person has a root or administrative level password.

Likewise, if a general user suspects that a password has been stolen or compromised, that user should change the password immediately and notify those in authority at the company.

Always use anti-virus software

Because viruses are such a persistent, annoying, and expensive problem, you'd be silly not to use anti-virus software to protect computers on your network. While anti-virus software isn't always 100 percent effective, it's better than no protection at all. Believe it or not but I've heard people say that they don't use anti-virus software because they've never been infected with a virus. Excuse me? If you don't have anti-virus software, then how do you know you've never had a virus? Most common viruses are not obvious to the user.

Anti-virus software consists of two parts: the *scanning engine* and the *signature files*. You need to regularly update both the scanning engine and the signature files on a regular basis or the anti-virus software will lose its effectiveness. The software program usually has an *update* command, or you can check at the vendor's Web site for updates.

The scanning engine tells the software how and where to scan, and the signature files are essentially a database of known viruses and their actions. The scanning engine compares files on your computer to the known viruses in the signature files. Anti-virus software is prone to false positives, but that's a small inconvenience for the protection it affords you.

When new viruses are found, anti-virus software vendors issue updates to their dat files to include the new strain. Occasionally, the scanning engine itself needs updating, too. If one part of the program is updated and the other part is obsolete, it simply won't work properly — but you won't know it's not working until it's too late.

For your anti-virus software to be most effective, you need to install it on individual workstations as well as on all the servers and other computers on your network. That is the only way to catch viruses at all entry points. All removable media, such as floppies and CDs, should be scanned before used on a system. Unfortunately, legitimate software CDs sometimes carry viruses, and floppies that people bring from home may also have viruses on them. I cover anti-virus software in-depth in Chapter 8.

If you install anti-virus software on your Internet gateway servers, the software can catch viruses coming in from outside connections.

Viruses: The biggest problem companies with Internet connections face

If your company is connected to the Internet, you are open to viruses. No ifs about it. One of the first major virus infection of the past few years was the I Love You bug. It was also the first virus to infiltrate U.S. classified networks. In a recent survey conducted jointly by CSI (Computer Security Institute) and the FBI, 94 percent of the respondents reported virus infections in 2001 for a loss of over $45 million. Only 40 percent reported system penetration. You're much more likely to be hit by a virus than by a hacker; anti-virus software is worth your time and money!

Although most viruses target the Windows operating system, you still need anti-virus software on Unix-based and Mac systems. A virus can travel across Unix and Mac systems and will not affect those systems. However, a virus can travel across those systems, and when it encounters Windows-based systems, the virus will start working. I've seen e-mail viruses that were perfectly harmless on a Unix-based e-mail server, but all the workstations were Windows-based. As soon as the mail was retrieved by the Windows-based computers, the computer starting infecting all the other Windows computers it could find.

Always change default configurations

Installing a system right out of the box and leaving it with the default configuration is probably one of the most common mistakes that people make when setting up a network. Default configurations often have default administrative accounts and passwords that hackers the world over know. This applies to routers, hubs, switches, operating systems, e-mail systems, and other server applications, such as databases and Web servers. I can't think of any software that is immune to this problem.

In addition to having known passwords on the computers, default configurations contain multiple security holes that you need to plug. Before you ever put any computer online, you should change the default account names and the passwords and apply all security patches. A little bit more time spent on a computer at this point can save you a lot of grief later. The fewer holes you leave on a network, the harder it is for someone to break into your system. I cover more on changing defaults in Chapters 12, 13, and 14.

Don't run services you don't need

Often you'll find that the default configuration of operating systems — servers in particular — have *services* or small programs running that you don't really need. The standard rule of thumb is to turn off anything you don't need because some of the default services have known security holes and they will introduce new vulnerabilities into your system. This rule goes hand-in-hand with the rule mentioned previously. If you don't accept the default configurations, then you'll often see that these services have been enabled. It's very easy to turn them off.

Some of the services I'm talking about are used primarily for remote administration. These include the "r" commands in Unix like *rsh and rlogin*. If you're not going to be using your machine as a Web server, then turn off the *http* or Web server program. The same applies for *ftp*. If you have no need to transfer files using ftp, then there's no reason to keep it running. There is a more complete list of dangerous and unneeded services in Chapter 12.

Immediately install security updates

The bad news is that almost all software contains security holes. The good news is that dozens of new alerts are listed daily in places like CERT and SecurityFocus. The person responsible for network security should be aware of these alerts and should subscribe to one of the many services that send e-mail alerts on specific problems. Many of these services allow you to sign up for alerts that only pertain to your situation. And, as soon as the alerts appear, you should obtain the fix and apply it to your computers. Although a time-consuming and possibly inconvenient practice, it's one of the best things that you can do to ensure your network security. All the firewalls in the world won't help you if you're leaving back doors open to hackers.

You should know that as soon as alerts are made public, hackers are searching for computers on the Internet that are vulnerable to the attack that made the alert necessary. As soon as hackers find those computers, they share the addresses with other hackers on IRC chat rooms and on Web sites.

Back up early and often

When an intruder trashes your system, the best recourse you have is to take your system offline and restore it from your backup. You *have* made a recent backup, haven't you? Good. Are you certain that the backup you've made is a *restorable* back-up? (I don't let up, do I?) Some types of backups are used for archival purposes only and aren't intended to restore a system to order. I've also seen people discover — too late — that their backup tapes were useless because of some corrupted data in the backup directories. You have to test your backups occasionally to make sure they are intact.

Backing up systems is like flossing your teeth: Everyone knows it should be done frequently and thoroughly, but few people do it often and even fewer people do it properly.

Hundreds of suppliers of backup solutions are out there, but I can't discuss all of them here. That could take another book! However, there is a method to the backup madness:

- ✔ The first day of every week you should make a *full backup* of your system. This includes every file on every computer.

- ✔ On subsequent days, you should make an *incremental* backup. This will include only files that have changed since the last full backup.

- ✔ Finally, once a month, you should store one of the full backups for archival reasons. This way, if you ever have to resort to restoring your system, you never have to go back further than one week.

One important thing to note is that you should never keep your backup media in the same location as your backup computers. If the location where your computers are suffers a physical disaster, such as a fire or tornado, then you haven't lost the back up tapes as well. If you keep your backups off-site, you'll be able to get back up and running.

Backups don't prevent hacks or intrusions into your network, but they can help you recover in the case of such events. Because Web servers are a common target for vandalism, many people keep a live backup or *mirror* in place just for that eventuality. If your Web site has been damaged, you can easily get the correct version running — that is, after you've fixed whatever problem enabled the intruder to access your system in the first place.

Protect against surges and losses

Protecting against surges and losses goes hand-in-hand with making regular backups. If you live in Lightning Alley, like I do, you'll quickly find that surge protectors and Uninterruptible Power Supplies (UPS) are indispensable. A rule of networking is keeping your system available, so having your network go down can be devastating in certain circumstances.

In any critical system you should have a certain amount of *redundancy* in place in case parts of your system start to fail. This is true in a hack attack or a natural disaster. For example, you can build a copy of your Web site on another machine. Then, if your main Web site suffers mechanical failures or a hack attack, you can unplug the bad one and plug in the redundant one. Your redundancy plan doesn't have to include top-of-the-line equipment. Equipment that you've slated for the dump can often serve you well in an emergency.

On one occasion, a partner's company was switching out their outdated system for a brand new installation. They physically took all the old computers out to the loading dock before firing up the new system. The new system had been extensively tested in the lab and everything had worked beautifully. Wouldn't you know it though, the entire system failed as soon as the new system was turned on at its new location. And all the computers that still worked were sitting hundreds of yards away. Not total disaster, but it was panic time in any case!

Know who you trust

Of course, you should know who is working with you in the office, but what about others on downline connections? Those are connections that go beyond the confines of your network to business partners or clients. Have you set up your computers to trust computers in other companies so that you can share data? Are you sure you have their IP addresses correct? Do you have a limit on the number of other networks you trust? Do you know who is remotely logging in to your network — if you allow such access? There are files on your network that list trusted connections. Make sure the addresses of those networks is correct. Also make sure that your firewalls and routers have the correct address information about your trusted connections. You should review all this information regularly to make sure there haven't been any mistakes made and that all the information is up to date and accurate. If you have terminated an agreement with another network, make sure that information is deleted as soon as possible and that all connections from that network will be blocked.

Physical access is also a concern. Can just anyone walk into your office? Are files left out in the open and computers left on at night? Do you think that the janitorial staff is above taking a peak at your data now and then? It's important that you have policies and procedures to handle visitors to your office. Sometimes it's a good idea to make sure that visitors have badges and have to be accompanied by an escort while they are on your property. If your employees regularly print hard copies of sensitive information — such as financial data — make sure that the printouts aren't left out in the open for prying eyes.

One last thought. What do you throw away in the trash cans? Are you sure you aren't throwing away paperwork with peoples' personal data? You could be breaking the law if you aren't protecting personal information about your employees. Take a look at what people are throwing away in their trash bins and you may be surprised at what you find. If you find that sensitive or otherwise important information is appearing regularly, you will need to set a policy that instructs all employees to either shred their papers or destroy them in some other manner. You don't want this information to fall into the wrong hands.

Hackers are known to engage in an activity known as *dumpster diving*. Hackers physically rummage through trash dumpsters looking for personnel files, network files, and anything else they can get their hands on — and use to hack their way into networks. Don't trust sensitive files to the trash. Shred them.

Chapter 2

Evaluating and Documenting Your Network Situation

In This Chapter

▶ Surveying your security

▶ Controlling locks and keys

▶ Keeping acccss under control

▶ Conducting interviews to gather information

▶ Considering the commonly overlooked assets

▶ Following the assessment cycle

▶ Documenting what you have

---

*B*efore you can start implementing network security, you have to know what you've got and what you're going to do with it. It's a bit like planning to landscape a new garden — what kind of soil do you have, how much space do you have to deal with, what plants do you already have, and what sort of new plants will do well in your climate? Like planting a garden, it's going to mean crawling around on your hands and knees a lot! You'll be looking under desks, behind computers, and making lots of lists. I've made most of this chapter in the form of a table with checklists to help you on your way. Feel free to adjust these checklists to suit your needs.

The Hands-On/On-Knees Network Security Survey

You can't protect what you can't count. Get ready to get out your flashlight and your clipboard and start filling out the checklist shown in Table 2-1.

These lists are also useful when it comes time to set up a journal in which you keep notes of changes made to hardware and software.

The hardware checklist

Table 2-1	Network Security Hardware Checklist		
Hardware	*Number of Items*	*Type*	*Password Protected? (Y/N)*
Dial-up modem			
Cable modem			
DSL modem			
Network interface card			
Workstations			
Notebooks/laptops			
File server			
Application server			
Mail server			
Web server			
Database server			
DNS server			
Firewall			
Intrusion detection			
Router			
Print Server			
Fax Server			
Employees' personal property			

Completing the hardware checklist

Following is some extra information to help you fill out the hardware checklist.

> ✓ **Dial-up modems:** List all dial-up modems you find in your office — the type and how many. You may find that some employees have brought in personal modems from home so they can dial up for their personal e-mail or so they can dial up the office from home.

Dial-up modems can introduce security vulnerabilities, especially if they are set up to answer incoming calls.

✔ **Cable modems:** Chances are that because cable modems make use of television cable service, you're not going to find any of these in an office — but it's not unheard of. Be sure to make note of the make and model as this makes a difference in the securing of these modems.

✔ **Digital Subscriber Line (DSL) modems:** Like dial-up modems, these use regular phone lines for hook up. Be sure to note the location of these and the make and model.

✔ **Network Interface Card (NIC):** You're not going to see this on the outside of the computer because it's located inside. You will see an RJ-45 plug stuck into the back of the box, however. The RJ-45 looks a lot like a phone jack, but the plug is fatter. The other end of the cable likely plugs into a wall outlet that looks like a phone jack, too.

✔ **Workstations:** These are the individual computers in people's offices or cubicles, another good place to look for modems or other Internet connections. (And while you're at it, make sure that a person's logon and password are not taped to the computer or under the keyboard.)

✔ **Notebooks/laptops:** These may be either corporate-owned or personally-owned computers. If they are corporate-owned, they should have identifying stickers or inventory tags on them to help identify them if they end up missing. If the notebooks/laptops are personally owned, the owner should have a written agreement with the company concerning their use. See Chapter 4 for more information.

✔ **File server:** Servers are usually stored in a central location with all the other servers. It's simply a computer that stores files that are to be shared with numerous users. Be sure to itemize what types of files are stored on this computer.

✔ **Application server:** Instead of storing files for shared use, an application server usually stores a program to be used by numerous users.

✔ **Mail server:** This computer is probably on its own somewhere in a closet or a server room and is the computer that handles all the e-mail for the company. Find out what sort of computer it is, and you'll also need to know its operating system and mail server software for the next checklist.

✔ **Web server:** This is the computer that displays the company's Web site to the outside world. Don't worry if you can't find a Web server — many companies have a Web-hosting company to host their Web site or a co-location provider to house their computers for them at an external site. Also make note of the operating system and the application software as well as anything else you have running on this computer.

✔ **Database server:** This computer can be anything from a single box running MS SQL to a number of huge computers running Oracle. Databases are often the heart of a company's operations and can contain personnel records, financial data, and customer files. Often these computers are kept separate from the rest of the company's computers — either in a closet or a dedicated server room. You'll need to know what operating system the server is running as well as which database application it contains.

✔ **Domain Name Server (DNS) server:** If your Internet Service Provider (ISP) is controlling your domain naming, you probably won't have a DNS server in your office. However, if your office has lots of computers on the network, you probably have one. This server converts domain names (such as "dummies.com") into IP addresses of individual computers.

✔ **Firewall:** This is usually a dedicated computer that is placed at the entry point of the Internet connection into the company. In this case, I'm referring to a software firewall and not a router. If this computer is not dedicated to the singular job of firewalling, it should be. Make note of the operating system and the firewall software, too. (There's much more on firewalls and routers and their differences in Chapter 9.)

✔ **Intrusion Detection System (IDS):** This computer is very similar to a firewall in some respects. The difference is that it is not meant to keep intruders out, but to warn you when intrusions are detected. This, too, should be a stand-alone computer. It is frequently monitored by another computer workstation somewhere in the office. More on IDS is in Chapter 10.

✔ **Router:** This is a box with lots of blinking lights that looks like it belongs in a science fiction movie. It can be large or small and is located at the entry point of your Internet connection, usually after the firewall. A router decides which way to send traffic much in the same way a railway terminal works. If one section is congested, it sends the traffic along a better route.

Routers are a frequent entry point for hackers who know how to fool them. See Chapter 9 for more about routers.

✔ **Print server:** This computer is used when there are a lot of network users and only a few printers. The print jobs are all sent to this computer and are printed out in a queue — generally in the order they are sent. This is not a huge network vulnerability, but I've included it to be thorough.

✔ **Fax server:** Similar to the print server, some fax servers are connected by modems to the phone line and also have network cards to connect to the rest of the network. Check the cables in the back of the machine to determine your set-up.

✓ **Employee equipment:** This is a very sticky area. If employees are allowed to bring their own equipment into the office, then their usage should have a written agreement and the equipment should be tagged. You don't want battles over equipment if something should happen to the original owner. You also don't want this equipment to be your weak link in the security chain.

The software checklist

Software is an all-important part of your network and should be checked and controlled. It's very easy to lose track of what software you have, especially when you have a number of different versions of the same software. If your employees have brought in their own software from home, this should be included in your list. (I cover employee agreements later on in this chapter.) Use Table 2-2 to track your software.

Table 2-2	Network Security Software Checklist		
Software	*Number of Copies*	*Version*	*Licensed? (Y/N)*
Operating System #1			
Operating System #2			
Operating System #3			
Operating System #4			
Mail			
Web			
Database			
Word Processing			
Spreadsheet			
Presentation			
Graphics			
Firewall			
Intrusion Detection			
Anti-Virus			
Other			

Completing the software checklist

Following is a list of some additional data in helping you fill out the software checklist. Note that on this checklist there is a column for the software license.

If you do not have the correct number of licenses for the number of applications you have, you are in violation of software copyright laws. Be aware of this as companies are audited and assessed huge fines for being out of compliance. If you are not sure about your licenses, talk to your software vendor.

- **Operating Systems (OSs):** The reason I included a number of lines for operating systems is that most networks have more than just one type. A typical corporate network uses Windows for its workstations and various flavors of Unix for its servers, but there are many Windows servers in use, too. Each computer's operating system should be noted and for security's sake, the versions should be standardized. This makes it much easier to apply security patches and upgrades when they become available. When OSs are changed or upgraded, notes should be made for future reference.

- **Mail server software:** Listing the various software packages for e-mail would be of use — during my last count, I found more than thirty different types! However, no matter which one you use, make sure that it is reputable and has available support. That support will come in handy if and when security vulnerabilities are found. Different mail servers operate on different operating systems, so you'll need to take that into account as well.

- **Web server software:** Just about every major software company has its own version of Web software. Even computers that are not considered Web servers can have a version running. For example, Oracle database software and DSL modems have Web servers running so those machines can be configured from another location. Web servers run on port 80 or port 8080, so you may need to do a port scan of your network to determine if you have any unauthorized Web servers up and running. You should disable Web servers that aren't needed. Because Web servers open big security holes in all networks, this is very important.

- **DNS server software:** There aren't as many DNS server software packages as there are mail servers, but there are still quite a few. Be aware if you are running BIND (which is a particular version of DNS) as that has been running high on the list of vulnerable programs.

- **Word processing applications:** Although this is usually bundled with other office products, I've listed it separately because it, too, has a number of vulnerabilities. This product needs to be patched just like any of the others. When Microsoft introduced the macro scripting language, it allowed office programs to interchange data automatically and seamlessly. They can even open other programs without the user's consent. A number of recent worms and viruses have taken advantage of these vulnerabilities. To date, only Microsoft products have been at risk, but that's not to say that other word processing programs might fall victim some day.

✓ **Spreadsheet applications:** If your spreadsheet can run macro programs, then it can be vulnerable to malicious code. Like the word processing programs, security patches should be applied.

✓ **Presentation/graphics applications:** Just recently I heard of a "proof of concept" virus that put a virus in a picture. (Proof of concept means that it can be done but isn't in common usage yet.) While there are no viruses that use pictures to infect computers yet, it seems like it's only a matter of time. I'm sure that anti-virus vendors will release updates to catch these viruses when the need arises. In the meantime, keep a list of the types of programs you use and their version numbers.

✓ **Firewall software:** Unlike a router used as a firewall, this computer is dedicated to detecting and preventing unauthorized entry into the network. Generally, the computer runs just an operating system and the firewall software. It's extremely important to keep this computer up to date with upgrades and patches, and it will frequently have strong vendor support. Any problems with the software should be reported to the administrator immediately.

✓ **Intrusion Detection System (IDS):** Like the firewall, this computer usually runs an operating system and the IDS software. It is also particularly important to keep this machine up to date.

✓ **Anti-virus software:** My favorite piece of security software! Nearly 96 percent of all attacks in 2001 involved at least one virus attack, according to the FBI. A/V software is in need of almost constant upgrading. I recommend at least once a week for the dat files and once a month for the scanning engines. Make sure you choose a reputable and certified vendor.

✓ **Application development programs:** Used to write programs. I'm talking about C++, Perl, and similar programs. If you have personnel who are writing programs for your company, it's important that they all use the same version and that they know how to write secure code. Writing secure code is beyond the scope of this book, but there are plenty of references available on the Internet.

Checking the Locks and Keys

Part of protecting your network involves knowing where everything is but also who can access the hardware and software and who controls the access. It's not unknown for equipment to "grow legs" and simply walk off the premises without anyone realizing it. What follows are some more items to add to your checklists.

✔ **Do your workstations have removable hard disks?** It's easy for someone to steal removable hard drives, which may contain important data. Hard drives should have hardware locks, and these locks should be controlled by a central authority.

✔ **Can the computer cases be opened without a key?** Random Access Memory (RAM) is a valuable asset and should be protected. It's usually very easy to open a box and steal the RAM and other chips and components from a workstation or server.

✔ **Do all pieces of equipment have inventory control labels?** This is a must to control theft of property. Don't forget to include such items as computer speakers and microphones.

✔ **Are the servers in a locked room?** It doesn't have to be a large room. Even if you only have one server, it needs to be protected so that access is limited to only those who have a defined need. This is not only to prevent theft of equipment, but also to prevent unauthorized changes to the configurations of the server(s).

✔ **Do all employees have IDs?** If you have a small office, you probably know everyone by sight and don't really need everyone to wear their ID tags. However, in offices with more than about ten people, I would strongly encourage the wearing of ID tags. The ID tags should also be color coded to indicate which areas they are allowed to enter. Visitors and repair personnel should have visitor tags and should not be allowed to roam around unescorted.

✔ **Is after-hours access controlled?** Do you have a guard who logs personnel who enter and exit after hours? What about your offices and server rooms? Are they all locked after hours? You need to have controls for logging access not only to prevent theft, but also to eliminate people as suspects if something goes missing at night or on the weekends. If you have a small office and an employee needs to go in after hours, that person should notify a superior prior to entering the office.

✔ **Who controls the keys?** I know of many offices that control the keys by putting them all in the manager's desk. Of course, the office and the desk are not locked, so anyone can get to the keys. All keys need to be labeled and their distribution kept in a log. Keys that aren't needed every day should be kept in a key locker or other safe environment.

✔ **Where are the back-up tapes kept?** If they are stored on top of the back-up computer, you're not following one of the tenets of safe computing. All back-up tapes should be labeled and locked away. Archived tapes should be kept off premises. I know of many companies who keep their archived tapes in bank safe deposit boxes. That solution is good because the bank keeps a record of all persons accessing the box.

✔ **Do you have security cameras in sensitive areas?** It's not a must, but it is something you should consider if you have the budget for it. Security cameras are good at deterring theft, and they keep a record of the comings and goings of staff.

Logical Access Controls

In addition to the physical access issues, the access to the computer systems also needs to be investigated.

Table 2-3 deals mainly with how your employees use their workstations. Because the major protection scheme for all workstations is the password protection, the majority of the questions here deal with passwords.

Table 2-3	Logical Access
Question	*Yes/No Answer*
Do all users have unique User IDs?	
Do all users have unique passwords?	
Are the screensaver locks enabled for all users?	
Are all users required to lock their screens when away from the desk?	
Do the screensavers automatically lock after a certain period of inactivity?	
Are users required to log out when away for a certain period?	
Do users log out at the end of the day?	
Are users allowed to share passwords?	
Are desks checked for written passwords?	
Does the system prevent a User ID from being used as a password?	
Are passwords required to be at least 8 characters long and to include upper- and lowercase letters, numbers, and special characters?	
Are passwords required to be changed every three to four months?	
Are passwords prevented from being reused for at least one year?	
Are administrative passwords kept in a locked file?	
Have all default passwords been changed?	

(continued)

Table 2-3 *(continued)*

Question	Yes/No Answer
Have all "guest" accounts been disabled?	
Have all administrative passwords been changed from the default?	
Are accounts allowed to have a null (blank) password?	
Are accounts locked out after a certain number of unsuccessful password attempts?	
Are unsuccessful password attempts sent to administrators in the form of an alert?	
Are system logs regularly reviewed?	
Can users request that new accounts be set up?	
Are controls in place for deleting user accounts?	
Are all removable media required to be labeled?	
Are confidential or proprietary printouts required to be labeled as such?	

Personnel Interviews

How your personnel perceive security is very important as to how well your security program is going to work. Conduct interviews with all your employees, regardless of position, from management to part-time, casual staff. Explain why you are conducting the interviews and that none of their answers will be held against them. This is their chance to be brutally honest without fear of attribution or retribution. Of course, after you have made these promises, you have to stick to them! Another method of conducting interviews is to use anonymous surveys. Many employees will be brutally honest when answering an anonymous survey whereas they feel intimidated by face-to-face encounters.

If your employees don't understand the need for security or how the security program works, they will do their best — even if unintentionally — to undermine your efforts. This is not because they are malicious; it's because security is usually seen as an inconvenience and a burden. If you ask for their help, they will usually give it to you. Listen to them, too. Very often they will be a source of good ideas.

Here is a list of some of the issues that should be covered in the interview:

- Is the employee aware of any existing security rules or policies?
- What are those policies?
- What is the employee's attitude towards security in general?
- What is the employee's attitude towards specific policies?
- Is the employee aware of any areas of vulnerability that need addressing?
- Does the employee know what to do if there is a security breach of any kind?
- Who does the employee think is in charge of security?
- Does the employee respect this person?
- What is the employee's workload like?
- Docs the employee feel that the present workload prevents him/her from following the security policies?

Assets You May Not Have Considered

How many floppy disks, CD ROMs, and other removable media do you have laying about the office. Do you know what is on every piece of this media? Although it may seem like a small thing, you'd be surprised at the amount of important data that is stored in such a manner. A lot of this data may be redundant to what is already stored on workstations and servers, but it still has value.

You should gather up all miscellaneous disks and check them out. Be prepared to find illegal software and other materials that you may not want to be in your office. If the disks belong to an employee, give them back and tell the employee to take them home and not to bring them in again. If they remain a few days later, physically destroy them. It's your office and you have a right to control what lives there!

If the data on the disks is important, treat it as such. All disks should be clearly labeled and stored appropriately.

The Assessment Cycle

You're not finished! Network security assessment is a beginning but it's never the end. But, you're on a good road and one that has been successfully traveled by many companies who have secured their systems. The network security assessment takes a look at where you are, where you need to be, and helps you determine what you need to do to get to the next step.

The steps towards total network security are as follows:

1. **Assessment.** Where you are and where you are heading (and what we've been doing so far).

2. **Policies.** Based on your findings, develop your policies and plans. The policies don't have to be perfect the first time around, but you do have to start somewhere. Your policies should be a "living document," meaning that they change as situations or requirements change.

3. **Implementation.** You've got your policies and plans, and now you have to put them into action. Again, this doesn't have to be perfect the first time around, but care should be taken so that you don't have to backtrack too often.

4. **Training.** Tell everyone what you're doing and why. Half the battle is getting people to go along with you. If they understand the how and why, they are more apt to follow the plans you've set.

5. **Auditing.** Check that everything is being done by the rules. Check the audit logs on the computers and ask questions of employees. Watch what people are doing. At this point you'll probably notice that some things need to be changed, and that brings you back to Step 1.

6. **Start from Step 1 again.** Chances are you'll have to go through this exercise once or twice to get everything working.

Document What You've Got

I can't emphasize this enough. We are human beings, and we keep far too much information in our heads. Our intentions are good and we keep meaning to write things down, but we never get around to it. Even if your documentation consists of sticky notes stuck in a notebook, prepare a central log and stick with it. You can always make it "pretty" later. The point is to get as much in writing as soon as possible.

Licenses and agreements

Software licenses are very important because you don't want to fall foul of the law. If you are ever audited, and companies frequently are, it helps to have all of your licenses in order. An easy way to accomplish this is to have a filing cabinet dedicated for this use. Create a folder for each piece of software owned and keep the licenses and agreements in the folder.

Who owns what

Sometimes one department has bought equipment or software out of their own budget rather than a general IT budget. If this is the case in your organization, it's best to keep these things in writing.

Do an equipment and software inventory and mark all physical equipment appropriately.

Employees' personal equipment should be marked separately from the corporate equipment.

Do you lease any computers or software? Be sure to keep these records on hand. They are very helpful when the lease expires.

If you have agreements on your hardware, it's best to keep those agreements in a central location as well. Hardware is always prone to failure and the rep who sold you the equipment may not be around when you have to deal with the vendor. If you have your agreements in order, it saves much time and energy when something needs to be fixed. Frequently these agreements cover such items as shipping costs and temporary replacements.

Employees' personal property

This can be a very sticky issue, and I would advise against letting employees use their own property at the office. If an item has been brought in from home by an employee, make out an agreement with the employee and keep it on file. The agreement should spell out under what circumstances the employee is allowed to keep the equipment at the office and who is liable if the equipment is lost, stolen, or broken. The liability clause should also say whether replacements are based on replacement costs or depreciated value.

More and more employers are giving their employees loans to purchase equipment for company use. You may want to have an attorney draw up these agreements. You need to cover such issues as:

- How is the loan repaid if an amount is outstanding upon termination?
- Can the employee keep the equipment if employment is terminated?
- Can the employee use the equipment for personal use?
- Who owns the data on the equipment?
- Who pays for repairs and upgrades?

Software is another issue altogether. If an employee brings in software from home for the company to use, the employee must sign over the license and all rights to the company. In other words, the employee no longer owns the software if the company uses it. That's the vendor's rules. Stay away from this practice of using an employee's software.

Chapter 3

Assessing the Risks

*W*hether you realize it or not, you take risks every day, and you do so with little or no conscious effort. For example, if you get in your car and drive to the store, you have unconsciously assessed the risk of injury or damage to you or your car. In all likelihood, you determined that the risk was low or manageable and drove away. Somewhere in your life as a driver, you learned to recognize the risks of operating a vehicle and how to manage them. Now you have to learn how to do the same for your computer and your network. It is important that you do a risk assessment, or you may end up operating under a false sense of security.

Doing a risk assessment is a bit like setting up an insurance plan. You list all your assets, figure out what those assets are worth and how much it would cost to replace them, and then decide how they need to be protected and how much that protection is going to cost. If you find that the protection costs more than the asset is worth, then you'll have to justify the expense of the protection or decide to do without it. You don't necessarily need to spend the money if you're not going to receive any benefit from it. For example, say you have Web server that runs on older equipment, doesn't contain elaborate content, does not gather customer data, and has no connections to the internal network. It's just a type of "cyber brochure" for the corporation. In this case the dollar value of the Web server is minimal and it probably wouldn't make sense to spend a lot of money on a firewall to protect it because it would be cheaper to simply rebuild or replace the Web server.

In this chapter, I show you how to interpret the risks and make a good evaluation of which ones apply to you and your situation. I also show you how to get a rough estimate of the dollar amount that damages and countermeasures will cost.

Risk Assessment Basics

You should do a complete risk assessment once a year or whenever major changes are made in your network or your assets. Basically, a risk assessment forces you to look at what you have to lose if the worst happens and all is lost.

Before you can start on your assessment, you first need to list all your assets and assign a dollar amount to them. The dollar amount should take into consideration not just the replacement cost, but also the loss of productivity, the man-hours required for repair, and any data that is lost or corrupted. Your assets are not just the hardware and software. You also have the time invested in creating data, your customers, your building and contents, and the value of your reputation. The following are some of the things that should be taken into consideration when assigning these values:

✔ The original cost of the asset

✔ The replacement cost if the asset is lost or damaged

✔ The value of intellectual property

✔ The value of lost productivity in man-hours and income

✔ Maintenance costs

✔ Liability costs if personal data is compromised

Some assets are a bit harder to give a hard value to. For example, customer confidence is a bit of an intangible. If your network were to experience a full outage for a day, that would undermine customer confidence in your ability to serve them. I've found that the best way to evaluate intangibles such as this is to go to the accounting department and get the figures for the average yearly sales per customer. Also, get the number of customers from the department.

As an example, say that each customer is worth $400.00 in annual sales and you have 1,000 customers. That makes your customer base worth $400,000.00 per year — or about $1,095.00 per day.

You can probably think of a lot more of these. Take a hard look at what you have and what you have to lose if the worst should happen and have fun playing with the numbers. The results may surprise you!

In a nutshell, a complete risk assessment consists of the following steps:

1. Decide what you are protecting. These are your assets. Include intangibles such as your reputation and customer confidence.

2. Assign a dollar value to your assets.

3. Examine the threats to your assets and your vulnerabilities to those threats.

4. Determine the cost of losses on an annual basis. This will be a prorated figure.

5. Determine the cost of protection and countermeasures against loss.

6. Do a cost/benefit analysis to decide if the protection or countermeasures are a good investment.

7. Start over from Step 1 on an annual basis or whenever you have a major change in your assets.

Vulnerabilities + Threats = Risks

I see the preceding terms used interchangeably in magazine and newspaper articles but at least in the world of computer security, they have distinct differences. A *threat* is a danger or something that can go wrong and the *vulnerability* is something that makes you more exposed to the threat. (If you think of vulnerability as a weakness, it may help you to keep the terms straight.) Marry the two terms and the result is the total *risk*.

For example, a threat to a wooden garage is fire. If you keep oily rags in a cardboard box on hot summer days, you increase your vulnerability to the threat of fire. Therefore, your garage is at high risk of catching on fire. Similarly, a common threat to networks is virus infections. If you have no antivirus software installed, you are more vulnerable to infection and the risk of damage to your system is high. The key to good network security is to either eliminate your vulnerability or employ protection mechanisms to reduce your vulnerabilities. This is called *risk management*.

Most people think of hacking attacks as the only threat to network security. Have you considered natural threats such as fire, storms, and earthquakes? There are also physical threats such as unauthorized access to your building or theft of equipment. Human error is also a threat because untrained staff can inadvertently cause damage. When you sit down and think about it, there are many things that can go wrong other than hack attacks.

Table 3-1 lists some threats and the associated vulnerabilities you need to consider when starting your risk assessment.

Table 3-1	Threats and Associated Vulnerabilities
Threats	*Vulnerabilities*
Fire	No fire suppression system in building
	Flammable material stored in hot area
	Lack of fire extinguishers in offices
	Building far away from local fire department
Water	Building located in flood-prone area
	Water sprinklers in rooms where electrical systems are stored (instead of chemical fire suppression)
Earthquake	Building located in earthquake prone area
Tornadoes and hurricanes	Building located in area prone to extreme storms
	Lack of protective covers for large windows
Electrical damage to equipment	Lack of surge suppressing equipment
Theft of equipment	No building security
	Unlocked doors
	Access to areas not controlled by badges, coded door locks, keys
	Equipment stored in open areas
	Lack of inventory control (meaning you won't know when and if something has been stolen)
Theft or damage of computer data and/or software (hacks and malicious code attacks)	Lack of access controls to network
	No firewall
	Uncontrolled modems connected to network
	No intrusion detection software to give alarms
	Access logs not monitored for access (meaning you won't know if and when something has been stolen)

Threats	Vulnerabilities
	No locks on hard drives to make sure they stay in the computer
	Security patches not applied to computers
	Operating systems not hardened against attacks
	Unnecessary ports open on network, which can allow unauthorized access
	Not knowing who is accessing your network or why they are doing it
	Not reviewing logs to determine if there is any unusual activity
	No security policies as to what people are allowed to do (if people don't know the rules, they won't be able to follow them)
	No anti-virus software — or no updates installed to antivirus software
	Uncontrolled use of floppy disks (a person could walk out the door with files in his pocket)
	Unlocked server rooms
	Back-up tapes left sitting in the open
	Insecure passwords or passwords written down and left out in the open
	Executable files available via download or as attachments to e-mail
Vandalism	Low employee moral
	Unsecured building in high crime area
Human error	Untrained, unskilled employees
	Frequent changes in operations
	High staff turnover
	Lack of written procedures

As you can see, there is a myriad of threats facing even the smallest of networks. However, not all of these threats may be applicable to you or your situation. For example, if you live in Vermont, the likelihood of hurricanes or tornadoes is pretty low, so you won't need extensive protection against these forces.

As to hack attacks, I think it's fair to say that your vulnerability depends on a number of factors. It depends on what you do and what data you store on your network. The size of your network is not necessarily a factor. You can have a very small network with a limited number of employees, but if you are doing contract work for the government, you are more likely to experience an attack than if you only host a high school reunion message board.

The following section looks at some of the factors that may leave you more vulnerable to hack attacks. I'm not putting virus attacks in this category because they are almost a given and can attack all systems, regardless of size or use.

How likely are the threats?

What is your profile on the Internet? Does your site appear at the top of the list in search engines? Do you do a lot of advertising on TV or in magazines? If your site were attacked, would it be a huge embarrassment to you? Do you connect to the Internet through an ISP or do you have a direct connection? These are just some of the questions you need to ask yourself because the answers will likely give you some idea as to how vulnerable you really are. However, this is an educated guess and not a scientific exercise. Things can still go wrong — we're human and can't foresee every eventuality.

Table 3-2 poses some questions to ask yourself about your network. For each "Yes" answer, give yourself one point. The higher the point value at the end of the list, the higher your Internet profile and the more likely you are to be a potential target.

Table 3-2	How High Is Your Internet Profile?
Question	*Yes/No*
Does your company do contract work for the government?	
Does your company have a high-profile Web site? (This could be a Web site that is controversial, is highly advertised and has lots of hits daily, or is a successful e-commerce site.)	
Does your Web site collect personal data and/or credit card numbers?	

Question	Yes/No
Is your network on a direct connection to the Internet that is always "on"?	
Does an ISP remotely host your Web sites? (Be sure you question your ISP about their security practices!)	
Does your Web site connect to a database without a firewall between the two?	
Do you allow modem connections to your network?	
Does your domain name evoke an emotional response or unusual claim? (Such as WeAreSecure.com)	
Do you share your network with other companies?	
Is your network part of a university or college?	
Do you offer online banking services or other financial services?	

✔ 1 or 2 "Yes" answers = Low vulnerability to hacks

✔ 3 or 4 "Yes" answers = Medium vulnerability to hacks

✔ 5 or more "Yes" answers = High vulnerability to hacks

As I mention previously, this is not a scientifically proven formula, but it is based on my years of experience in the field of computer security. Use this table to give you a rough picture or an educated guess.

Figuring out the likelihood of attack is subjective, but there is some hard data to consider. Each year the FBI and the CSI (Computer Security Institute) do a report entitled "Computer Crime and Security Survey." The 2002 report shows that 42 percent of the respondents experienced at least one security related incident and 74 percent of those incidents came through the Internet. Bear in mind that almost all of the respondents had antivirus software and firewalls, too. This is a very interesting and enlightening report, and I would urge you to read it if you get the chance. You can request a copy at www.gocsi.com — click the links to the requests form.

Based on this report, here is a list of the most likely attacks, rated from the most prevalent form of attack to the least:

✔ Virus attack

✔ Insider abuse of Internet access

✔ Laptop theft

✔ Denial of service attack

- Unauthorized access by outsiders (system penetration)
- Unauthorized access by insiders
- Theft of proprietary information
- Financial fraud
- Sabotage
- Eavesdropping (snooping)

Of course, there is a very effective method of determining your vulnerability level to attacks and that is to perform a *penetration test*. A penetration test is usually conducted by professional testers who use software, including hacking tools, to attempt penetration of your network from the outside. When the test is completed, the testers should provide a written report listing the vulnerabilities and the level of risk associated with each. A good test report will also include a list of countermeasures to be employed to either eliminate or reduce the risk. Remember, however, that changes in your network configuration can change the results of a penetration test. Therefore, the results of a penetration test are only reliable for a short period of time after the test was completed. If you make changes to your system to alter your vulnerabilities found by a test, you should run the test again to make sure that the changes have worked and that you haven't introduced other vulnerabilities as a result of your changes.

Non-professionals should never attempt penetration tests with hacking tools. You can seriously damage your network if the tests are not conducted properly. Even the professionals run into problems sometimes. Therefore, it's also important to have a written agreement with the testers that spells out the parameters of the tests and responsibilities if damage should occur.

When you are ready to assess your risk level, Figure 3-1 helps you in determining your level of risk. You should use this graph to plot the risk level for each asset to help you to decide what need protecting. As you can see, if you have a low level of threat but a high level of vulnerability, you have a medium level of risk.

How often can threats occur and what will it cost me?

Bad things happen and sometimes there's not anything you can do to stop them. The best you can do is try to guess how often it may happen and then place dollar amounts on what you could lose if bad things occur. There's an entire industry based on these guesses and it's called the insurance industry. By taking a cue from insurance companies, we can use some of their formulas to extract dollar figures. These dollar amounts may open your eyes.

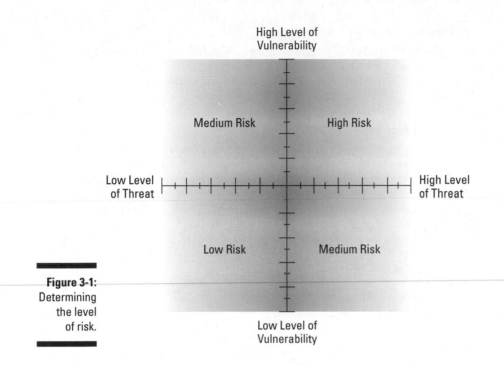

Figure 3-1:
Determining
the level
of risk.

Annualized rate of occurrence

There are some things that are fairly easy to put a number to and others aren't so cut and dried. For example, if you live in Florida, the likelihood that you will experience a devastating hurricane is once every 30 years. In risk assessment, you use an *annualized rate of occurrence* (ARO). This value represents the estimated number of times something will happen within a one-year time span. In the example of a major hurricane, the ARO is .03 times per year (one year divided by 30 equals .03). If this were to happen every year, your ARO would be 1.0 and if it happened 5 times a year, the ARO would be 5.0. (If something happens more than once a year, you multiply that number times one year rather than divide it.)

The ARO for the threats shown in Table 3-1 varies from company to company. It depends on the safeguards you already have in place and the exposure level shown in Table 3-2. Again, these figures are subjective and they change from year to year. Your best bet is to refer to reports such as the FBI/CSI survey (available at `www.gocsi.com/forms/fbi/pdf.html`) to give you some indication as to the prevalence of attacks. It's probably a good bet that you will experience one or more virus infections a year.

After you have your ARO, multiply the value of the asset by that number to give you the amount you could lose per year without protection. If your building is valued at $90,000.00 and you live in a hurricane zone, then the result of your ARO would be $2,700.00 per year.

Exposure factor

The next item to look at is your *exposure factor* (EF). The exposure factor is the percentage of loss that would occur if you experience an attack. If you estimated that an attack would affect half of your network, your EF would be 50 percent.

Annualized loss expectancy

Now that you have a rough idea of how often an attack might occur and what each occurrence will cost you in losses, you can move on to calculate your *annualized loss expectancy* (ALE). This formula gives you a dollar amount of the losses you can expect per year, per asset, per threat. When you add up all the potential losses, then you have a good idea of your financial standings. This figure also helps you determine how much, if any, you should spend on countermeasures to prevent or reduce your risk.

The formula for this is (result of ARO) x (EF) = ALE

I'll use the example of hurricane damage to illustrate. The ARO is ($90,000.00 x .03) and the EF is 75 percent of the building:

$2,700 x .75 = $2,025.00

Now you have a figure to play with. If you spend less than $2,025.00 per year on hurricane shutters and storm insurance, you're ahead of the game!

Now that we have the basic formulas to look at, let's look at how you would put them together for a risk analysis spreadsheet (see Figure 3-2).

The cost of countermeasures

After you have completed your risk assessment spreadsheet, you will have a rough idea of what your annual security budget should be. You'll need to add the cost of salaries for security-related positions and the cost of security training as well. I know it will look like a huge number and, believe me, most companies do not even come close to spending that figure. That's because few companies can see the return on investment and security does not generate any income — it's pure outgo. I read a report in the *Washington Post* a few years ago that stated that companies spend more each year on their coffee service than they do on security!

To determine how much you should spend on security requires a *cost/benefits analysis,* which is not hard to do at all. Simply look at each of the figures on your spreadsheet and then research the costs of protections or countermeasures. For example, say that the cost of a sophisticated firewall costs $20,000.00. (And yes, they can cost that and more!) Your spreadsheet shows that your annual loss from data theft could be $80,000.00. In this case, the cost of the protection is far less than the potential loss, so, as Martha Stewart says, "This is a good thing." A cost/benefit analysis report is effective in getting upper management to approve your security budget.

Remember that the benefits of adding security aren't just in the reduction of risks. Adding security to your system may allow your organization to benefit through an increase in ability to serve your customers. For example, you may be able to take credit card orders online and provide secure online ordering. The benefits of your increased capabilities need to be considered in doing your cost/benefits analysis.

It's going to take a fair amount of research on your part to come up with the exact prices for your countermeasures because there are so many different products and services and each company needs to customize security to meet their own needs. There is no such thing as "one size fits all" in network security. Some countermeasures won't cost you anything except your time (such as installing security patches). In most cases, you should contact the vendor to negotiate prices, especially if you have a medium to large network. The vendors are happy to have your business and you shouldn't feel intimidated by asking for a special deal. Ask about a "site license," which is, in essence, a volume discount.

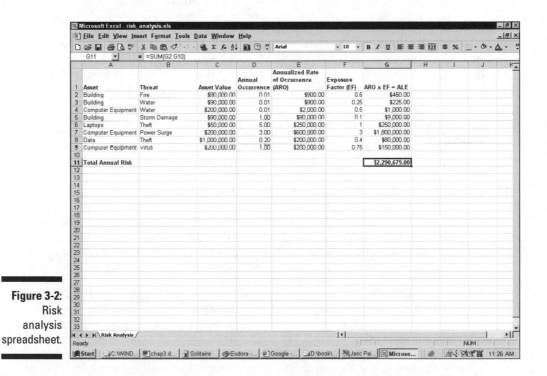

Figure 3-2:
Risk
analysis
spreadsheet.

Risk Mitigation versus Risk Avoidance

The simple definition for risk mitigation is prevention. You want to prevent bad things from happening if at all possible. The countermeasures and protections you put in place are the way you mitigate and manage your risk. There are three reasons for employing risk mitigation:

1. The cost of the prevention or countermeasure is trivial or non-existent.

2. Mitigation is required by law. (Such as protecting social security numbers from release.)

3. The company can't afford the loss or destruction of a particular asset.

There are some trade-offs in security, however. Generally, a highly secure network is going to be costly to implement and maintain, and your users may have to endure decreased functionality or inconveniences. This may be required if you are running a top secret network, but usually a company makes a decision to reduce the level of some security measures in favor of speed and ease of use.

An example of this is the encryption of all the information in a database. Whenever the records in the database are retrieved, the process of decrypting the data takes a lot of processing power and it creates a delay in the amount of time it takes before the operator sees the result of the request. This delay may frustrate the database operator and make him or her think there is something "wrong" with the database because it takes so much time to pull up the information. Is it more important to protect the data with encryption or is it more important that the database operators be able to work quickly?

You have to make these determinations for yourself. No network can be completely secure, but you must decide when your security is "good enough." The more experience you have, the easier this becomes. Keep abreast of new products and new threats when deciding to change your countermeasures.

Education of your users is key in maintaining your protections as well. If your users understand why protection is needed and how it works, they will work with you instead of against you. I know of plenty of instances where users managed to disable anti-virus scanners on their machines because they didn't understand the importance of the protection. They didn't realize that an infection on their machine could spread through the entire network.

If risk mitigation is like establishing a fortress against the enemy, risk avoidance is like deciding not to go into battle at all. In some instances, this may be a preferable choice. For example, if your company has a Web site just for the sake of it — the site doesn't generate any income and isn't updated very often — then why have one? Web servers introduce many vulnerabilities to your network and if you don't really need one, you can avoid the risk by not having one. Simple, huh?

Chapter 4

Planning and Implementing Security Policies and Procedures

. . . .

In This Chapter

▶ Deciding what policies need to be written

▶ Creating good policies

▶ Sample policies

▶ Putting the policy team together

▶ Implementing policies

▶ Using education

. . . .

Simply put, security *policies* are the rules that everyone must follow and the *procedures* are how the rules will be put into place and enforced. One does little good without the other. Security policies and procedures define the who, what, when, where, and how of your security mechanisms:

✔ Who is responsible?

✔ Who needs access?

✔ What needs to be done?

✔ When do the policies apply?

✔ Where are there dangers?

✔ How are policies implemented and enforced?

Policies don't need to be a complex manual full of legalese and incomprehensible language. In fact, they need to be kept as simple as possible so people can understand them. Often a simple one page memo will suffice for each policy. The same goes for procedures. The important thing is to keep all the policies and procedures organized and in one place, which goes a long way in reducing the risk of sending out redundant or conflicting policies. Remember that all policies should be "living" documents — meaning that they adapt to changes.

In this chapter, I tell you how to write policies that work and are accepted by management and staff alike. I also discuss some particular policies and provide you with some simple examples. Last, but not least, I discuss your implementation of the policies.

Deciding on the Security Policies

Decisions. Decisions. Decisions. There's no getting around it, planning and implementing security is full of important decisions to make. Just putting firewalls and anti-virus programs in place is not enough. You also have to decide how the protection mechanisms are going to be configured, who's responsible for maintenance, and how and when the users should report violations. That's just a few of the decisions you have to make. The good news is that you don't have to make them all at once. You should do as many as possible during the first pass, but you can always change policies and add more later as the need arises.

Make the policy reasonable

Remember that you are dealing with human beings, and in general we hate to be told what to do. You have to make the policies fit with human behavior and attitudes. If your policies are unreasonable, you will be met with resistance every step of the way. That's because unreasonable policies make everyone's job harder. Here are some examples of the same policy — you decide which is reasonable and which is not:

> *All staff must change their passwords weekly. Each password shall consist of at least 12 characters and must include upper- and lowercase letters and at least two non-sequential numbers and special characters.*

> *All staff must change their passwords once every six months. Each password shall consist of at least eight characters and must include both upper- and lowercase letters and a number or special character.*

I think you'll agree that the first policy is a bit too much to bear. The second policy, although strict, is much easier to follow.

Here are two other examples for you to consider:

> *All staff must shut down there computers whenever they will be away from their desks for longer than 15 minutes.*

> *All staff must activate their password-protected screen saver whenever they will be away from their desks for longer than 15 minutes.*

Again, the second policy is more likely to have followers and is easier to enforce than the first policy.

Make the policy enforceable

We've all heard funny tales of stupid laws that are nearly impossible to enforce. For example, in Indiana there is a law on the books that makes it unlawful to bathe during the winter. Not only is this law totally ridiculous, but it is unenforceable as well. The police cannot monitor every home during the winter and cite those they find bathing. Even if they could, no court would seem justified in either fining or incarcerating a winter bather!

The same holds true for security policies. If you are going to make a rule, not only do you have to consider whether or not you can actually enforce the rule, but do you have the manpower to enforce the rule and will upper management support it? Common sense should prevail. Take a hard look at your policies. I heard a story of a company in California that uses the "Dilbert Test" for all of their policies. If the policy they want to put in place can be parodied in a Dilbert cartoon, they don't use it. Sounds good to me.

Be consistent

One of the biggest criticisms I hear of security policies is that they are not consistent. Different departments are held to different standards. The biggest culprit is upper management. They often feel they are above the rules or that exceptions should be made according to status. This leads to dissent and the breakdown of the entire process. Good policies apply across the board.

The other problem with policies are contradictions or confusing directives. This is particularly true when changes are made to old policies. If you don't read through the old policies, you may miss these contradictions. A good example is password length. A few years ago, six characters were deemed good enough for a password. Now the prevailing attitude is that eight characters should be implemented. If you cross-reference the policies and note that the new one supercedes the old one, you go a long way in eliminating possible confusions.

Even the best-written security policies are unable to cover every eventuality. You may want to implement a new process that doesn't meet the requirements as defined in the policies. In that case, a waiver must be obtained before the process can be implemented. The process of obtaining a waiver should be included as a policy itself. In any case, if you find you are giving out too many waivers for a particular policy, then it's probably time to change the policy.

Sample Policies

If you do a search on the Web for "security policies", you will be inundated with hits! There is a growing industry to provide businesses with security policy templates. Some of these templates are free and others are bundled with security auditing software. Writing policies is not necessarily hard, but it can be a bit tedious. It's not like writing a best selling thriller! To give you an idea of what policies entail, I'm providing two basic policies that your organization should have.

Appropriate Internet usage

This first policy describes what is considered appropriate use of the Internet while at work. If you have a direct Internet connection for your employees to use, you don't want them using all your time surfing the Net and conducting personal business. However, to deny them all personal access to the Internet is probably unreasonable. Feel free to use this policy as your own and make as many changes as you deem necessary!

Internet Acceptable Use Policy

Overview

All Internet related equipment, including but not limited to computer equipment, software, storage media, electronic mail, and Internet connections are the property of <Company Name> (also referred to as "Company"). These systems are to be used for business purposes and in the course of normal daily operations. It is the Company's best interest to make sure that these resources are protected and used appropriately.

Purpose

The purpose of this policy is to outline the acceptable use of computer equipment for Internet usage at <Company Name>. These rules are in place to protect the users and the Company. Inappropriate use exposes the Company to risks including virus attacks, compromise of network systems and services, and legal issues.

Scope

This policy applies to employees, contractors, consultants, temporaries, and other workers at the Company, including all personnel affiliated with third parties. This policy applies to all equipment that is owned or leased by the Company.

Policy
General Use and Ownership
1. Users should be aware that the data they create on the corporate systems is the property of the Company. Because of the need to protect the Company's network, management cannot guarantee the confidentiality of information stored on any network device belonging to the Company.

2. Employees are expected to use good judgment in their daily use of the network and computer equipment. No restrictions are placed on the use of the internal network. However, Internet usage is restricted to Company-related business such as e-mail and research on the Web. Personal use of the Internet is restricted to before business hours, after business hours, and during the lunch period. Personal use of the Internet can be rescinded at any time.

3. The Company reserves the right to audit networks and systems on a periodic basis to ensure compliance with this policy.

Security Information

1. Keep passwords secure and do not share accounts. Authorized users are responsible for the security of their passwords and accounts.

2. All computers should be secured with a password-protected screensaver with the automatic activation feature set at 15 minutes or less. Users who will be away from their desks longer than one hour should log-off (control-alt-delete for NT and Win2K users).

3. Postings by employees from the Company e-mail address to newsgroups should contain a disclaimer stating that the opinions expressed are strictly their own and not necessarily those of the Company, unless posting is in the course of business duties.

4. Employees must use extreme caution when opening e-mail attachments received from unknown senders, which may contain viruses or Trojan horse code.

Unacceptable Use

The following activities are, in general, prohibited. Employees may be exempted from these restrictions during the course of their legitimate job responsibilities.

Under no circumstances is an employee of the Company to engage in any activity that is illegal under local, state, federal or international law while utilizing Company-owned resources.

The following lists are activities that fall into the category of unacceptable Internet use:

1. Unauthorized copying of copyrighted material including, but not limited to, photographs from copyrighted sources, copyrighted music, and copyrighted software for which the Company does not have an active license is strictly prohibited.

2. Revealing your account password to others or allowing use of your account by others.

3. Using the Company's computers to actively engage in procuring or transmitting material that is in violation of sexual harassment or hostile workplace laws in the user's local jurisdiction.

4. Sending unsolicited e-mail messages, including the sending of junk mail or other advertising material to individuals who did not specifically request such material (e-mail spam).

5. Creating or forwarding chain letters, Ponzi, or other pyramid schemes of any type.

6. Posting the same or similar non-business-related messages to large numbers of Usenet newsgroups (newsgroup spam).

Enforcement

Any employee found to have violated this policy may be subject to disciplinary action, up to and including termination of employment.

Revisions

(Any revisions are listed here along with the date of the change.)

Anti-virus policy

This policy should be a standard in any organization — large or small — because the threat of virus infection is huge and there are new viruses appearing every day. Just having anti-virus software in place is not enough. The staff must understand why the software is in place, who is in charge of it, and what to do if a virus is detected. This policy also educates the user as to where the dangers lie.

Anti-Virus Policy

Overview

All Internet related equipment, including but not limited to computer equipment, software, storage media, electronic mail, and Internet connections are the property of <Company Name> (also referred to as "Company"). These systems are to be used for business purposes and in the course of normal daily operations. It is in the Company's best interest to make sure that these resources are protected and used appropriately.

Purpose

The purpose of this policy is to outline the anti-virus use policy at <Company Name>. These rules are in place to protect the employee and the Company. Inappropriate use exposes the Company to risks including virus attacks, compromise of network systems and services, and legal issues.

Scope

This policy applies to employees, contractors, consultants, temporaries, and other workers at the Company, including all personnel affiliated with third parties. This policy applies to all equipment that is owned or leased by the Company.

Policy

All Company computers must have the Company's approved anti-virus software installed and scheduled to run at regular intervals. It is the responsibility of the IT Department to maintain the anti-virus software and to ensure that the virus pattern files and scanning engines are up to date on all computers. The IT Department is also responsible for setting and maintaining the virus-scanning schedule on all computers.

It is the responsibility of the Users to report any viruses found on their computers to the IT Department. If a virus is discovered on a computer, that machine is to be removed from the network until it is verified as virus-free by the IT Department.

Users should never download files from unknown or suspicious sources. If a file must be downloaded and its source cannot be verified, the file must be scanned prior to its storage on a file server. If the file will fit on a floppy disk, download the file to the floppy first, and then scan that disk.

Users should never share floppy disks that have not been virus scanned. After a floppy is found to be free of viruses, the date of the scan and the initials of the User must be printed on the floppy label.

Users should never attempt to disable their virus-scanning software on their computers. If problems arise, the User should contact the IT Department for assistance.

Any attempt by a User to create and/or distribute malicious programs into the Company's network (such as viruses, e-mail bombs, worms, Trojan horses, and so on) are prohibited. Any User who engages in such activity is subject to disciplinary and/or legal action.

Enforcement

Any employee found to have violated this policy may be subject to disciplinary action, up to and including termination.

Revisions

(Any revisions are listed here along with the date of the change.)

Employee agreement

After an employee has read the security policies, he or she should sign an agreement to uphold the policies. This agreement should then be kept in the employee's personnel file for future reference. This agreement eliminates the "I Didn't Know" excuses.

Network User Agreement

I,_____, <User Name> have read and understand the Security Policies of <Company Name> and agree to uphold those policies. I understand that I must report any misuse or violations of policies by any persons to my immediate supervisor or department head. I also understand that any misuse or violations by myself can result in disciplinary action, termination, and possible legal action.

_____   _____

Signed   Date

Writing the Security Policies

As you can see from the examples of the policies given, you need to put some time and thought into the writing of them. There are many bases to cover and a lot of circumstances to take into consideration. Don't fall into the trap of trying to get everything written at once before you release the policies. If you do that, you run the risk of developing *shelfware* — an unfinished folder of policies that sits on the shelf and never gets used.

Who's in charge?

Who in your organization is going to be in charge of setting the policies? Is it someone from upper management? The IT Department? Or an appointed security officer? If at all possible, one person should be in charge. If your company is medium to large in size, it's best to appoint a security officer whose main job is to oversee and manage security. In many cases, this is seen as an unjustifiable expense and security responsibilities are given to someone as additional duty. But if your company is serious about security, it should be viewed as a full-time job with full-time responsibilities.

Regardless of whether the security officer is a full-time or a part-time job, the position must have the support of upper management. Often, staff treat security personnel with suspicion and disrespect because staff are not sure where security comes in the pecking order of the company, and no one from upper management has told them how important it is to cooperate with the security staff.

If you are trying to choose who in your organization is the best person to serve as security officer, make sure that the person has the necessary skills to do the job. This may seem like a no-brainer, but you'd be surprised at the number of security officers I've met whose previous duties consisted of little more than data entry. People in these circumstances can quickly be overwhelmed by the job and will lose the respect of the rest of the staff.

Here are three minimum requirements for choosing a security officer:

✔ The person must have a firm grasp of technology. Just being able to work at a computer is not enough.

✔ The person must be able to understand the repercussions of threats to security.

✔ The person must be able to communicate well.

Of course, if you're really serious about getting a top-notch professional security officer, you should look for someone with the right credentials. There are certifications you can check for. One of the most respected is the *CISSP* (Certified Information Systems Security Professional). People who hold certifications have a minimum number of years experience in the field and have passed an arduous test of their ability. However you choose your security officer, this, too, must be written into the policies, which should elaborate on the roles and responsibilities.

Security by committee — really!

Security policies affect everyone and, therefore, everyone should have some say in the policies. That's not to say that everyone should be involved in the actual writing of the policies — that could result in a bureaucratic mess! If you have more than a couple employees, I suggest you create a team to write security policies. It doesn't have to be a large team — just a few people with a cross-section of skills and backgrounds. This team should have the authority from upper management to do the work and the resources and support to do so.

The reason team writing is important is that different people may have valuable insights into the way the company actually operates. For example, the IT department may know of inadequacies in procedures that can result in data theft or other security violations. The Human Resources department may have specific ideas about how to authorize access to various parts of the network. These insights and points of view are important in writing good policies that work.

If you don't have a security officer, then one person must be "in charge" of the group writing the policies. This person should keep the group focused and should have the authority of ultimate decision-making. The group should assemble all the necessary data such as the risk assessment report and input from personnel. The personnel input can be in the form of a formal question-naire or informal interviews. When the team and the data are assembled, you can begin the actual task of writing.

Information gathered from personnel within your company can help you gauge the level of security awareness and competence within your organization. Here are some examples of questions you might want to include in your questionnaire.

- ✔ **Are you aware of the company's security policies?** If people answer "no" and you do have policies, obviously you are not doing enough to educate your staff.

- ✔ **What, in your opinion, is the most important resource on the network to protect?** The answers may surprise you. Most staff are concerned with protecting resources that make their jobs easier — such as online hourly timesheets.

- ✔ **What breaches in security do you see as possible?** Again, the answers may surprise you. Some answers will point out the obvious while others may highlight obscure problems you may not have considered.

- ✔ **Which security policies are hardest for you to follow?** This may high-light policies that are contradictory in wording or hard to understand.

- ✔ **What would you do if your computer were infected with a virus?** Questions like this help you to understand whether or not your staff understand procedures.

- ✔ **What do you see as being your responsibility towards security?** Many staff see security as being "someone else's problem" and not their own. The answers can tell you whether or not your messages are getting through and can help you develop education for your staff.

Some key policies

Starting security policies from scratch can seem a daunting task. Where do you begin? Luckily, the Internet abounds with examples of policies. Most are not copyrighted and you are free to use them and change them as you see fit. One of my favorites is the SANS Institute Security Policy Project at `www.sans.org/newlook/resources/policies`. While you won't find every policy there, you will find quite a few to at least get you started. If you don't use any of the policies on the Internet, I suggest that you do read some of them. If nothing else, they can give you some ideas for your own policies.

There are also policy templates you can buy on the Internet and policy-making software. I don't have a lot of experience with these programs and would urge the buyer to beware. See if you can find any reviews of the pro-grams in the major computer magazines and see if you can get demo copies before you buy. In many cases, I think you'll find it's just as easy to write the policies yourself. At least if you write the policies yourself, you really know what's in them!

Here are some policies I consider "must have's":

- ✔ **Roles and Responsibilities** — Describes each position in the organization along with the particular security roles and responsibilities for that position.

- ✔ **Physical Access** — Covers who is allowed onto the premises and in what areas and how to you handle visitors and vendors. Details ID requirements as well.

- ✔ **Network Access** — Spells out who is allowed to access which parts of the network along with any exceptions. Explains how to handle access for visitors and how is access approved?

- ✔ **Password Policies** — Details the acceptable password length and composition as well as how often passwords need to be changed.

- ✔ **Appropriate Internet and E-mail Usage** — Covers who is allowed to access the Internet and under what conditions along with any exceptions. Covers about personal use as well (the example given in this chapter answers some of these questions).

- ✔ **Anti-Virus and Malicious Code** — Goes over how to work with the anti-virus software, who is responsible for maintenance, and how viruses should be reported (an example of this policy is given in this chapter).

- ✔ **Configuration and Maintenance of Computing Systems** — Explains if everyone is required to have the same software and the same versions along with any exceptions. Covers if staff can use personal pictures on their computer desktops and who is allowed to make changes to software.

- ✔ **System Back-Ups** — Dictates how often back-ups need to be done and who should do them, if they are all full back-ups or incremental back-ups, and where the back-up tapes are stored.

- ✔ **Configuration and Maintenance of Security Mechanisms** — Describes how security mechanisms such as routers, firewalls, and intrusion detection systems are to be configured and how the configurations are to be maintained and documented. Also details how and when changes are allowed to be made and who should make the changes. Included in these policies are how and when security patches are to be applied and who is in charge of making sure that patches are applied. Details who gets security alerts generated by the security mechanisms and the rules for responding to these alerts.

Of course, there are many other policies you may want to use. The key is to tailor them to your workplace. If you have only a five-person staff, then you probably don't need a detailed physical access policy and ID badges, but you should still have a policy.

Ready, Set, Implement

Let's imagine that you've written all of your security policies and they've been approved by upper management. You're all finished and you can sit back and relax now. Right? Well . . . not exactly. Now you have to put the policies into action. (And here you were looking forward to a day sitting by the pool, huh?)

The next step is to write the Security Procedures (sometimes called the Security Plan). These procedures follow the policies and go one step further to explain, in detail, who does what and when. A policy may state that the IT department is responsible for making back-ups of the systems. The procedures spell out how the back-ups should be conducted, who should do them, and what to do if something goes wrong. It's nothing more than standard operating procedures, only these procedures deal specifically with security issues.

An example of a security procedure for handling the discovery of a virus on a workstation:

Security Procedure for Virus Reporting

1. The IT department shall prepare a red folder for every workstation that contains the following:

    • A copy of this procedure

    • Notice on red paper which states, "This computer is possibly infected with a virus. Do Not Disturb!"

    • Phone numbers of anti-virus support personnel

2. If the user suspects a virus has infected the workstation, the user will immediately stop using the computer.

3. The user will place the red notice on the monitor of the infected workstation.

4. The user will immediately contact one of the personnel listed on the support sheet.

5. The user will write down the time of the occurrence, the type of activity seen, and what actions proceeded the activity. (Was an e-mail with an attachment opened or a new program started, for example?)

6. The anti-virus personnel will unplug the workstation from the network to prevent further infection.

7. Anti-virus personnel will ensure that the anti-virus program is up to date and running properly.

8. Anti-virus personnel will follow the security procedures for removing the virus and check the rest of the network for infection.

9. Once the danger of infection is over, the anti-virus personnel will reconnect the workstation to the network and remove the red virus notice from the monitor.

10. Anti-virus personnel will make a report of the infection and submit it to the security officer and the IT manager.

Who does what?

In your security policies, you describe the roles and responsibilities of the staff positions. Building on that, you can go on to describe how these people are to assist in the actual implementation of the policies. Some people may have a proactive role such as configuring the firewall while others may have reactive roles such as reporting violations. You may have a security officer, but that person cannot be and should not be expected to be responsible for all duties. Superman doesn't exist except in comic books!

Here's a simple look at the some of the policies for a few roles. The listings of responsibilities is not meant to be all-encompassing; it's just to give you an idea of some of the considerations to be made in writing your own procedures.

- ✔ **Upper Management** — Responsible for providing an annual budget and other resources required to implement security policies. Must provide visible support for security staff and encourage compliance with policies. Signs-off on all policies and changes. Meets with Security Officer at least monthly.

- ✔ **Security Officer** — Responsible for ensuring compliance with written security policies. Conducts security audits of all departments at least annually. Reviews the configuration of all security mechanisms at least monthly. Conducts investigations and security reviews of all breaches. Meets weekly with department heads to discuss security issues.

- ✔ **IT Department** — Responsible for configuring and maintaining all computer systems and security mechanisms. Reviews configurations of all security mechanisms at least monthly and keeps a log, noting any changes. Backs-up all servers daily and stores tapes in a locked safe. Notifies the security officer of security alerts and breaches and responds to events accordingly.

- ✔ **All Users** — Responsible for following the security policies and reporting any breaches or violations to the department head or the security officer. Responsible for protecting their passwords and not sharing them with others.

Buy-in, education, and awareness

Probably one of the toughest jobs in implementing security is getting staff and management to buy-in to the process. As I mentioned previously, people don't like to be told what to do and security procedures are often ridiculed and met with resistance. However, if you involve people in the process, they will be more apt to cooperate. What do I mean by that? Well, the people who helped to write the policies were involved, and they can help explain the policies to others and the justification for putting those policies into action. Create incentives or awards for following the rules or by making suggestions to improve the rules. And, when you get ready to start your education and awareness program, involve others in setting up the theme and materials. Because security is everyone's business, give them a vested interest in it to help it succeed.

It's only money

Sometimes the only thing management understands is money. If you can show upper management that a good security program will actually save them money, that helps with their buy-in. How can you convert an intangible such as security into dollars and cents? By looking at the cost of manpower and potential lost sales.

Imagine that you have at least one virus infection a year that requires you to take the network off-line for one day. You have to pay the IT staff overtime to take care of the problem. You may also suffer the loss of important data — an important asset with a real value. Chances are that the rest of the staff wil wander around twiddling their thumbs for an entire day and speculate endlessly about what is happening instead of working. That is essentially a paid holiday at work for all employees. Then imagine that you lost ten potential sales because the clients couldn't connect to your network for a day. If you roll all these costs together and present them to management, they will have a hard time ignoring your request for support.

While working as a security officer, I became involved in a major virus infection threatening my network. The rate at which the infected files grew was huge, and my only recourse was to take the entire network off-line while we went through every server and every workstation to delete the infected files. While I had good management support in obtaining the staff needed to get the job done, the management would not allow me to conduct an all-hands meeting to tell the users what was happening. The staff knew I was the reason that they couldn't use their computers, but they didn't know *why*! Had I been allowed to convey the problem, the speculation would have ended, and the supervisors would have found other things for the staff to do while the computers were down. I hate to think what the salaries for 300 staff for four days of lost work was worth!

Schooling the masses

Part of the buy-in process involves the education of the non-technical — this includes management and staff. If you think about it, most people have gotten their education about network security from CNN reports of viruses and myths reported via spam e-mail. Remember the "Good Times" virus hoax from the mid '90s? The hoax warned that your computer would get infected if you simply read the words "Good Times" in an e-mail message. Ironically, users often *included* the phrase "Good Times" in the subject line of their own warning messages about the virus. This hoax is *still* one of the most widely disseminated virus myths.

A security education and awareness campaign doesn't have to be fancy (see Figure 4-1), but it should be fun and interesting. There's nothing worse than being given a packet that is about as interesting as medical benefits and told to read it. Do we ever read all that stuff? Here are some examples of ways to make your education and awareness a little less boring:

**Like a helmet,
Your password is your
Protection**

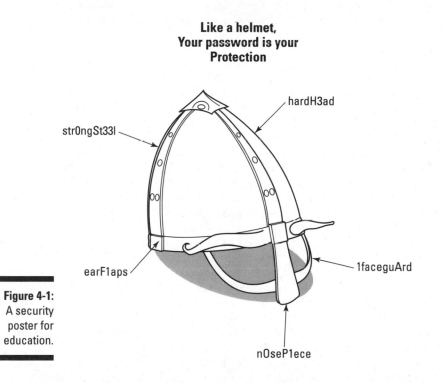

hardH3ad

str0ngSt33l

earF1aps

1faceguArd

n0seP1ece

Figure 4-1:
A security
poster for
education.

✔ **Make posters.** The posters should be comical with a topical message. Posters should be changed and/or rotated often because people stop seeing them after they have been in place for too long without any changes.

✔ **Mousepads.** Distribute mousepads that have a policy or procedure written on them. Or, you can print helpful hints and phone numbers on the mousepad.

- ✔ **Friendly reminders.** Send around reminders in envelopes but make the contents really strange or funny. I once sent around envelopes full of confetti with the notice "This is what your data will look like if you don't protect it!" I would also send out notices once a month to remind users to back-up their files to one of the back-up servers.

- ✔ **Questionnaires/games.** Send out simple games or silly questionnaires about security policies. The key is to give out a prize to the winner — money, paid lunch, or a half-day off, for example.

First of all, your program should consider the target audience. Are they technically aware? You wouldn't give the same talk to general users that you would give to network administrators in the IT Department. How sensitive is the audience be to the opinions of others? You may want to think about having separate departmental meetings. Consider your resources as well. If you have a small company, then Web-based security training is probably beyond your budget.

Whatever you do, do NOT base your security training on e-mail messages! Why not? Most users are so inundated with e-mail that they don't read all of it and rarely read a message in its entirety. Many users set filters for messages they consider to be "junk" to go straight to the trash bin. You don't want your well-constructed messages to end up this way!

Think of your education and awareness program as an advertising campaign. The job is to get the message to the people and get them to remember it. That may be easier than it sounds! Think about the number of bad commercials you saw on TV last night and you'll see what I mean. You can always do a cheap video that parodies a commercial or a TV show. The staff love to see themselves on videos and the others will enjoy making fun of them.

Here are some guidelines for a successful education and awareness campaign:

- ✔ **Start out your campaign with something fun and unusual.** Don't bore your audience. This is a good time to hand out 3D promotional items such as mousepads or note cubes that contain a message.

- ✔ **Use creative logos, themes, artwork, and giveaways.** You may even start a contest to come up with the best logos and artwork. There is a ton of copyright free artwork available on CDs or on the Internet.

- ✔ **Teach through example.** People love "war stories." Use real-life problems and solutions to get your point across.

- ✔ **Be humorous.** Tell funny stories and jokes that illustrate your point.

- ✔ **Use analogies.** Often techno-speak is incomprehensible unless you put it in laymen's terms.

✔ **Keep the message simple.** Don't try to bombard the staff with too much information. If you have a lot of information to cover, you may want to give it in multiple short sessions instead of one long one.

✔ **Challenge the audience's beliefs and expectations.** This is a great way to dispel old myths and teach the facts. Use urban myths and examples of hoaxes to illustrate your point.

✔ **Keep the subject matter current and credible.** It makes no sense to talk about threats if they don't apply to you or are out of date.

One more thought: Participation in education and awareness should be a requirement for everyone regardless of position or status. Contractors and frequent visitors should also be part of this program. Your education policy needs address the length of time new hires have to complete the program and how often employees need to attend refresher briefings. Last, but not least, after an employee completes the program, he should sign a statement indicating that he has received the training, understands it, and will comply with all rules. This agreement is separate from the others that the staff may have signed. If you want to limit the number of agreements that you keep on file, you may want to award the staff with certificates of completion of the training instead.

Part II
Your Network Is Your Business

The 5th Wave
By Rich Tennant

"Someone want to look at this manuscript I recieved on email called, 'The Embedded Virus That Destroyed the Publisher's Servers When the Manuscript Was Rejected.'?"

In this part . . .

Without your network, your ability to conduct business is hampered. Your network is probably one of your most important company assets and should be protected as such. But how do you decide on your priorities and what are things going to cost?

Before you can jump into the fray wielding your security sword, there are important business considerations to delve into. This is the part that those bean counters in your organization love — it's how to deal with the dollars and sense of securing your network!

Chapter 5

Choosing Controls without Breaking the Bank

In This Chapter

▶ Helping you decide which solutions are best

▶ Defining your security requirements

▶ Looking at security mechanism pros and cons

▶ How to deal with vendors

▶ Deciding who does the security work

▶ Considering consultants and outsource companies

Security controls and mechanisms have become big business. Everyone from the major accounting firms to Joe Blow down the street are out to get your security business. The vendors are out in force, too. If you read the trade magazines, it seems like new products appear on the market almost daily. Finding information on security products can be a very confusing road to travel. A recent survey by SecurityFocus.Com shows that, on average, security professionals spend over two hours a day researching security products and methods on the Internet. That's one-quarter of a work day.

Much of the advertising focuses on security mechanisms themselves as the answer to all of your problems. If you were to accept all of the marketing propaganda, you'd believe that intrusion detection systems were all-knowing and all-seeing and that XYZ Company's new system is the last security product you'll ever need. Sorry, but that's hardly ever the case. The trouble with security mechanisms is that you cannot just install them and then leave them alone. The key to all security mechanisms is people. You need people to configure them, maintain them, and to respond to the alerts the machines produce. There's not an automaton that can do those jobs yet.

This chapter takes a look at what you really need to protect your network. I discuss how to set your requirements and how to decide on the security mechanisms that suit your needs. I describe some of the pros and cons of the security mechanisms in general and how to deal with the vendors. I also give you some questions to ask a consultant if you decide that your best route is to outsource your protection.

The Good, Fast, Cheap Triangle

This is my favorite trick for choosing almost anything from washing machines to firewalls. The trick is this: You have three possible solutions, but you can only choose two! What does that get you? I call it the "Good, Fast, Cheap Triangle" as shown in Figure 5-1. Read on to find out more:

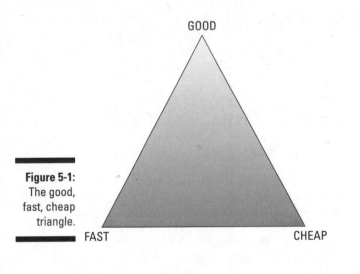

Figure 5-1:
The good, fast, cheap triangle.

GOOD

FAST   CHEAP

  ✔ If it's good and fast, it's not going to be cheap.
  ✔ If it's fast and cheap, it's not going to be good.
  ✔ If it's cheap and good, it's not going to be fast.

If you think about it, that just about covers everything. Give this picture to your teenager the next time he or she starts talking about a new car!

It will be totally up to you to decide which of the two meet your needs. I'm not really saying that any of the two combinations are bad. It's more that you just have to realize that no security solution is going to be perfect and accept the fact that every solution will have its drawbacks.

Remember this trick when you are wading through the piles of vendor sales literature. Take all their promises with a grain of salt. I have yet to find the perfect firewall, antivirus program, or intrusion detection system. They all have their drawbacks in cost, speed, efficiency, maintenance, or ease-of-use.

Setting Your Requirements

Before you can decide which security mechanisms to put into place, you have to decide what you really need. Your needs can be drawn from the results of your risk assessment. The higher a risk is rated, the more important it is to implement security and that, then, becomes a requirement. For example, if your organization decides that equipment theft is a high risk, then measures must be made to reduce that risk. Your security requirement would be to control access to the areas where equipment is stored.

It is important to be as specific as possible in your requirements in order to reduce the number of choices available to you. If you simply state that you need antivirus software, you'll have tons of products to choose from. If you state that you need antivirus software that automatically scans e-mail attachments, then your choices are reduced. When you have defined your basic requirement, you next need to define the extended requirements to see if what you need fits what the vendors have to offer.

Remember that we're not just talking hardware and software security, either. You also have to protect your building, your equipment, and your staff. Anything that can be considered an asset needs to be reviewed for its security requirements.

In setting your requirements and reviewing the products, you may find that you don't need a new product; you just need to make the best use of what you have. For example, if you have determined that your network is at low to medium risk of unauthorized entry by intruders (hackers), you may want to enforce stronger password rules and increase the level of filtering on your routers. You may find that you are spending a bit more in labor costs this way, but you have saved yourself an outlay for more equipment.

Table 5-1 shows how you may go about describing your requirements and possible solutions. This is not a complete and comprehensive list but is intended to get you started. Chances are that you will have a lot more of these than I have listed.

Table 5-1	Defining Your Security Requirements		
Area of Concern	*Requirements*	*Extended Requirements*	*Possible Solutions*
Viruses	Keep viruses from entering systems	E-mail servers scan attachments	Disallow all e-mail attachments
			Anti-virus software
			Content filtering and examination of files
		Desktop systems scan files and floppy disks	Anti-virus software on all desktops
		Ability for updates to be sent to desktops without having to physically visit each machine	Antivirus software on all desktops
			Antivirus software on servers that can automatically download updates and "push" them to desktops.
Web server security	Keep intruders from entering network through Web server	Allow only trusted guests and customers to access Web server	Disable guest accounts on Web server
			Password protect access to server
			Harden Web server operating system against attack
			Set up static IP addresses for access; all others denied
			Use SSL to secure the connections

Area of Concern	Requirements	Extended Requirements	Possible Solutions
Accounting department servers	Prevent unauthorized access from internal network	Segregation of accounting network from rest of company	Enforce internal access controls via user permissions and passwords
			Harden servers against attacks
			Router to segregate main network from accounting
			Use static routes and filtering rules on routers
Theft of equipment	Prevent theft of equipment	Control inventory	Sign-out process for equipment
		Track equipment in building	Equipment stored in locked rooms with controlled access
			Inventory control tags
			Central database of equipment for inventory control
			Radio transmitters in equipment that can be tracked on receivers
Server room protection	Prevent unauthorized access	Allow authorized personnel in but keep unauthorized personnel out	Keyed locks or cipher locks on all doors
			Guard located at desk at entrance to server room
			ID tags for employees and guests that indicate if access is allowed

The Pros and Cons of Products

In this section I list some of the most popular security products and their pros and cons. This is not a complete list as there are new products appearing at an amazing rate. However, there are a number of resources on the Internet to help you wade through the chaff to get to the wheat.

Antivirus scanners

Antivirus scanners consist of two parts: the software (called the *engine*) that does the scanning, and the virus files, which is a database of known viruses. In order to get the best out of these systems, you have to make sure that you have the most recent version of both parts. The software doesn't get updated very often, but the virus files are almost continually updated. Get into the practice of checking for updates for the virus signature files at least once a week in order to catch the most viruses.

Pros

Antivirus scanners are essential to catching viruses. Without them you won't catch anything at all and you'll never know when or if you are infected. They can prevent the destruction of data and potential loss of productivity. Most are very easy to install.

Cons

Many antivirus program lack good documentation, and it's not necessarily clear how scans need to be configured. Also, software can catch only existing viruses or programs that contain the properties of viruses previously seen. Both the Melissa virus and the ILOVEYOU virus got past many scanners because they were a new type of virus not previously recorded. The scanners can catch only what they know — they're not good at guessing what might be a new virus.

If you set the antivirus programs to scan intensively, they can be disruptive. For example, if you set it up to scan floppies every time one is placed in the drive, the scan can hog all the computer's resources and bring other programs to a screeching halt. Sometimes e-mail scans can screw-up your e-mail program. In the past I have seen that anti-virus programs that scan e-mail upon receipt have changed the POP3 (Post Office Protocol) configurations of the e-mail program. This results in errors in the e-mail program being able to retrieve mail. These problems cause people to disable the software and risk infection. You may have to test your anti-virus software to see if it causes any conflicts with your e-mail program. If it does, you will either have to change the e-mail program you use or not enable that particular feature of the anti-virus software.

In addition, not all antivirus scanners actually work as they advertise. The best thing to do is to check their ratings at the Virus Bulletin. They maintain a list of programs that have been tested and rated. These ratings can be found at `www.virusbtn.com/vb100/archives/products.xml`.

Packet-filtering routers

A *router* is a device or a computer that sits between your direct connection to the Internet and the rest of your network. It examines the traffic coming in from the Internet and then uses a database of routes and rules to send the traffic to the correct section of your network. Traffic can be filtered by originating IP addresses, destination IP addresses, and/or ports. Traffic that is not allowed is simply dropped at the router. Routers range from very simple PCs that you can build yourself to complex and sophisticated machines. It can be a tiny box on small networks to refrigerator-sized machines on large networks. Some of the more sophisticated routers now support Virtual Private Networks (VPNs).

Pros

Most routers have rules that allow you to control what traffic comes in and what traffic goes out. These rules are referred to as *filters* or *access control lists (ACLs)*. This means that the rules are set to filter who or what can have access or what is allowed in or outside of the network. For example, you can deny *incoming* telnet access on port 23 (the port telnet uses), but allow *outgoing* telnet access. The same goes for Web browsing. You can allow *outgoing* HTTP access on port 80 for Web traffic, but deny *incoming* traffic on that port. Routers maintain logs of successful and failed connections so you can check for intrusion attempts. Many routers also have Web-based interfaces to make configuration easier.

Cons

While routers are an essential part of the Internet, they aren't without their problems. If you have a very large network, the large routers can be very expensive and complex. Training is imperative and is expensive for almost all routing products. It is very hard to correctly configure the routing tables, filters, and ACLs and misconfigurations can go unnoticed for long periods of time: sometimes even too late. In addition, there are many known bugs in the routing software and hackers who are familiar with particular types of routers are very good at defeating their defenses. Taking care and maintaining routers takes a lot of time and time costs money. However, since your routers are often the first (and sometimes only) security mechanisms between your network and the Internet, it's vitally important that you don't cut corners here.

Firewalls

To begin with, there are many, many different types of firewalls — each with their pluses and minuses. You see routers referred to as firewalls in some literature, but I prefer to keep them separate.

Firewalls work by examining the network traffic and applying rules as to what is allowed and what isn't. In most cases, firewalls can look more deeply into the traffic content than a router can. They can also look deep into the *headers* and other parts of the packets to check for irregularities. The header of the packet includes such information as the origin and destination of the packet, the size of the packet, and what types of data the packet consists of. Here are the major differences in the way firewalls work:

- **Stateful inspection.** This gives arriving traffic (packets) the third degree. This is the "Grand Inquisitor" of firewalls and nothing comes in or goes out that isn't thoroughly inspected. Not only are all packets inspected inside and out, the application, the user, and the transportation method are all queried and verified. That information is maintained so that all future transmissions are inspected and compared to past transmissions. If both the "state" of the transmission and the "context" in which it is used deviate from the norm, connection is refused.

- **Application proxies.** These firewalls can examine an entire stream of data and not just the packet itself. Based on the content of the stream, the firewall makes a decision as to which application is being used to transmit the data. It then starts a version of the application, like telnet or FTP, but it's a more restrictive version of the application in which rules are set as to verify the user and the destination. When the user has been authorized to use telnet, for example, the proxy telnet then completes the connection.

- **Hybrid firewalls.** As its name implies, these firewalls use a combination of scanning methods to create a hybrid of its own. Hybrids typically include hard circuits between networks that are not inspected, various levels of packet filtering, and more granularity in the stateful inspection and application proxies. These are very adaptive firewalls and require a large amount of skill and training to run them.

Firewalls and their uses

As there are so many types of firewalls, it's best to define your use before you even consider checking out the vendors. You'll find that some firewalls are smaller than a breadbox while others resemble a normal PC. I've found that Network Computing does a great job of comparing the different firewalls so you can narrow down your choices. Their guide is at www.networkcomputing. com/ibg/Guide?guide_id=292. In the following bulleted list, I cover a few of the different types of firewalls.

✔ **PC firewalls.** Also known as personal firewalls, these are a relatively new entry to the field. They are designed to protect a single home computer or a home connection with just a couple of computers. They work by having you identify which programs you want to be able to access the Internet and alert you if your computer is being scanned or attacked from the outside.

✔ **SOHO firewalls.** SOHO stands for *Small Office/Home Office* and these firewalls are intended for networks with less than 50 computers. These firewalls are often a single box (appliance firewall). The box may look like a router rather than a standalone PC. Some of these firewalls also include Web servers, e-mail servers, and DNS servers. They are easy to install and configure and are good if you don't have a dedicated IT staff to take care of such things.

✔ **Enterprise firewalls.** Unless you have the need for Internet, *intranet*, and *extranet* services, these firewalls are probably not for you. An intranet is a network that offers many Internet-based services such as Web pages and e-mail, but is self-contained and accessible only by people inside the firewall. An extranet, on the other hand, is very similar except that it allows certain outsiders to access it. You'll often find extranets in *business to business (B2B)* enterprises. Enterprise firewalls are large, complex, and expensive, but very cool. They are usually hybrid firewalls that can support multiple networks and a vast number of rule sets.

Pros

Firewalls are very good at examining your Internet traffic and keeping unwanted traffic (and intruders) out. Often, an intruder cannot see a firewall on your network. When problems arise, the firewall can send out alerts, and the logs it maintains are helpful in trying to locate attacks. They are also good at controlling how your staff uses the Internet.

Cons

Firewalls are not foolproof. Any attacker with in-depth knowledge of your particular type of firewall can defeat its defenses. Firewalls are also known for sending out a lot of false alarms, which can be troublesome if the staff gets into the habit of ignoring the alarms. The logs are hard to understand because they contain a lot of complex data and the format is difficult to read. If the firewall administrator hasn't been properly trained, he may miss important clues about possible attacks. Configurations on the sophisticated systems can be difficult and confusing, and training is a must for those systems. Like routers, they key to firewalls are the filters and ACLs. It's very important that these filters be properly configured or your firewall will not do the job it was intended to do.

Intrusion Detection Systems

Intrusion Detection Systems, or IDS, are a relatively new entry into the arena of security mechanisms. They can be set up to examine the traffic on a single machine or on the entire network. In simple terms, the machine examines traffic and compares it to a database of known attack methods and then sends alerts when these conditions are met. More complex IDSs can look for anomalies in network traffic — a condition that might indicate an attack — and attempt to prevent the attack. The market is growing and new features and abilities are added to IDSs as the technology matures.

Pros

If your network is deemed at high risk of possible attack, this mechanism can help you identify when those attacks might be occurring. An IDS can look at all the traffic and draw a conclusion based on various factors — it's not just limited to certain types of traffic, but can look for patterns and changes. IDSs also send alerts and reports to the administrators based on what they are finding and the administrators don't have to rely upon deciphering log entries to be able to tell what is going on. They are fairly easy to install and maintain and there are many products on the market.

Cons

There are literally hundreds of ways to defeat an IDS and they are all well known and documented on the Internet — thanks to IDS hackers. Because the IDS is comparing traffic to known patterns in a database, if your attacker is using a method not found in the database or an unknown pattern of attack, there's a chance the attack won't be seen. An IDS is also expecting the attack to come at a certain pace. If the attacker sends the data very slowly, for example, the IDS won't necessarily see the pattern. IDSs are capable of sending zillions of different kinds of alerts and reports and, if you are not careful about what you ask for from your system, you may be flooded with too many to be able to effectively respond.

Dealing with Vendors

Let's face it — the vendors you deal with are sales people whose goal is to move boxes. They can resort to high-pressure sales and scare tactics to get you to buy, but many are knowledgeable professionals. Don't be afraid to ask them to tell you why their product is better then their competitors' and what benefits there are to buying one over the other. If they are good at their jobs, they will help you understand the technology and product and help you to choose the solution that is best suited to your needs.

Sometimes it seems the hardest thing of all is to get a firm price out of some vendors. It drives me crazy when I have to send in a request form for a quote when all I really want to know is if they are in my price range. However, there are online and on-the-shelf computer magazines that do price comparisons for your benefit. Do some researching before you start shopping around. And don't forget training. In addition to purchasing the product, you often need to buy training for your staff. Don't skimp when it comes to the training because it's usually well worth the cost. Don't forget the Good, Fast, Cheap Triangle!

When you have narrowed down your choices, or to help you narrow down the choices, reviews are all important. Check the online magazines listed here. You'll find essential information from people who have actually used the products and/or tested them in labs. Because products and their features are ever-changing, I can't possibly list them all here. What I can give you is a list of Web sites and Usenet groups you can contact for more information (which I highly recommend).

- ✔ `www.cnet.com` — An online magazine with hardware and software reviews
- ✔ `www.techweb.com` — An online magazine with hardware and software reviews
- ✔ `www.zdnet.com` — Another very good online magazine with reviews
- ✔ `http://comp.security` — Computer security newsgroup
- ✔ `http://misc.security` — Newsgroup with various security-related subjects

Negotiations

If you are a small organization, there is probably not much you can do about product prices, and you'll probably end up paying whatever the market will bear. That's because you won't have the volume of business needed to negotiate special pricing. However, if you are in a position to buy a number of products or services, you may have some negotiating power under your belt. Vendors are less likely to discount products unless you are buying in volume or unless you can promise them X amount of revenue over X number of years. Resellers, however, are a bit more flexible. In any case, it's always best to ask for a discount. The worst they can do is say no.

If you are buying training for the product in question, you may be able to get a price break on either the product or the training. For example, if the vendor needs two people to fill up a class they are giving next week, it's worth it to them to offer it to you at a discount rather than have to cancel it because they don't have the minimum number of people required. Sometimes they can work out a special deal to do your training in-house as opposed to a distant location. In terms of the product, sometimes a vendor has a large inventory of a particular item he is willing to discount. It may not be exactly the model you were looking for, but if it meets your requirements, it may be worth considering. Sometimes support comes at an additional cost, too. Don't forget to ask if it's extra. Maybe the vendor will throw in free support if you buy within a certain time frame.

Buying big-ticket security products is like buying a car. You want to buy, but there are lots of models to choose from. You have an interest to get the best product at the best price and the seller has an interest to sell as many as he can per month so he can make payroll. Do your research on pricing, know your requirements well, don't succumb to pressure, and you'll do well.

Bells and whistles

If you haven't heard of this term before, I'm going to wonder where you've been all of your life! Bells and whistles are those cool little extras that make you believe that you've just *got to have* _____ (fill in the blank). They're like the pop-out drinks holders in your car — really nice to have, but not totally necessary. When it comes to buying security products, the vendors and resellers will expound with great delight on all their bells and whistles.

One such feature I often hear of is the *Graphical User Interface (GUI)*. This means that you can configure the product on a Web browser from any machine on your network. Frequently the only protection of this feature is a password. In order for this feature to work, a Web server must be running on the product. Ask yourself — is this really needed? Because Web servers are inherently insecure, this feature will need its own protection. So, if the vendor is trying to sell you the next model up because it has this feature, maybe what you really need is the more basic model with a simple command-line interface.

Often you'll run into the situation that one person in your organization wants the product with all the extras and others don't. In that case, you'll need to do a cost/benefit analysis to see if the extra cost is worth it. On the other hand, if the model you want comes with features you don't need, see if these features can be disabled. One of the basic rules of network security is to not run what you don't need.

Who's Going to Do the Work?

With all these new security mechanisms coming into your workplace, have you considered who is going to be responsible for them? Many companies assume the work is over when the systems are installed but they couldn't be further from the truth. The work has only begun. Security isn't a "do it once and forget it" process. Security systems and mechanisms have to be installed correctly, maintained and updated, and someone has to respond to the security alerts and read the logs. If you have a dedicated IT Department, is the work going to be spread over a number of different people, or is one person going to be responsible? One thing for sure, these security protections can be very labor intensive.

You'll have some hard decisions to make here. Do you want to have one person in charge of all of your security or will you have a dedicated team? Many companies give dole out security responsibilities without any real thought. Often, security duties are additional responsibilities given to staff who are expected to do security in their spare time. For example, it's not uncommon to find that a network administrator, whose main job is to make sure that the network stays up and running, is also responsible to read the firewall logs and install anti-virus updates. The fact of the matter is that the poor network administrator often has her hands so full of the job at hand, that she never gets the time to read the logs or install the updates. Since security is seen as adjunct duty, it's given a low priority. In other cases I've seen security duties given to people who are wholly unprepared for the job — such as the office manager who is great with people but possesses no technical skills.

In a Utopian situation, you'd have a Security Manager and a number of Security Administrators who worked together as a team to run the network security. The Manager would be responsible for running the entire security program, from establishing policies and procedures to making sure that things get done and the Administrators would be getting their hands dirty with router and firewall ACLs, keeping the systems updated and patched, and a myriad of other duties. Maintaining the security posture of a network is a full time, highly skilled job and effective and experienced staff would make things run well.

Unfortunately, most companies can't be run as Utopias and strict budgets often limit the number of security personnel employed to do the job. Often one person is asked to do the job of many. This doesn't mean the effort is doomed to failure, however. It just means that the security personnel need to understand the demands of the job and the company should be prepared to provide temporary support personnel when required.

Whichever your situation happens to be, just remember that it's best to employ security professionals whenever possible. If you ask inexperienced personnel to take on the job, be prepared for mistakes to be made. Can you afford these mistakes and will the overall security of your network suffer?

In regards to training security personnel for new mechanisms or new technologies that are to be deployed, please make sure that the staff has the training they need *when* they need it. Often, people are sent to training months before the system they have been trained on actually comes in the door. By that time, they may have forgotten most of what they learned in class and it will take them some time to become accustomed to the new equipment.

Outsourcing and Consultants

Sometimes your only option is to outsource some or all of your security duties. Outsourced security is a relatively new market generally serviced by telecoms, ISPs, and *managed security services (MSS)*. While security outsourcing companies may have the technologies and the staff to help you, the market is still maturing and the failure rate of new companies is high.

Most outsourcers focus on firewall and intrusion detection management with managed VPNs coming in a close second. Some of them offer one-time specialized services, such as configuring your routers. They usually meet with you, do a risk assessment, and offer services to match your needs. The costs for their services ranges from $300/month to $30,000/month, depending on the amount and type of services you need and the size of your network. This may seem like a lot of money, but it may be cheaper than buying the equipment and hiring staff yourself.

People are still wary of letting outsourcers take control of their security. While consultants and security services have the skills and experience, they don't promise 100 percent reliability — nothing in security has that sort of success rate. But, you have to wonder, if they make a mistake, will they try to cover it up so they can keep your business, or will they come clean with you? It's a big jump of faith to put this much trust in someone.

Here, then, are some questions you need to ask and some advice on picking an outsourcer.

Questions to ask

- Does their philosophy about business and security match yours?
- Do they have all the experienced staff they need, or do they occasionally outsource jobs themselves? (Be suspicious if they answer "yes" to this one!)
- How much experience do they have? Beware of statements such as "Our staff has a total of 100 years of experience combined." What does that really mean? Do they have 100 employees with one year each?
- What will they do in a disaster?
- What will *you* do if they go out of business?
- Will they sign a nondisclosure agreement? (So details about your company's security aren't given to others.)
- If they don't seem to be communicating well with you, how well can they be communicating your needs to their staff?
- Do they have references and clients you can talk to?

Some advice

- ✔ Ask for a written proposal. The proposal should detail everything you could possibly think of.

- ✔ Compare proposals from other companies.

- ✔ Beware of bargains. If it seems too good to be true, it probably is!

- ✔ Check out their operations by visiting their offices. Be wary if they offer excuses as to why they don't want you to visit.

- ✔ While visiting their offices, ask if you can speak to some of the staff.

- ✔ Don't buy what you don't need. If they try to tell you that "everyone" buys a certain service, maybe they aren't customizing their service to your needs.

- ✔ Demand a strong *service level agreement* (SLA) that spells out all roles and responsibilities. There should be no questions left unanswered.

- ✔ Trust your gut feelings. If something tells you that this company isn't right for you, walk away.

Chapter 6

You Could Be Liable If . . .

*I*f you pick up a major newspaper on any given day, you're likely to see a story about computer crime. The computer has replaced the brandishing of a gun and note formerly used to rob a bank. Credit card numbers and personal data are frequent targets, and identity theft has become big business for international crime groups. Trade secrets and intellectual property is stolen and sold to the highest bidder.

Legislators in the United States and abroad struggle to adequately define computer crimes and to set appropriate punishments. It's difficult for them to describe technologies that some of them barely understand themselves. Prosecution becomes a problem when countries cannot even agree that a crime has taken place. This was the case with the writer of the Melissa virus. Although his virus attacked computers in the United States, where it violated federal laws, he lived in the Philippines, which has no computer crime laws. He has never been prosecuted of any crime.

Laws involving computers can be confusing at best, and jurisdictions are sometimes difficult to establish. In America, ignorance of the law is no excuse. Therefore, it's not only important to know the laws — which are there to protect your assets — but you also have to be aware of what you have to protect in order not to run afoul of the law yourself.

One subject on which there has been much talk in the media lately is the concept of *downstream liability*. This means that if your network security is breached and your network is then used to attack another, you may be held liable for damages. It's a bit like having your gun stolen by someone who then commits a crime with it. It's your responsibility to make sure that your property is protected against unauthorized use and damage. I haven't heard of any successful court cases dealing with this yet, but I think it's only a matter of time.

U.S. Computer Laws

Few, if any, laws are perfect, and this is especially true when complex technologies come into the equation. Legislators have had to struggle to come up with acceptable definitions of the technologies and broad descriptions of what constitutes criminal use.

In the United States there are three different types of laws: criminal, civil, and administrative:

- Criminal laws are to protect the general public and violators usually face a jail sentence.
- Civil laws protect the individual or companies from damages or loss. Civil cases usually result in fines and restitution instead of jail time.
- Administrative laws are regulatory standards written by government agencies. Some of the administrative laws I use in this chapter come from the Federal Trade Commission (FTC).

The text of all of the criminal laws below can be read in their entirety at `www.usdoj.gov/criminal/cybercrime`.

The laws I've listed in the following section are *federal* statutes. Please remember that the state and local laws may (and do) differ.

Fraud and abuse

18 U.S.C. §1029 — Fraud and Related Activity in Connection with Access Devices

Only the government would define a credit card as an "access device"! Yet, that's what this statute protects. It's illegal to steal credit cards, but only if you have at least 15 cards or have charged at least $1,000 worth of goods in a calendar year. Of course, if you store credit card data on your system, it's up to you to provide adequate protection against theft.

18 U.S.C. §1030 — Fraud and Related Activity in Connection with Computers

This is the grand-daddy of all federal computer laws. The first person convicted under this statute was Robert Morris, Jr., who released the infamous Morris Worm in 1988.

This law prohibits access to a computer without authorization or to exceed authorized access. Government computers and financial institution computers are mentioned in particular, but the law goes on to include computers "used in interstate or foreign commerce or communications, including a computer located outside the United States that is used in a manner that affects interstate or foreign commerce or communication of the United States." That definition seems to include any computer connected to the Internet and any private computer system that crosses state lines or international boundaries.

One key element to this law is that damage in excess of $5,000 must have occurred. However, damage can be defined as the costs involved in bringing the system back to its original state or the costs of an investigation. What this means is that a hacker who only enters a system and has a look around cannot be prosecuted under this law. Of course, that person must be physically present in the United States or located in another country in which we have legal agreements for him to be charged and prosecuted. This is the case with all federal statutes.

18 U.S.C. §1362 — Communication Lines, Stations, or Systems

At first reading, this law seems to protect the destruction of telephone lines and equipment. However, the law also states that whoever "willfully or maliciously interferes in any way with the working or use of any such line, or system, or willfully or maliciously obstructs, hinders, or delays the transmission of any communication over any such line, or system" shall be prosecuted. It could be argued that because the Internet is carried over telephone lines, this law applies. Perhaps a person who carries out a Denial of Service attack would be guilty of violating this law.

18 U.S.C. §2511 — Interception and Disclosure of Wire, Oral, or Electronic Communications Prohibited

This law is mainly about wire taps, but because the Internet is used to transmit "electronic communications," computers are also protected. This would seem to protect e-mail communication and makes network "sniffers" illegal. Of course, the owner of the system is allowed to intercept, but outsiders or unauthorized persons are not. Not only is the interception illegal, but the disclosure of any data gathered is also illegal. What's not so clear in this statute is what constitutes an "interception." Is reading an e-mail over your co-worker's shoulder illegal?

18 U.S.C. §2701 — Unlawful Access to Stored Communications

Simply put, this law seems to make it illegal to access and alter anything on disk drives unless you have authorization. It's also illegal to make the data inaccessible to others who previously had authorized access. Perhaps this means that hackers can be convicted if they install hacking tools (thus altering the media) and changing the permissions so the administrators can't access the machines.

18 U.S.C. §2702 — Disclosure of Contents

Again, this one seems pretty simple. Companies that provide electronic communications services may not divulge the contents of the communication or the information about the subscriber. If an Internet Service Provider (ISP) is hacked and this information is stolen, the company may be held liable for not adequately protecting this data.

Intellectual property

There are literally dozens of laws that cover the protection of intellectual property, and I can't go into all of them here due to the sheer number and complexities. However, intellectual property covers copyrights, trademarks, trade secrets, offenses to the integrity of IP systems, and misuse of dissemination systems.

Basically, these laws don't look at right/wrong as a black and white issue. Instead, they look at whether or not a company tried to protect the intellectual property, how they tried to protect it, and what damage was done by the theft or destruction of the property.

17 U.S.C. §501 — Infringement of Copyright

Copyrights are a big deal, as the owners of Napster have discovered! This statute makes it illegal to reproduce or distribute copyrighted material. Actually, there are 13 different statutes under this code, but I'm not going to cover them all here. It's important to remember to copyright your material and to give the correct credit (and permissions!) for copyrighted materials you use.

If a hacker enters your system and then uses your system to store and distribute illegal software, you may be held liable, too. Also be careful of any artwork that you use on your Web site — make sure that it is free of copyright. And one last thought: If you only have 10 licenses for word processing software and you have that software installed on 11 machines, you are in violation of copyright laws.

Trademarks

Again, there are dozens of statutes here, and we all know that we should use trademarks appropriately. However, I did find one section of interest that deals with the registration of Internet domain names. The rule reads: "Any person who registers a domain name that consists of the name of another living person, or a name substantially and confusingly similar thereto, without that person's consent, with the specific intent to profit from such name by selling the domain name for financial gain to that person or any third party, shall be liable in a civil action by such person."

A few years ago, it was a popular ploy to buy up hundreds of domain names and then offer them for sale at hugely inflated prices. I haven't seen as much of this lately since this ruling came into effect. I did check today and found that www.johnsmith.com is still available but www.johndoe.com is taken!

Trade secrets

The Uniform Trade Secrets Act of 1985 was an attempt to bring all the federal and state laws into line with one another. "Trade secret" is defined as information, including a formula, pattern, compilation, program, device, method, technique, or process. However, for a trade secret to qualify for protection under the law, it must provide some competitive advantage or value for the company. This is particularly true if the secret in question required a large expense in research and development to make it. A trade secret must also be shown to have been protected against theft or loss. If a company does not tell its employees that something is secret and makes no attempt to protect it, then the person who reveals the secret cannot be prosecuted.

Privacy laws

Privacy laws are a big bandwagon in Washington, D.C. and everyone seems to be jumping on board. There are arguments on both sides — whether to increase or decrease the protection of privacy. The government can read your e-mail if it thinks you are a terrorist but, at the same time, banks and medical institutions must comply with new laws that limit the amount of personal information they can collect and disseminate.

You may have noticed that many Web sites contain a link to their "privacy policies guidelines." Check out www.cnn.com/privacy.html and www.microsoft.com/info/privacy.htm for some good examples. While there are no laws governing what can and cannot be collected from adults visiting a Web site, there is a limit as to what can be collected from a child. What is interesting, though, is that if you publish a privacy policy on the Web and then violate it yourself, you can be held liable. There have been a number of successful court cases over this issue. The sites in question were convicted of false and deceptive advertising and not strictly for invasion of privacy.

15 U.S.C. § 6801-6810 — Financial Privacy

These statutes are also known as the Gramm-Leach-Bliley Act, which places restrictions on financial institutions on when they may disclose a consumer's personal financial information to nonaffiliated third parties. It must be noted that "financial institutions" has a broad definition under this act. They include, but are not limited to, mortgage lenders, "pay day" lenders, finance companies, mortgage brokers, non-bank lenders, account services, check cashers, wire transferors, travel agencies operated in connection with financial services, collection agencies, credit counselors, and other financial advisors, tax preparation firms, non-federally insured credit unions, and investment advisors that are not required to register with the Securities and Exchange Commission.

This act says that financial institutions must tell their customers what they plan to do with personal data and to give customers an opportunity to "opt out" of having their data passed on to other companies.

This act also dictates that the senior executives of financial institutions are personally responsible for security. They need to have written security policies in place and ensure that security measures have been implemented and tested. Additionally, all staff must be trained on information security issues. I read recently that corporate officers can be fined up to $290 million dollars if they do not comply with this law.

Children's Online Privacy Protection Act (COPPA)

This is a rule from the FTC on the collection and distribution of information gathered from children under the age of 13. It states that there must be a means of verifying a child's age and that parental consent must be given to collect the data. All data concerning children must be protected and, in addition, networks that target children must desist from using unfair and deceptive advertising practices. This act was the result of complaints filed against Web sites that targeted children with games and contests.

Health Insurance Portability and Accountability Act (HIPAA)

Another biggie! Although you wouldn't guess it from the name, this federal law (Public Law 104-191) creates security and privacy standards for medical information. This came about because the government wanted to make it easier for people to transfer health insurance coverage between jobs. To help offset the increased costs for insurance companies, the government agreed to set standards for computerized medical payment systems, which potentially could save the healthcare industry a lot of money and help reduce fraud. That meant that more people's medical records would be put on computer, which resulted in standards that would need to be established to protect this sensitive information. The HIPAA Privacy Rule imposes fines — from $100 per violation up to $25,000 per year — for illegal disclosure of what is referred to as *Protected Health Information (PHI)*, even if the disclosure is accidental. Knowingly leaking or stealing PHI bumps up the penalty to $50,000 and one year in prison, while offering the information for sale can result in fines up to $250,000 and longer stretches in jail.

Although HIPAA was originally passed in 1996, the rules that implement it are still evolving. Because of this, and the fact that some parts of HIPAA are very complex, you should check out the details to see if your network needs to comply with the rules. If your network handles any kind of medical information, there's a good chance that this law may affect you.

The definition of "medical institution" is quite broad, too. Almost anyone who deals with medical information is included, such as pharmacies, doctors' offices, medical supply companies, healthcare consultants, insurance companies, billing agencies, and many more.

Like the Gramm-Leach-Bliley Act, it imposes restrictions on how data is to be stored and protected. As things stand, most covered entities must comply with the HIPAA Privacy Rule by April 14, 2003. This means they must have:

- Someone in charge of privacy
- Established acceptable privacy policies and procedures
- Created appropriate safeguards for PHI
- Signed agreements with organizations with whom they share PHI
- Trained all personnel who handle PHI to do so with great care and in compliance with the law

The main page for HIPAA at the US Department of Health and Human Services is at `http://aspe.dhhs.gove/admnsimp`. There are links to HIPAA legislation, HIPAA FAQs, and implementation guidelines. With what is probably the biggest tongue-in-cheek joke, some of the most complex parts of HIPAA are called "Administrative Simplification."

State and Foreign Laws

State laws differ from federal laws in many ways. Due to the intrastate nature of computers, jurisdiction is often difficult to decide upon. Generally, an attack originates in one state but the attacked computer is in another. The same concept is true with countries. In the case of international attacks, the country of the origin of the attack has usually takes the lead. There are also laws in foreign countries that vary greatly from those in the United States. This is particularly sticky in the area of privacy.

States

For this section I had originally intended to summarize the state computer crime laws as not all states have such laws and the ones that do vary greatly. However, during my research, I discovered that much of the data was either out of date or unreliable. So, rather than give you incorrect information, I've assembled a list of laws I could find. Please consult your attorney for interpretations of these laws or to see if any of these laws have been changed.

Computer crime laws

- Alabama: AL Code §§ 13A-8-100 to 13A-8-103
- Alaska: Statute §§ 11.46.200(a)(3), 11.46.484(a)(5), 11.46.740, 11.46.985, 11.46.990, 11.81.900(a)(46) & (52)
- Arizona: Statute §§ 13-2301(E), 13-2316
- Arkansas: Code §§ 5-41-101 to -107
- California: Penal Code §§ 484j, 499c, 502, 502.01, 502.7(h), 503, 1203.047, 2702
- Colorado: Statute §§ 18-5.5-101 to 18.5.5-102
- Connecticut: Statute §§ 53a-250 to 53a-261
- Delaware: Code Ann. tit. 11, §§ 931-939
- Florida: Statute ch. 775, 815, 934
- Georgia: Code Ann. §§ 16-7-22, Code Ann. §§ 16-9-90 to 16-9-94
- Hawaii: Statute §§ 708-891 to -893
- Idaho: Code §§ 18-2201 to -2202, 26-1220, 48-801
- Illinois: Statute, ch. 38, §§ 16D-1 to -7
- Indiana: Code § 35-43-1-4, 35-43-2-3, 35-43-4-1, 35-43-4-2, 35-43-4-3, 35-43-5-1, 35-43-7-3
- Iowa: Code §§ 716A.1 to 716A.16
- Kansas: Statute Ann. § 21-3755
- Kentucky: Statute Ann. §§ 434.840 to 434.860
- Louisiana: Statute Ann. §§ 14:73.1 to 14:73.5
- Maine: Statute Ann. tit. 17-A, ch. 18, §§ 431-433
- Maryland: Code Ann., Crim. Law §§ 27-45A, 27-145, 27-146, 27-340
- Massachusetts: Gen. L. ch. 266, §§ 30, 60A
- Michigan: Laws §§ 752.791 to 752.797
- Minnesota: Statute 609.52, 609.87, 609.88, 609.89

- Mississippi: Code Ann. ch. 45

- Missouri: Statutes §§ 569.093 -.099

- Montana: Code Ann. §§ 45-1-205(4), 45-2-101, 45-6-310, 45-6-311

- Nebraska: Statutes §§ 28-1341 to -1348

- Nevada: Statutes §§ 205.473 -.477, 205.481, 205.485, 205.491

- New Hampshire: Statute Ann. §§ 638:16 -:19

- New Jersey: Statutes Ann. §§ 2A:38A-1 to -6, 2C:20-1, 2C:20-23 to -34

- New Mexico: Statutes Ann. §§ 30-45-1 to 30-45-7

- New York: Penal Law § 155.00, 156.00, 156.05, 156.10, 156.20, 156.25, 156.26, 156.27, 156.30, 156.35, 156.50, 165.00, 165.07, 165.15, 170.00, 170.05, 170.10, 170.15, 170.20, 170.25, 170.27, 170.30, 170.35, 170.40, 170.45, 175.00, 175.05, 175.10, 175.15, 175.20, 175.25, 175.30, 175.35, 175.40, 175.45

- North Carolina: Statute §§ 14-453 to -457

- North Dakota: Central Code §§ 12.1-06.1-01, 12.1-06.1-08

- Ohio: Code Ann. §§ 2901.01(J), (M); 2901.1(I); 2901.12; 2912.01(F), (L)-(R), (T); 2913.04 (B), (D); 2913.42; 2913.81; 2933.41(A)(7)

- Oklahoma: Statute Ann. tit. 21, §§ 1951-1958

- Oregon: Statute § 164.377

- Pennsylvania: Statute § 3933

- Rhode Island: Gen. Laws § 11-52-1 to 11-52-8

- South Carolina: Code Ann. §§ 16-16-10 to 16-16-40

- South Dakota: Codified Laws Ann. §§ 43-43B-1 to 43-43B-8

- Tennessee: Code Ann. §§ 39-14-601 to 39-14-603

- Texas: Penal Code Ann. §§ 33.01 - .05

- Utah: Code Ann. §§ 76-6-701 to 76-6-705

- Virginia: Code §§ 18.2-152.1 thru 18.2-152.14

- Washington: Code § 9.26A.100, 9.26A.110, 9A.48.070, 9A.52.110, 9A.52.120, 9A.52.130, 9A.56.010, 9A.56.020, 9A.56.030, 9A.56.040, 9A.56.050, 9A.56.262, 9A.56.26, 9A.56.266

- West Virginia: Code §§ 61-3C-1 to 61-3C-21

- Wisconsin: Statute §§ 943.70

- Wyoming: Statute § 6-3-401, 6-3-501 to 6-3-505

Spam laws

Believe it or not, many states are on the side of the consumer when it comes to e-mail spamming, making it illegal to alter the headers in e-mail messages. Other states make it illegal to send adult content via spam. If your company deals in direct marketing messages, you should be aware of your state's regulations concerning spam. Check out Table 6-1 for state-specific spam laws.

Table 6-1	Spam Laws
State	*Spam Ruling*
Arkansas	Illegal to send unsolicited email using a third party's domain name without permission, misrepresent the sender or point of origin, or contain falsified routing information
California	Unsolicited commercial e-mail messages must include instructions and contact information, and opt-out requests must be honored. Certain messages must contain a (like "ADV:ADULT" for adult content) at the beginning of the subject line.
Colorado	Prohibits the sending of unsolicited commercial e-mail that uses a third party's Internet address or domain name without permission, or contains false or missing routing information. Unsolicited commercial e-mail messages must contain a label at the beginning of the subject line, and must include the sender's e-mail address and opt-out instructions; opt-out requests must be honored.
Connecticut	Illegal to send unsolicited bulk e-mail containing falsified routing information.
Delaware	Illegal to send unsolicited bulk e-mail containing falsified routing information.
Idaho	States that unsolicited bulk commercial e-mail messages must include an e-mail address for opt-out requests and requires senders to honor opt-out requests. Such messages may not use a third party's name for the return address without permission, and must contain accurate routing information.
Illinois	Illegal to send an unsolicited commercial e-mail message using a third party's domain name without permission; containing falsified routing information; or with a false or misleading subject line.

State	Spam Ruling
Iowa	States that unsolicited bulk commercial e-mail messages must include an e-mail address for opt-out requests and requires senders to honor opt-out requests. Such messages may not use a third party's name for the return address without permission, and must contain accurate routing information.
Kansas	Commercial e-mail messages may not contain falsified routing information, use a third party's domain name without permission, or have a false or misleading subject line. Senders of commercial e-mail messages must include opt-out instructions and honor opt-out requests. Unsolicited bulk commercial e-mail messages (500 or more recipients) and advertisements for sexually explicit content must contain a label at the beginning of the subject line.
Louisiana	Illegal to send unsolicited bulk commercial e-mail to more than 1,000 recipients if the e-mail messages contain falsified routing information.
Maryland	Illegal to send a commercial e-mail message that uses a third party's domain name without permission; that contains false or missing routing information; or with a false or misleading subject line.
Minnesota	Prohibits commercial e-mail that uses a third party's domain name without permission, contains false routing information; or has a false or misleading subject line. Such messages must contain opt-out instructions and contact information. Unsolicited commercial e-mail messages must contain a label at the beginning of the subject line.
Missouri	Requires unsolicited commercial e-mail messages to contain opt-out instructions and contact information.
Nevada	The first state with spam legislation! It is illegal to send unsolicited commercial e-mail unless it is labeled or otherwise readily identifiable as an advertisement and includes the sender's name, street address, and e-mail address, along with opt-out instructions. The law prohibits all unsolicited e-mail that contains falsified routing information.
North Carolina	It is illegal to send unsolicited bulk commercial e-mail containing falsified routing information.
Oklahoma	It is illegal to send unsolicited bulk commercial e-mail containing falsified routing information.

(continued)

Table 6-1 *(continued)*

State	Spam Ruling
Pennsylvania	Requires unsolicited commercial e-mail messages containing explicit sexual materials to contain a label at the beginning of the subject line.
Rhode Island	States that unsolicited bulk commercial e-mail messages must include an e-mail address for opt-out requests and requires senders to honor opt-out requests. Such messages may not use a third party's name for the return address without permission, and must contain accurate routing information.
South Dakota	Prohibits sending commercial e-mail that misrepresents or obscures its point of origin or routing information, or contains a false or misleading subject line.
Tennessee	Unsolicited bulk commercial e-mail messages must include opt-out instructions and contact information, and opt-out requests must be honored. Certain messages must contain a label at the beginning of the subject line.
Utah	Unsolicited e-mail and sexually explicit messages must disclose the sender's name and physical address, and the point of origin of the message and must include a label at the beginning of the subject line, along with opt-out instructions. The law also prohibits the falsification of routing information.
Virginia	Illegal to send unsolicited bulk e-mail containing falsified routing information.
Washington	Illegal to send a commercial e-mail message that uses a third party's domain name without permission; that contains false or missing routing information; or with a false or misleading subject line.
West Virginia	It is illegal to use a third party's domain name without permission, misrepresent the point of origin or other routing information, have a false or misleading subject line, or contain sexually explicit materials. Each message must include the sender's name and return e-mail address, along with the date and time it was sent.
Wisconsin	Unsolicited commercial e-mail messages that contain obscene material or depict sexually explicit conduct must include the words "Adult Advertisement" in the subject line.

Overseas laws and safe harbor

The European Commission's Directive on Data Privacy went into effect in October,1998, and prohibits the transfer of personal data to non-European Union nations that do not meet the European adequacy standard for privacy protection. While the United States and the European Union share the goal of enhancing privacy protection for their citizens, the United States takes a different approach to privacy from that taken by the European Union. The United States relies on a mix of legislation, regulation, and self-regulation while the European Union relies on comprehensive legislation. The European model requires creation of government data protection agencies and registration of databases with those agencies. As a result of these different privacy approaches, the Directive may have significantly hampered the ability of U.S. companies to exchange data with European companies, even if they were offices of the same company. In order to bridge these different privacy approaches, the U.S. Department of Commerce, in consultation with the European Commission, developed a "safe harbor" framework.

Companies that decide to participate in the safe harbor must comply with the safe harbor's requirements and make a public declaration. The company must contact the Department of Commerce in writing each year and state that it agrees to adhere to the safe harbor's requirements. The company must also state in its published privacy policy statement that it adheres to the safe harbor. Because the requirements are self-regulatory in the United States, many privacy advocates are quite critical of this program.

Organizations must comply with the seven safe harbor principles. The principles require the following:

- ✔ **Notice.** Companies must notify individuals how and why they collect information about them and how they intend to use it. They must provide contact information for inquiries or complaints.

- ✔ **Choice.** Companies must give individuals the opportunity to opt out on whether their personal information will be disclosed to a third party or used for some other purpose than originally authorized. For sensitive information, an opt in choice must be given.

- ✔ **Transfers to Third Parties.** To disclose information to a third party, companies must apply the Notice and Choice rules (previous). If the company wants to transfer information to a third party that is acting as an agent, it may do so if it makes sure that the third party subscribes to the safe harbor principles or is subject to the Directive. As an alternative, the organization can enter into a written agreement with such third party requiring that the third party provide at least the same level of privacy protection as is required by the relevant principles.

- ✔ **Access.** Individuals must have access to personal information about them that a company stores and be able to correct, amend, or delete that information where it is inaccurate.

✔ **Security.** Companies must take reasonable precautions to protect personal information from loss, misuse, unauthorized access, disclosure, alteration, and destruction.

✔ **Data Integrity.** Personal information must be relevant for the purposes for which it is to be used. An organization should take reasonable steps to ensure that data is reliable for its intended use, accurate, complete, and current.

✔ **Enforcement.** In order to ensure compliance with the safe harbor principles, there must be:

- Readily available and affordable independent recourse mechanisms for individual complaints and disputes. These must be able to be investigated and resolved and damages awarded where the applicable law.

- Procedures for verifying that the safe harbor principles have been implemented.

- Obligations to remedy problems arising out of a failure to comply with the principles. Penalties must be strong to ensure compliance. Companies that fail to provide annual self-certification letters will no longer appear in the list of participants and safe harbor benefits will no longer be assured.

Privacy and Monitoring

In our litigious society, anyone can sue anyone else for just about anything. Cases brought before civil courts are often not held to the same rules and regulations as they are in criminal courts. In the O. J. Simpson case, he won in a criminal court but lost in a civil court. Cases involving computer technologies are heard in civil courts, too. Often, the cases have involved invasion of privacy.

Companies are increasing the amount of monitoring they do of their employees' e-mails and Web surfing. Companies are wary of employee abuse of the equipment, and they don't want to get caught in the middle of a battle when an employee sends out a racially sensitive joke, for example. The courts have ruled that computer equipment belongs to the company that furnishes it and, therefore, they also own the data on all those computers. Thus, employees should have no expectation of privacy of anything they store or transmit on a company system.

The laws on computer abuse support the company, but the language can be confusing and misleading. In order for a company to stay within the law, they should have a clear, written company policy governing the monitoring of electronic communications and computer files and what it considers to be appropriate use of the system. Some companies go so far as to change the banners on the logon screens which state that an employee agrees to any monitoring when they log on.

Sticky Wickets — Ethics

Laws are often seen as black and white; right or wrong. That's pretty amazing when you consider that many laws are based on ethics, but you can't legislate ethics. That's because ethics consist of shades of gray, and cultural and religious upbringing often change perceptions of what is right or wrong. Here are some cases involving computers and ethics. I'll let you decide what should be done. There are no right or wrong answers here.

Case one

You're working as a network administrator for a company and you discover that a friend of yours, who has moved to another company, had installed hacking tools on the system. Your company has a rule that hacking tools are not to be placed on the system, even for vulnerability testing. You know where your friend works and still talk to him. Do you tell him what you found? Do you tell your current employer? Do you tell your friend's employer?

Case two

You're the e-mail administrator for a company. All the e-mail that has been incorrectly addressed gets dumped into one of your mailboxes, and your job is to go through that mailbox and forward the e-mail to the correct person. In reviewing e-mails, you discover that your boss and a co-worker are having an affair. Do you forward the e-mail and say nothing? Do you just delete the e-mail? Do you mention the e-mails to one of them?

Case three

Your company has bought a cool software program for you to use. The software license says that you are allowed to install an extra copy on your laptop that you use to do your work at home. But, when you get home, you decide that you'd like to have the software on your desktop machine in your office, too. Do you put it on the desktop machine and delete it from your laptop?

Case four

You're the boss of a busy department. You suspect that one of your employees is getting ready to jump ship to another company and may be giving the new company some proprietary data. Your company doesn't have any policy on monitoring employees' computer use and you have no software to audit his use. You ask the employee who sits in the next cubicle to spy for you by listening in to his conversations and read e-mails that are sitting on his screen. Is there any other recourse? Do the ends justify the means?

Contacting the Authorities

Although many networks are successfully hacked each year, only a small percentage of the intrusions are actually reported to the authorities. That is because companies don't want the adverse publicity and they are often unsure of who to call in for help. What they don't realize is that this allows the hacker to attack someone else.

Law enforcement authorities have come a long way in dealing with computer crime. While not every office may have the capabilities of investigating the crime, they do know who they can contact for help. If you suspect that you have been hacked, especially if there is potential for loss, you should start with your local law enforcement. They will discuss the details with you and decide whether they can handle it or if it should be bumped up to another agency.

There is a relatively new government program that is managed by the FBI and the *National Infrastructure Protection Center (NIPC)* called *InfraGard*. This program was set up to share information and incident reports between organizations and the government agencies. You can report incidents to them without fear of publicity at www.infragard.net/ireporting.htm. You have the option of calling them, sending them a fax, or sending them a secure e-mail about the incident. All incident reports are sanitized so that anyone reading or responding to the report has no knowledge of who the company is. You can also become a member of InfraGard and that information is also available at their Web site. You may also want to check out the NIPC information at www.nipc.gov.

After the authorities decide to start an investigation, they can and will start collecting evidence. That means that computer files and equipment can be taken. If you plan on cooperating with them, as the owner of the system, you can simply give them what they ask for without the need of a search warrant. Often, the backup tapes you have created will suffice, and they won't need you to take your network offline.

Of particular interest to the authorities is child pornography. There have been cases where an employee was found to be using a company's system to store and distribute this sort of material. Be very careful in cases such as this. The federal authorities will become involved and most of your system will be examined.

Chapter 7

Building a Secure Network from Scratch

*W*hat if you could do it all over again and build your network from scratch? If you're like most companies, security has always been an afterthought and the solutions have been like repairing potholes — a patch here and a patch there with fingers crossed that more holes don't appear. This ad hoc approach doesn't provide consistent and reliable security and adds to the pain of troubleshooting problems on the network.

Security always gets a lot of attention when there's something big on the news or if your network has recently suffered from some sort of attack. But memories are short and the resources that were available in the heat of the moment quickly vanish into thin air. When you build security into your network design, however, that's one less thing to go wrong, and you don't have to beg for money for new security devices later.

Getting Layered

A good security infrastructure looks at your network as three separate components or, as I refer to them, *layers*:

- ✔ **Network** — Consists of all the things that make the network work — network cards, routers, switches, hubs, and so on.

- ✔ **Platforms** — The different operating systems that your servers and desktop machines use to run.

✔ **Processes** — The applications and the way they move data around to different machines.

Most security designs only look at one layer — the network layer. Usually, filtering routers, firewalls, or intrusion detection is added to this layer and the network is considered "secure." That's a fallacy. I call it the "M&M Security Model." It consists of a hard, candy outside and a soft, gooey middle. That is, all the protection is put into surrounding the network, and there's nothing to use as a defense if the perimeter is broken.

A more effective security design adds security to each layer. That way, if one level of defense is breached, there are other fail-safes to at least limit the amount of damage (or intrusion) that can be done. The network can be secured with security mechanisms such as firewalls and routers for the first layer, the operating systems of all your computers (including your firewall!) can be hardened against attack for your second layer, and the applications themselves can be configured to defeat common vulnerabilities as your third layer. Each layer supports the other, but is not totally dependent upon the other for all of its security.

Securing Your Network Components

Before you start laying in your defenses, you'll need to look at all the various components that make up your network. This includes the machines that make the network work, the services that make machines and data available, and how you connect to the outside world. Each of these pieces of the puzzle needs to have its appropriate security measures in place in order to create the layers of security. The bits and pieces I'm mentioning here are common to most networks, but are not an exhaustive list.

Routers, switches, and hubs

The first piece of equipment from the Internet to your network is usually the router. A router is like an AAA Triptik — it knows all the available routes to the destinations (computers) on your network and all the available routes back out again. If there is congestion or outages in the network, the router routes around them. A router has some security measures built-in such as being able to deny certain types of traffic. By default, routers allow all traffic, but you can configure them to filter out protocols that you won't be using.

Routers come in various sizes and robustness depending on how much bandwidth and traffic they are supposed to handle. Some are the size of a slice of bread and other are as large as a refrigerator. All routers have an internal operating system that has been configured at the factory to a certain level of security. However, sometimes these operating systems have security holes, so check with your vendor for security patches. Routers also come with default administrator passwords used for configuring the rules for allowed traffic.

Be sure to change the default password because every hacker in the world knows, or has access to, those passwords.

Hubs are used to connect separate networks. They are dumb repeaters with no routing information and are not used as security devices. They are usually used to connect two or more networks to a router.

Switches are like hubs except their job is to maintain an even level of bandwidth among networked computers. They are not used as security devices, either.

DNS

DNS stands for *Domain Name Service* and is the service that translates domain names into IP addresses (like www.xyz.com into 192.0.0.10) and IP addresses into domain names. If you have only a couple of machines connected to an ISP, then your ISP probably handles this for you. However, if your network many computers, you need to have a DNS server. Often, companies have two DNS servers: one to handle the addressing for all the computers on the internal network and another to handle Internet addressing.

Your DNS server's operating system should be hardened and the appropriate security patches applied. The DNS application (frequently *BIND* — Berkeley Internet Name Domain, or the proprietary version built into your operating system) is subject to security flaws and should be patched. Internal DNS and external DNS should be on separate machines so that your internal network isn't visible to the entire outside world.

E-mail

Will your network need a lot of internal communication between machines and the occasional connection to the outside for e-mail? Are you handling your e-mail or is your ISP doing all of that for you? If your ISP is handling all of your e-mail (inbound and outbound), then you probably don't have a need for an e-mail server. However, if your business is heavily reliant upon e-mail, you will probably have a high volume of e-mail traffic. In that case, you probably want two e-mail servers: one for inbound traffic and one for outbound traffic.

Your e-mail servers need to have their operating systems hardened and security patches applied. The e-mail application needs to have any appropriate security patches applied as well. You also need anti-virus protection on the e-mail servers because most viruses enter through this path.

Web

If you use your Internet connect for occasional Web surfing, there are no special requirements for equipment. You simply use your Web browsers on your desktop machines to connect to the Internet. But if your company has the need for a Web site, then you need at least one Web server, depending on the amount of traffic you support.

Your Web server should have its operating system hardened and security patches applied. The Web server application needs to be configured for security, which means disabling guest accounts, limiting access to directories, and applying necessary security patches. Web servers are notoriously easy to hack and it's important to keep the security patches up to date on these machines.

Databases

If your Web server offers dynamic content (content that changes on the fly), or if you are using it for e-commerce, you will also need at least one database server to hold and serve up the data to the Web server. The database server and the Web server should always be on separate computers. The reason for this has to do with the fact that Web servers are easily hacked and databases are usually full of important information. If you put the Web server and the database on the same machine, that makes it easier for a hacker to steal the data on the database. When the two machines are separate, you can place more security on the more important machine — this also creates an important, additional layer of security.

In order for databases and Web servers to exchange data, you need to run small programs called *scripts* or be running a type of middleware that does the translation for you. (One type of popular middleware is Cold Fusion.) These scripts or middleware can also contain security holes. Examine the scripts themselves for holes or apply security patches to the middleware. Of course, your database operating system should be hardened and the security patches applied. The database application itself will also need to have its own security patches applied.

Remote access to internal network

Many companies have a sales force that uses a Web connection to the internal network to accomplish such tasks as entering customer orders and checking on inventory. Other companies allow employees to dial-in to their internal network to use specific applications or to upload data such as timesheets. If your users are dialing-in for access, you'll need to have a bank of modems to handle the calls. If you're not using modems, then they'll normally connect to one machine that then allows them to enter the rest of the network.

In either case, modem connections or direct connections, you want to have some very strong security. The data passing between a remote connection and your network will be in the clear, so you may want to consider setting up a *VPN* (Virtual Private Network), which includes encryption. (VPNs are discussed in depth in Chapter 16.) Additionally, you want some form of strong authentication because logon IDs and passwords are easily cracked. Security tokens, digital certificates, and biometrics are some solutions to look at. They are cumbersome and complicated, but they may be worth the effort if your company can afford them.

If your company is using remote control software such as PCAnywhere, be sure that the appropriate security patches are applied and strong passwords are used.

Application and file servers

If your company allows outside access to your internal network, you may want to have application or file servers specifically for their use.

If you are allowing file transfers from outside your network, consider which applications you will permit for these transfers. The most common application used is *FTP* (File Transfer Protocol). If you plan on using FTP, remember that most Web servers also allow FTP transfers.

Whether you have file servers or application servers, both need to have their operating systems hardened and the appropriate security patches applied. An application server needs to have security patches applied for the different applications that you run. (A database is actually an application server, but I cover it separately.)

Setting Levels of Trust

After you have decided on all the bits and pieces that make up your network, you then need to decide how much trust you're going to give the various components. The level of trust is usually determined by how likely that machine is exposed to threats from the outside and how likely that machine is to suffer an attack. Usually, all machines on the internal network are highly trusted, those outside the firewall are not trusted, and those that sit in the middle have a limited level of trust. Take a bank for instance. Those who work inside the bank are trusted and those who are outside the bank are not trusted. The customers who come into the bank have limited levels of trust. The amount of trust you give a machine is controlled by rules and security devices.

In addition to establishing the level of trust, you have to decide how important the machines (and the data and applications stored on them) are to your company's business. Usually, you don't expose the most important machines to outside threats. If the important machines need to be connected to the outside, you must increase the level of protection in relation to their importance. The risk assessment you have done helps you with these decisions.

In other cases, you may find that it's important to connect a machine to the outside, but it doesn't need a high level of protection. A good example is a Web server that contains public information but no critical data. This machine can be placed on its own network segment with protection measures between it and the internal network, but little or no protections between it and the outside. This sort of placement is called the *sacrificial lamb*. The use of a sacrificial lamb is not meant to appease the network gods, however. It's more like the fact that damage or disruption to it doesn't bother you that much. Of course, always keep back-up tapes of these machines so that rebuilding them is easily carried out!

Sacrificial lambs aren't always hung out of the network with no protection. One effective way of protection is to set them up in a *DMZ*. Yes, that's demilitarized zone. It's effectively a "no man's land." There's not much in the way of protection in a DMZ. One example of a DMZ architecture is shown in Figure 7-1.

In this case, the data flow and the protection scheme is as follows:

- The DMZ is offered some protection from the Internet by being behind the router. The router is configured to allow only HTTP, FTP, and DNS traffic through to the DMZ.

- The machines in the DMZ also employ practical security — their operating systems have been hardened and application software patches have been applied. (Note that sacrificial lambs should also have their operating systems hardened and patches applied.)

- The firewall doesn't allow any machine to connect to the internal network unless the connection request originates from the inside. In other words, the machines can't communicate with the inside without being asked to first.

✔ The firewall also restricts the type of traffic allowed to pass from the Internet to the internal network and back out again. Your security policies go towards setting up these rules on the firewall.

Another way to set up a DMZ is to put both the internal network and the DMZ behind the router and the firewall, but the networks are still kept separate. Figure 7-2 shows an example.

The setup in Figure 7-2 gives the DMZ more protection from the outside. You can also add another router on the internal network side of the firewall for an additional layer of protection between the DMZ and the internal network.

Now the question is, "Why the two choices?" The answer has to do with both performance and security.

Firewalls tend to be very labor-intensive machines. They are constantly churning away, filtering, and examining traffic. When the traffic is really heavy, the firewall can become a bottleneck and slow down traffic. A router in front of a firewall does a bit of pre-screening to help out the firewall. Because Web servers tend to handle high traffic volumes, it usually makes sense to put the Web server in a DMZ in front of the firewall so it doesn't add to the workload of the firewall.

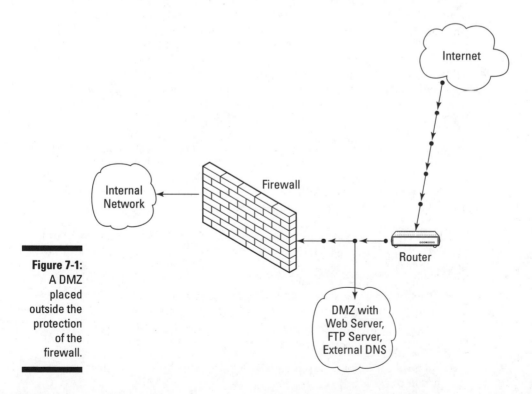

Figure 7-1:
A DMZ placed outside the protection of the firewall.

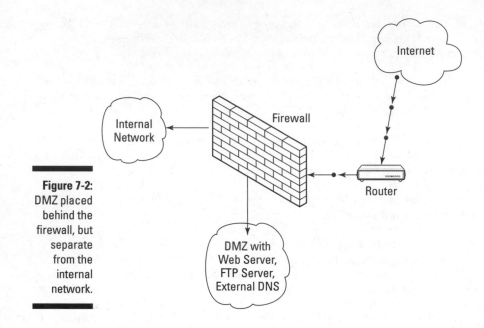

Figure 7-2:
DMZ placed
behind the
firewall, but
separate
from the
internal
network.

On the other hand, maybe your Web server needs a little more protection than just what the router offers. In that case, you can put the Web server in the DMZ behind the firewall. This is a good news/bad news scenario. The good news is that the DMZ now has more protection. The bad news is that the firewall now has more holes in it. Firewalls filter and examine the traffic via the rulesets. Each rule opens or closes little holes (communication channels) for the traffic to pass through. When you have lots of machines with different types or traffic behind a firewall, you have to open up lots of little holes. If you're not very careful, your firewall could become Swiss cheese!

Each of the DMZ architectures has a trade-off, and you have to decide which is the better risk worth taking. Of course, the risk assessment you did (Remember? Risk assessment was covered in Chapter 3) will help with your decisions on how much protection your machines need and where they ought to be placed in these architectures.

The DMZs I've shown you aren't the only solutions; they are just the simplest ones. They do, however, illustrate the layered concept that I talk about at the beginning of the chapter:

✔ The networks (internal and DMZ) are protected with security devices (router and firewall).

✔ The platforms are all protected by hardening their operating systems and having security patches applied.

✔ All applications on all platforms have the appropriate security patches applied.

Therefore, if the network protections fail, the platforms are protected from some attacks because their vulnerabilities have been mitigated with the security patches. If the platform security fails, then the applications are protected against some attacks because of their security patches.

Of course, no security is perfect. Unfortunately, many people have bought the myth that firewalls provide the ultimate protection. They don't. Firewalls can be defeated by talented hackers who know the firewall system you are using. If you think about it, the firewall in your car between you and the engine is not intended to keep you safe from fire — it's there to give you some protection so you have time to get out of the way. Look at your computer firewall the same way. It's there to protect you but you'd better have another plan ready to go if it fails. (See Chapters 19 and 20 for incident response and disaster recovery.)

Part III
The All-Important Security Mechanisms

The 5th Wave   By Rich Tennant

COMPUTER SCIENCES LAB

"I'm sure there will be a good job market when I graduate. I created a virus that will go off that year."

In this part . . .

It's time to assemble those locks, chains, fences, and barricades to your network! After you've looked at your potential weaknesses and decided upon your plan of action, it's time to decide how and where to install the mechanisms to ensure security.

The chapters in this part look at how the different mechanisms work and helps you to decide the best implementation for your network security. These chapters aren't so technical as to dry your eyes out but just technical enough. They may not end up being your favorite bedtime stories, but they can help you sleep better at night!

Chapter 8

Anti-Virus Software

• •

In This Chapter

▶ Understanding how anti-virus software works

▶ Looking at a typical virus scan

▶ Finding out if anti-virus programs work

▶ Considering content filtering software

▶ Using your e-mail program to filter out some viruses

▶ Looking at anti-virus do's and don'ts

▶ What to do in a virus emergency

• •

*V*iruses. Ugh! As I was writing this book, I was getting approximately 100 messages a day that were infected with the Klez virus. Although I have anti-virus software running and was fortunate not to have been actually infected, it still took time to respond to the alerts and to find and delete the infected files. What a waste of time!

It's difficult to get an exact number of viruses or infections because there is no central agency responsible for collecting such data, and viruses themselves are often known by a number of different names. One company in the U.K. that filters all of its subscribers' e-mail for spam and viruses has reported that in the early months of 2001, only one out of every 1,053 e-mails traveling through the company's gateways had a malicious attachment. A year later, the frequency had jumped to one out of every 325 e-mails. That's a huge increase any way you look at it.

Viruses cost businesses money, and the threat is not going to go away any time soon. The interoperability between applications only makes it easier for virus writers to release viruses that can spread quickly and quietly without the user's knowledge.

Understanding Anti-Virus Software

It's amazing how few people actually understand how anti-virus programs (also known as *AV scanners*) detect and eliminate viruses from their systems.

This is due, in part, to the vendors' lack of easy-to-understand documentation. Therefore, anti-virus programs are often misconfigured and out-of-date and do little or nothing to protect the systems on which they're installed.

All AV scanners, including products like Norton and McAfee, work with a database that contains information about viruses; this information is called the virus *fingerprint* or *signature*. The database needs to be updated frequently so that it contains the most up-to-date virus information. Did you know that anti-virus vendors generally offer updates well ahead of a mass infection? That's because viruses are often detected and reported several weeks to months before end-users are aware of them. However, because people do not keep their scanners updated, a virus can quickly reach epidemic proportions. Then there is the inevitable mass scramble to get to the vendors' Web sites to download the updated files, which sometimes overwhelms the Web sites and further delays updates.

Of course, some virus epidemics have been due to the fact that the virus exhibited completely new code and behaviors that the scanners did not have in their database. The database is based upon existing viruses and behaviors previously seen. This is a significant weakness of AV products that vendors try to overcome with the use of *hueristics* — a method of anticipating and examining behaviors that is explained later in this chapter.

AV scanners also suffer from a lack of support from upper management. They're often given a low priority in the security budget because management doesn't see the immediate return on their investment. And because AV scanners need constant updates, management doesn't want to invest in the labor costs of keeping the product working. Add to this the plethora of anti-virus products from which to choose, and many system administrators despair. They'll install just about anything and call it "good enough."

AV scanner basics

AV scanners are a bit like police cruising the beat. But instead of watching your neighborhood, they're watching action in your computer. They look out for suspicious behavior and attempt to intercede when they think something bad is happening or about to happen. Both the police and AV scanners look for patterns and behaviors they know to be troublemakers and leap into action when a suspect crosses a predetermined threshold of acceptability. Like the police, however, AV scanners sometimes reach the wrong conclusions. This is usually caused by insufficient data or new behavioral patterns.

How and when your AV scanner actually scans for viruses depends on the product you use, which features you have installed, and how the administrators have configured it to act. By default, most scanners work in the background without you realizing it.

Virus detection is an inexact science, and it is impossible to create an AV scanner that is 100 percent accurate. Because viruses attempt to look like normal computer operations, the AV scanners have to examine code and how it operates. However, it is simply not possible to know how every bit of code that enters a computer is going to operate, and it is not feasible to test every bit of code before it executes. To do so would demand so much of the processing power of the CPU that normal programs would not be able to execute when the AV scanner is working. The best a scanner can do is to look for clues.

The engine and the database

The AV scanner actually consists of two parts: the scanning engine and the database. The engine provides the user interface and a library of commonly used functions. The engine functions consist of dozens of complex searching algorithms, CPU emulators, and various forms of programming logic. The engine determines which files to scan, which functions to run, and how to react when a suspected virus is found. However, the engine knows absolutely nothing about the viruses themselves and is useless without the signature database.

In addition to containing the virus signature files, the database also contains the rulesets used in the heuristic scans. The word *heuristic* comes from a Greek word meaning "to discover." A scanning database contains heuristic algorithms that make certain assumptions about what a virus may look like. The database analyzes a program's structure, its attributes, and its behavior. After completing the analysis, if the database concludes that it looks like a duck, walks like a duck, and quacks like a duck, it's probably a duck — or a virus in this case.

Because the distinction between the scanning engine and the database is not obvious to most people, many religiously update the signature files for the database but are unaware that the engine also needs updating. Checking for updates or upgrades for the scanning engine when you look for signature updates is very important.

If you have the correct signatures in your database but the wrong version of the scanning engine, there's a good chance that your anti-virus program won't catch important viruses. And because it won't be apparent to you that it's not working correctly, you won't know it until it's too late!

A typical scan

AV scanners have a number of tricks they use to prevent virus infections, find infections, and disinfect programs and files. They use three basic methods of operation:

✔ They look for infections by known viruses using the database of signature files.

✔ They monitor changes, or attempted changes, to files and programs.

✔ They scan for suspicious activity by using rules-based logic.

Using the database of signature files

When a virus copies itself from one file to another, it leaves bits of its code in the infected file. The *sequence* of that code is specific to each virus and is part of what make up the fingerprint of the virus. When the scan is run, and a sequence or fingerprint is found, the AV software does what you had configured it to do: notify you, attempt to disinfect the file, quarantine the file, or delete it.

Monitoring changes

When a virus infects a program, it generally changes the size of that program. To track those changes, the known size of each executable program is computed and stored in the database when the anti-virus product is first installed. These sizes are called *checksums*. When a scan runs, it compares the stored checksums to the current checksums. If the checksums vary considerably, the AV scanner runs other routines to investigate further. If the change in the size of the program can't be attributed to a known virus found in the database, a generic disinfection routine is run to see if it can restore the program to its original state.

Scanning for suspicious activity

This type of scan is the "looks like a duck" heuristic mentioned earlier. The heuristic scan uses its algorithms to look at programs and files and give them an overall "score". If the score is high, there is a good likelihood that a virus is present. What happens from that point varies from product to product, but many AV scanners then attempt to emulate what the suspected virus may do. Rather than examining the logic of the suspected virus code, the scanner runs a simulation of a virus in a virtual environment. This simulation has also come to be known as the "sandbox" emulation. This is a very effective technique for attempting to identify new viruses that don't appear in the signature database, but it can also cause many false-positive reports.

Do AV programs really work?

Until the early 1990s, there was no way for end-users to ensure that anti-virus products actually did what they claimed to do. Many anti-virus vendors marketed their products by claiming that "Brand X Anti-virus works better than Brand Z because we check for more viruses!" This was misleading because no one knew exactly how many viruses existed. There was no central "storehouse" of viruses, and vendors used their own names for viruses (it's still common for one virus to be known by several names). The anti-virus vendors also disagreed on how AV scanners should operate in principle. Some vendors felt that AV scanners should look only for new viruses, and others felt the scanners should search both old and new viruses.

Two things happened to change the AV scanner market. In 1993, Joe Wells, a research editor with a business magazine, began collecting viruses from around the world and created a "library" or central clearinghouse of viruses. He called this library of viruses the "Wild List" and made it available to legitimate anti-virus researchers. His list divided viruses into those known to have infected systems (*in the wild*) and those that had been written but were not actively infecting (*in the zoo*). He also created a naming convention of viruses to maintain an efficient and searchable database.

The other notable event was the development of commercial anti-virus testing and certification by a company known as the National Computer Security Association (NSCA, which later became ISCA.net and is now called TruSecure Corporation). Dr. Richard Ford, a noted virus expert, created a virus testing lab for NCSA in which vendors could submit their products for testing. His lab environment tested the AV scanners to see if they could detect all the viruses in the WildList. Although the original test results were dismal (many scanners failed to detect more than 80 percent of the viruses in the list), a standard testing method had been created — and the AV vendors could prove that their products worked as claimed. Other commercial and independent test labs continue this effort today in an attempt to help the user find reliable AV products.

Believe it or not, there is no industry standard for AV scanners. There are, however, commercial and independent labs that test AV software to see if they catch all the viruses they are supposed to. The two best labs are the Virus Bulletin at `www.virusbtn.com/vb100` and the ISCA Labs at `www.icsalabs.com/html/communities/anti-virus/index.shtml`. Both of these labs let you see whether the various anti-virus products have passed or failed the latest testing. Check them out, and you'll likely be surprised at the number of products that fail.

Content Filtering

In the early 1990s, content filtering made its debut in the form of family-oriented, Web-surfing filters that made it possible to block sites parents found offensive from family viewing on home computers. Soon libraries began installing these filters to prevent users from accessing porn sites. (Some libraries have been taken to court over this matter, but that is a different story.) Content filters have grown-up. The technology has matured and the programs can do much more now than just block Web sites.

But how does content filtering relate to viruses? If you think about it, many of the newer viruses have been distributed via e-mail. Those infected e-mails often contain a common phrase in the subject line or the message text. If you can catch those messages before they reach the recipient, you can save your network from potential infections.

Filtering software

Content filtering software is able to search the contents of network traffic for messages or programs you don't want to come in. The software is installed on a server at the gateway (entrance) from the Internet and can look at all SMTP (mail) or HTTP (Web) traffic that moves in and out of the network. You set up the rules for what you want the filter to search for and what it should do when it finds a match. The rules are extremely flexible, and they are what create the filters. You can tell the software to search for text strings in messages and/or to inspect all e-mail attachments. Although you can specify file extensions such as "exe" or "vbs," the more sophisticated content filtering programs also examine the structure of the files.

Say, for example, there is a new virus circulating in which the phrase "Look what I found" is in the subject header and the attachment has the file extension of "zyx." Using the program's interface, you can set up a rule that tells the program to look for both the subject header and the attachment type. You can also tell the program what to do when it finds one of these e-mails. You have many choices:

- Delete the e-mail and attachment.
- Quarantine the e-mail and attachment for an administrator to view.
- Forward the e-mail and strip the attachment for deletion or quarantine.
- Send the e-mail and attachment to the recipient with another e-mail sent to the administrator that a possible virus has been found and sent onward (This step not recommended because it could send the virus onward!).
- Bounce the e-mail and attachment back to the sender.
- Send an e-mail message to the sender that a possible virus has been found in the e-mail he or she just sent.

There are many more options to chose from and they depend largely on the product you are using. Check with your user's manual or the vendor's Web site for all the available options.

Some *content filtering* programs also work in concert with anti-virus programs (which are installed separately) to give you another level of protection.

In addition to providing a level of anti-virus protection, many companies are finding that content filtering can help protect against the leakage of company secrets and proprietary information. You can set up the filters to look for key words that indicate a message with a forbidden subject is being sent, which prevents the message from coming in and sends a notice to the administrator. Government agencies find this sort of software useful when looking for words such as Secret or Top Secret.

As with many security mechanisms, the choices among vendors is staggering, and there are a few drawbacks as well. Although some of the rules are re-configured, others are created manually. The primary problem is that if your rule is not defined correctly, the offending traffic won't be caught. For example, if you specified the file extension "vbx" instead of "vbs," there's a chance the filter won't work. Some programs allow you to use wildcards such as the asterisk (*), but you must be careful where you use them or you may filter too much traffic. Additionally, when there is a heavy load of e-mail traffic or a lot of big attachments to examine, the program can delay the delivery of e-mail from several minutes to several hours. And last but not least, you have to assign an administrator (or someone of authority) the responsibility of examining quarantined messages and responding to problems. Some administrators see these tasks as trivial, and the messages quickly stack up.

Filtering in e-mail programs

Did you know that most e-mail programs have the ability to filter messages on their own? That comes as a surprise to many people who have never learned the intricacies of their e-mail programs. These filters can be used to move personal messages to specific mailboxes, move spam messages to the trash, and to quarantine suspected virus bearing messages.

To set up filters against viruses, you need to use the specific phrases found in the e-mail subject header and message body. This is important because generics won't work. Two sites I use to get specific information on virus are

- ✔ **Symantec** at `http://securityresponse.symantec.com/avcenter/vinfodb.html`
- ✔ **F-Secure** at `www.f-secure.com/v-descs`

Once you have the specific phrases used by current viruses, you can create rules or filters that will look for messages containing these phrases in either the subject line or in the body of the message. You can tell the rule to filter out these messages upon receipt and either store them in a special folder you have created, or delete them upon receipt. You can get the instructions for creating rules or filters in the different e-mail programs — such as Outlook, Outlook Express, Netscape Mail, or Eudora — by clicking on the *Help* command and entering a phrase such as "creating rules." Each of the programs handles the creation of rules or filters differently.

Be aware that by simply creating a filter or a rule to catch messages with possible viruses is not a fool-proof method. Ideally, this should be considered a short-term fix to use until you have updated your anti-virus signature files.

In addition to the filters, the newer versions of Outlook and Outlook Express use *Security Zone Security Settings* to further assist in preventing viruses. These settings can be found under the Tools⇨Options menu. Figure 8-1 shows this Options dialog box.:

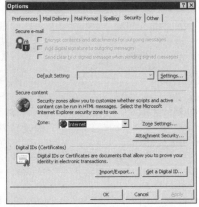

Figure 8-1:
Security
Zone and
Attachment
Security for
Outlook 2000
(v 9).

Your version of Outlook may look slightly different as changes are made in the different versions. If you have trouble finding it in yours, look in the *Help* section for the program and type in "attachment security."

Anti-Virus Do's and Don'ts

I wish I could give you a simple list of how to set up your anti-virus program but, given the number of different products on the market, that isn't feasible. I can, however, give you some basic rules to follow.

✔ Do have a written anti-virus policy that details the responsibilities of management and staff, how anti-virus is to be maintained, and specific instructions on what to do in an emergency.

✔ Do make sure that anti-virus software is installed on every machine, even if the machine is not capable of running e-mail. Viruses can sit undetected in files on any machine.

✔ Do update anti-virus signature files and scanning engines regularly. I recommend at least a weekly update, although daily is better. If your company has a central anti-virus server, it can install updates on other machines on the network. However, a computer must be turned on for this to work. If a machine was not turned on at the time of the update, it will have to be updated manually.

✔ Do run the anti-virus program in full-time, background, automatic, auto-protect, or similar mode.

✔ Do enable scans of the memory, master and boot records, and system files upon start up of every machine. It doesn't take long for an anti-virus program to complete these scans and it's just plain silly not to enable these features.

✔ Do configure the anti-virus program to scan *all* files — not just executable programs. Viruses come in all sorts of files and just scanning executables is not enough.

✔ Do enable the anti-virus heuristic controls (if they are available). A heuristic scan takes longer, but not so much longer that it makes much difference to users.

✔ Don't allow Windows Scripting Host (WSH) to run on machines that don't need it. Although some Windows programs need WSH to run, most machines can have this removed without harm. WSH controls the Visual Basic Language and many viruses have been written with it. By removing WSH, the virus can't operate. You can get good instructions for removing WSH from `http://www.sophos.com/support/faqs/wsh.html`. This site lists the methods of removing this feature on Windows 95, 98, NT, and 2000.

✔ Do enable Macro Virus Protection in all your Microsoft Office programs.

✔ Do disable the Preview Pane view in Outlook and Outlook Express. Some viruses can be launched by simply previewing them, even if the message is never opened. Disabling this feature saves you a lot of grief.

✔ Do not enable JavaScript for e-mail. Although there are no JavaScript viruses, it's only a matter of time before they appear, too. There are other vulnerabilities in JavaScript other than viruses, so it's a good idea to disable this feature in any case.

✔ Don't allow your e-mail programs to "auto open" attachments.

✔ Don't open attachments from people you don't know or attachments that seem suspicious.

✔ Do configure your e-mail programs to display messages in plain text only if HTML formatted e-mail isn't necessary. This is especially true for Web-based e-mail as there have been a number of vulnerabilities found in using HTML-enabled e-mail.

✔ Do educate all your users on the dangers of e-mail attachments and viruses in general. Also educate users about virus hoaxes and how to tell the difference between real and imagined threats.

✔ Do use the security features that come with the product. This includes preventing general users from being able to make changes in the program. Some users try to turn off the virus detection and you don't want them to be able to do that.

✔ Do educate your users about the anti-virus program you are using and how it works. This helps eliminate confusion, and staff will be less likely to try to disable the anti-virus program on their desktop machines.

Virus Myths

I'll be so glad when I stop receiving messages from my friends with the subject line: "Dangerous new virus!" Almost without fail these messages come from a friend of a friend of a friend who *heard* that this particular virus is a problem. Some examples of these well-meaning messages have included warnings about the *Flaming Monitor Virus*, the *Sound Card Virus*, and the famous *Budweiser Frogs Screen Saver Virus*. Without fail, all of them turned out to be elaborate hoaxes.

Who dreams up these hoaxes? I have no idea and I doubt that any one of them can be traced back to just one person. That's probably one of the biggest differences between a real virus alert message and a hoax — the real alert message will probably have a link to a URL about the virus and the person sending the alert will accept responsibility for the alert.

So how can you tell which alerts are real and which are hoaxes? There is an excellent Web site called *Virus Myths* and you can find it at www.vmyths.com. You can check to see if your alert is listed there and, if it isn't, there is an e-mail address you can send your alert to and they will check it out for you. Whatever you do, don't turn around and bombard all your friends and family with copies of the message until you can vouch for its veracity. There are some other indications of hoax alerts you should be aware of to help you tell the difference:

✔ The e-mail shouldn't contain chaotic details about the virus and how it works. It should only contain a summary of the virus and provide a link to a known and accepted authority on the subject — usually one of the anti-virus sites.

✔ The e-mail shouldn't quote false authorities or non-experts. Often these hoax messages come from the sales department, the accounting department, or from someone who once worked as a PC repair technician. Ask yourself: "Does this person really have the experience to know what he is talking about?" Just because the message came from upper management doesn't mean that the person knows the difference between a real virus and a hoax. Don't be afraid to question their authority. A real virus alert will come from someone who's *sole* job is computer security.

✔ Is the message part of a chain letter? That should be a tip-off. Does the message offer rewards for forwarding the message to others? A real virus alert would never do that.

In addition to being an annoyance, perpetuating virus myths is a disservice to the community. It's like "crying wolf". People become immune to these messages and then discount all of them — even the real ones. The best thing to do is to not distribute mass mailings about questionable virus alerts. If you do find a real virus, send out an e-mail worded like this:

To: Friends and Family

From: (your e-mail address)

Subject: Virus information at www._____.com

I've recently become aware of a virus that is making the rounds quite quickly. It's called "_____" virus and you can find more information about it at the URL in the subject line: www._____.com.

Please update your anti-virus program and its signature files immediately. You can get this information at your anti-virus vendor's Web site. Please be patient if you find it difficult to get to the Web site as there are a lot of people trying to get the update.

Regards,

This message should suffice. You don't need to resort to scare tactics, just inform them that the danger is there. Hopefully, they'll all act responsibly and update their anti-virus programs. On the other hand, if you have sent out an alert that turns out to be a hoax, **admit your mistake**. Send a note out and simply state that you were mistaken. This happens to lots of people, so you shouldn't be ashamed to admit it. You may just prevent a mass hysteria if you act responsibly yourself.

Emergency! What to Do

Okay. The worst has just happened and you think your network has been infected with a virus. The first rule is **don't panic!** A virus infection has happened to others and was bound to happen to you at some point. Hopefully you anticipated this and have an *Emergency Response Team* ready to operate. An Emergency Response Team should be part of your Security Policies and is comprised of experts who can take over in an emergency. To get the complete scoop on these teams and dealing with disasters, please refer to Chapter 19 and Chapter 20.

If you don't have an Emergency Response Team, don't panic! Here's what you do:

1. **Identify what infection you have.**

   You may have to do some research on an anti-virus Web site if your anti-virus program can't specifically identify which virus has entered your system. If your anti-virus program has all of its updates, it should be able to identify the virus. If your anti-virus program has not been updated recently, do that immediately.

2. **Locate the source of the infection.**

   Scan all machines on your network to pinpoint which machines have the infection.

3. **Quarantine all infected machines.**

   Take them off the network so the infection can't spread. That could mean physically unplugging the offending machines from the network or, if the infection is rampant, taking the entire network offline. You don't want to risk infecting others inside or outside of your network.

4. **Eliminate or "cure" the infection.**

   Run your anti-virus program on all infected machines. Sometimes the anti-virus program can't reverse the infection, which means that you'll have to manually disinfect all machines. To manually disinfect a machine, you have to change registry settings or reinstall a portion, if not all, of the operating system. The anti-virus vendor's Web site should have specific disinfection instructions. If there is no information on the Web site, don't hesitate to give them a call.

5. **Don't bring the machines or the network back online until you are sure all traces of the virus are gone.**

   This means scanning all machines AGAIN.

6. **Have a staff meeting and tell everyone what happened, why it happened, and what you had to do to fix it.**

   Make this a "lessons learned" excursive and not a meeting to point fingers and place blame. You may discover a whole bunch of things you did correctly, too. View this as an opportunity to make sure it doesn't happen again.

Chapter 9

Firewalls and Brimstone

· ·

· ·

1 wish I had a dollar for every executive who said to me, "Won't a firewall fix our security?" I wouldn't be rich, but I could certainly buy that new car I've been lusting after! Since their entry into the security market, buyers have viewed firewalls as the ultimate in network security. While they can be very powerful protection mechanisms, they cannot protect a network that is full of security holes. That would be a bit like putting a steel gate on a chain link fence that is only three feet high. The door may be scary looking, but anyone who looks past it can simply go around it.

A firewall is like the security checkpoint at an airport. Everyone who wants to enter is like a packet traveling to the network — all must go through the checkpoint and be examined. Non-ticket holders are turned away and told they cannot enter — those are dropped packets. The security personnel are like the firewall rulesets. They can do only what they are told to do. If they are given incorrect information or if they didn't understand the instructions, they can let the wrong traffic pass through. The security personnel can also send out alerts and communicate problems to superiors much like the auditing logs in a firewall do. The only exception to this analogy is that, in an airport, the traffic is examined in only one direction. A firewall examines traffic in both directions. Of course, we know what the problem is with security checkpoints — long lines and waits. The same can happen with firewall traffic. However, the delay, which is usually negligible, is worth it for the protection you get in return.

How a Firewall Works

Before you can understand how a firewall works, you need to understand the concepts of *ports* and *services*. Imagine the highways and roads that run into and out of a city. They have numbers and run in certain directions and they don't all start and stop in the same place. These roads are the *ports* in your network. They are not physical ports like your printer port; they are software instruction channels.

Now imagine the traffic that travels on the highway into the city, but pretend that the number of the highway determines the *type* of traffic that can travel on that road. Say that only 18-wheelers are allowed to travel on Highway 101 and only motorcycles are allowed to travel on Highway 80. The restricted traffic are the *services* that are allowed to travel on a given port.

A packet of information traveling to your network from the Internet has the port and service information imbedded in its *header*. The header is like a shipping label in that it includes information about the sender and the recipient, contents of the package, the size of the total shipment, and so on. When the network receives the packet, it opens the port so the packet can travel through. In all, there are 65535 ports, but not all ports have an assigned service. I've included a graphic of all the information included in a packet header in Figure 9-1.

Ports and their associated services have been assigned by the IETF (Internet Engineering Task Force). This is a group of mainly volunteers who have worked out the descriptions of ports and services. Although these descriptions are not necessarily industry standards, for the most part they are accepted as such and the vendors code their networking software accordingly. For example, here are the accepted methods of use for the established ports:

- **Ports 0–1023 are *well known ports*.** The services associated with these ports are well established and accepted. They are used by common programs that need a high level of access privilege. The ports for Telnet, FTP, SMTP, and so on. fall within this range.

- **Ports 1024–49151 are *registered ports*.** Vendors have gone to the IETF to get specific ports registered for use by their software. Generally, these ports don't have a high level of access privilege.

- **Ports 49152–65535 are *private* or *dynamic ports*.** These are generally ports used for a short term connection and are chosen at random by the software requesting the connection.

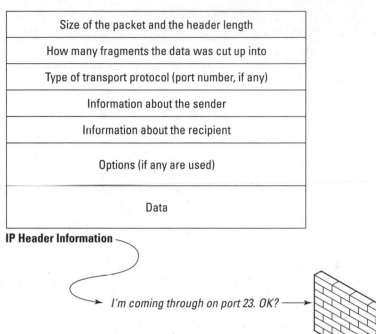

| Size of the packet and the header length |
| How many fragments the data was cut up into |
| Type of transport protocol (port number, if any) |
| Information about the sender |
| Information about the recipient |
| Options (if any are used) |
| Data |

IP Header Information

I'm coming through on port 23. OK?

Figure 9-1:
An example
of the
information
contained in
a header.

The preceding explanation of ports and their assignments is a bit simplistic, but you need only to understand the basics at this point. Firewalls do a majority of their work at the port and service level. They examine the ports and services in three basic ways: packet filtering, stateful inspection, and application proxying.

Packet filtering

All network traffic is segmented into little pieces called *packets*. Because each packet has a header full of information, it's relatively easy to use this information to sort and forward the traffic. All routers use this information to send the packet on to its final destination, and some routers have packet filtering capabilities. Firewalls also use this technology as the first level of its defense.

Packet filters are essentially plain text rules that the administrator writes and then stores on the firewall. The rules can allow or deny traffic based upon its origination, destination, port, or service. Each firewall has a default ruleset that consists of one of the following:

✔ **Deny All** — All traffic that is not *expressly allowed* is denied. This means that nothing is allowed through unless it is given permission.

✔ **Allow All** — All traffic that is not *expressly denied* is allowed. This means that all traffic is allowed through unless a rule has been set to deny its entry.

You have to know which default setting your firewall uses in order to correctly set up the rules. This should be relatively easy to determine by referring to the user's manual or the setup program.

The formats for rules vary from vendor to vendor and I can't give you examples of all of them. Table 9-1 shows you one way you may see the rules as they appear in the firewall's user interface. In this case the rules are telling the firewall how to handle requests for traffic to and coming from port 23 (telnet).

Table 9-1			Examples of Firewall Rules for Telnet Use				
Rule	*Direction*	*Source Address*	*Destination Address*	*Protocol*	*Source*	*Destination Port*	*Action Port*
1	In	External	Internal	TCP	>1023	23	Permit
2	Out	Internal	External	TCP	23	>1023	Permit
3	Out	Internal	External	TCP	>1023	23	Permit
4	In	External	Internal	TCP	23	>1023	Permit

The preceding rules allow traffic on port 23 (telnet) in or out of the network. The rule doesn't give you any protection against a hacker using port 23 to attack your system. This rule assumes that everyone coming in on port 23 is trusted. You need a more complex rule to allow only trusted addresses to use specific ports.

Most firewalls now have good administrative interfaces to help you set up the rules. However it's still very easy to set up incorrect or conflicting rules. This is probably one of the biggest reasons that firewalls are defeated. I've certainly seen my share of improperly configured firewall rules. In one case, all the rules were backwards — nothing was allowed out, but everything was allowed in!

It's also important to remember that the services running on ports are bi-directional — they communicate in both directions. Therefore, it doesn't do you any good to allow a port in one direction and then deny it in the other. For example, if you allow outbound telnet but deny inbound telnet, you can send commands to another machine, but you won't see the results on your computer monitor.

Stateful inspection

While packet filtering looks at all packets traveling in and out of a firewall, stateful inspection gives the packet the third degree. This is the "Grand Inquisitor" of firewall defense, and nothing comes in or goes out that isn't thoroughly inspected. Not only are all packets inspected inside and out, all applications coming through the firewall, the user, and the transportation method are all queried and verified. The information is maintained in a "state table" so that all future transmissions are inspected and compared to past transmissions. For example, if someone from inside the firewall requested a Web page from outside the firewall, the request is logged in the state table. When the page attempts to come back through the firewall, the firewall checks to see if a request for the page has been made. If there has been no request for the page, its transmission is denied.

Some firewalls also compare the state of the connection and the context in which the connection request was made. The context is sort of like the *situation* of the connection. If a connection was made from various machines at the same time, that would be an abnormal context. If both the state of the transmission and the context in which it is used deviate from the norm, the connection is refused and the packet is dropped. As an additional security measure, all firewalls using stateful inspection keep all ports closed until a specific port is requested.

Stateful inspection also supports connectionless protocols such as *User Datagram Protocols (UDP)*, something that routers can't do. This is done by tracking the port numbers used by these routines and caching them for future comparison.

As with packet filtering, stateful inspection is set up according to the ruleset on the firewall. Again, you have to specify whether traffic will be allowed or denied and what conditions have to be met for the traffic to be allowed.

Application proxying

A proxy is something done on the behalf or request of another. For example, in shareholders' meetings, a person who is not able to attend will give someone else his proxy to vote. In a firewall, a proxy is a transparent intermediary that works between two connections (see Figure 9-2). In the example of a telnet connection, Computer A on the outside initiates a request for a telnet connection. The connection is intercepted by the firewall, determined to be legitimate, and the firewall repackages the data and sends the data on to Computer B on the inside. In addition, the firewall hides Computer A's real address from Computer B. Neither Computer A nor Computer B know or see the firewall's intervention and they don't realize that the telnet session has been, in effect, hijacked and restarted. All they know is that they can communicate with one another seamlessly.

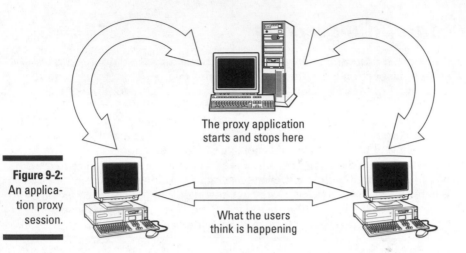

Figure 9-2:
An application proxy session.

The proxy application starts and stops here

What the users think is happening

This method of protection is very effective because it ensures that nothing funny happens during the communication session. The application proxies are more restrictive than the applications on the users' machines. Those restrictions are set by the rules and can verify the user and the destination, for example.

One problem with application proxies is that not all applications have proxies. There are proxies for the commonly used applications such as FTP, HTTP, telnet, and so on, but there are no proxies for custom Web applications. In some cases, companies have written their own custom proxies for applications they have to use, but the programming of a proxy can be difficult, depending on the firewall. Some firewalls have neat new interfaces for creating custom proxies Firewalls using proxies require an enormous amount of RAM to be able to run the applications and handle all the other jobs they are doing at the same time.

Filtering the rules

Now that you have a basic understanding of what a firewall looks at as traffic passes through, you need to understand how the firewall actually decides which rules to apply. As I mentioned, setting up the rules can be tedious, tricky, and confusing. And if setting up the rules is hard for you, imagine how hard it is for the firewall to interpret them. Firewalls use two basic methods of selection: first available and best available.

The first method of selection, *first available,* means that when a packet comes in, the firewall goes through the list of rules, and the first rule that looks like a match is used. This works well for fast transactions, but the firewall won't know if there was a better rule farther down the list.

Which brings us to the second method of rule selection, *best available*. When a packet reaches the firewall, the firewall looks at all the rules that may be a match and then chooses the one it considers to be the best. You have to check with the firewall vendors to see which way a certain firewall works. It's not always evident from their product descriptions.

The downside of firewalls

Sorry, but I never promised you that one security mechanism would do it all. There are always cons to go with the pros, and here are some of the basic disadvantages of a firewall:

- A firewall can be seen as a "single point of failure." If you're relying on a firewall for all of your protection and the firewall fails or is breached, then you effectively have no more security.

- A firewall may not be able to examine encrypted traffic. Therefore, if a hacker sends an encrypted attack, it could get through.

- A firewall can be a bottleneck to the flow of network traffic, which makes your network seem slower.

- Firewalls are extremely restrictive towards certain types of traffic that users want. For example, it's difficult to set up firewalls to accept streaming audio and instant messaging (IM) traffic securely.

- Most firewalls do nothing to stop viruses. You still need an anti-virus program or add-in to catch viruses.

- Firewalls do not protect modem connections. If you have remote users who dial-in to your network, you need another security mechanism.

- A firewall with a poor set of rules (or default settings) is just as bad as no firewall at all.

- Firewall security logs are difficult to read and interpret. If you're looking to see if your security has been breached, you may go crazy reading the logs for clues unless you use a specialized log reporting application.

Personal Firewalls

Companies spend a lot of money on their firewalls but do little to ensure the security of their remote users. Laptop users should have personal firewalls installed on them to help keep their connections secure. For example, a personal firewall could be set up to only allow connections to and from a certain set of IP addresses. This could help to deter a hacker from possibly *hijacking* the connection. You can also password protect personal firewalls so if unauthorized users try to make any changes to the password rules, they won't get very far.

In my opinion, personal firewalls are one of the greatest recent inventions in network security. Finally, a pretty good protection mechanism that is easy to set up and, in some cases, free! Personal firewalls can be used on home computers, very small networks (like for home offices), and remote users' laptops.

WARNING!

One note, however: Don't rely upon a personal firewall for all your security! Continue to use good passwords, apply security patches, and use anti-virus software, too. A firewall is just one tool; it isn't a total security package.

A lot more home users have "always on" connections nowadays like DSL and cable modems. Generally, home computers are much more vulnerable to attack than corporate networks because the average consumer knows little to nothing about securing a computer. I have found two useful Web sites that users can use to check the security settings of their computers. The two sites do a simple port scan to see what information they can discover about your system, which is the first thing a hacker does before deciding to launch an attack. Here are the two Web site addresses:

  ✔ **Sygate Online Services** — http://scan.sygate.com/prestealthscan.html

  ✔ **Gibson Research Corp.** — https://grc.com and click Shields Up!!

Both of these sites give the user an immediate report as to what the scan detected and what the information may mean to a hacker. If you have a personal firewall installed, this is a good way to test it. If your personal firewall fails the test, then it is either misconfigured or you need to try another product. Many computer magazines have done comparison tests of the different products, and these are available online. CINet has a very good price comparison section of their magazine at www.cnet.com. Another very good magazine of the same type is ZDNet, which is available at www.zdnet.com/reviews.

One product I have used for a couple years now and am very pleased with is ZoneAlarm by Zone Labs (www.zonelabs.com), shown in Figure 9-3. ZoneAlarm uses packet filters to allow or deny traffic and also uses what I call "application filters" to control which applications can be used to contact the Internet. The program maintains an internal database of some of the specifications of common applications so Trojan horse programs can be effectively blocked. For example, one common Trojan horse program is called BackOrifice. If a hacker renamed it "iexplore.exe," which is the program name for MS Internet Explorer, ZoneAlarm would know that the program masquerading as Internet Explorer isn't really that program, and it would be blocked from use on your system.

The ZoneAlarm firewall also closes vulnerable ports by default and can alert you in real-time when an unknown computer tries to connect to yours. It uses dialog boxes to check with you when an application on your computer tries to connect to the Internet and asks if it should never allow the connection, allow it all the time, or allow it just this once. ZoneAlarm provides some protection from dangerous e-mail attachments, and the newest version can suppress those annoying pop-up ads that appear when you're browsing the Web. The basic version of ZoneAlarm is free to home users (Wow!), and the full version is relatively inexpensive. Although it may not be clear to average users how to configure the advance settings, a good tutorial is included.

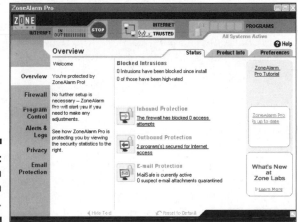

Figure 9-3:
ZoneAlarm
Pro's main
menu.

Of course, there are other products available other than ZoneAlarm but not all of them are free. BlackICE is a good product with a strong following and also works as a small intrusion detection system. It will react more strongly if it thinks your computer is under attack. You can find BlackICE at `www.securelab.com`. Secure Lab is an online store in which you can buy many different security products.

Another good product is Norton Personal Firewall, which is sold by Symantec. There product also includes a year's free intrusion detection service when you buy their firewall. McAfee also makes a good firewall called Personal Firewall Plus.

Not-Your-Kitchen Appliance Firewall

Appliance-based firewalls are hardware devices operating on your Internet connection's front end. Appliance firewalls are called such because you get all you need in one little box, or appliance. Instead of a computer and a monitor, most appliance firewalls have a small screen on the front of the box that you use to move through configuration menus. The operating system is specially built and secured, and there's nothing to install and little to configure. They are about as close as you can get to a plug-and-play firewall.

When these firewalls first appeared on the market, most were little more than intelligent routers. Now, most of them use packet filtering, stateful inspection, and at least a few application proxies. The most common proxies are for FTP, telnet, HTTP, and SMTP. Many of them also support VPNs (which I discuss in Chapter 16).

What's important to consider when looking at appliance firewalls is the number of connections or users it can support. Some of these devices are able to support fewer than 25 users and are more effective in a small office/home office environment than a big corporation. However, there are appliance firewalls built expressly for thousands of users and very fast networks.

Big Boys' Firewalls

So you got a large network, multiple offices, and thousands of users. If that's the case, you'll want a firewall like the Big Boys use. These are also known as *enterprise* firewalls, and they are complicated and very expensive. When you're considering these types of firewalls, you usually need more than one, and you'll also need full-time dedicated staff to operate and maintain them. This is a very serious security investment.

Enterprise firewalls usually look like big computers or servers, and that's just what they are. They come from the vendor or reseller with the operating system installed, but the hard job comes in the configurations and learning how to use the management consoles. You can't learn how to use these systems from a manual — you have to attend the training classes, and some can take a week of your time. The manuals are helpful if you've had experience with firewalls before, but if you are new to firewalls, I strongly suggest you taking a class.

One reason to choose an enterprise software is when you have a requirement for high availability. That is, your network must be available 99 percent of the time and you can't afford any failures of your firewall(s). This usually means that you'll need redundant pairs of firewalls. You can build what's called a *firewall sandwich* or you can rely upon *session failovers*.

✔ A firewall sandwich is two firewalls with a machine operating as a load balancer between them. Both firewalls work all the time, but if one fails, the other takes all the load. The downside of this solution is that whatever data the dead firewall had is lost and connections must be reestablished.

✔ With session failovers, both firewalls exchange session-state information over a dedicated private link; when one firewall fails, the other takes over without session interruption.

The cost of enterprise firewalls tends to run into the tens of thousands of dollars. And because most vendors won't deal with you directly, you'll also be up for the reseller's fees and consulting time. Add to that the dedicated firewall staff, and you have a very expensive proposition. However, you don't normally spend that much money on security unless you have an awful lot to lose, so it's better to get the best system you can afford.

Firewall Management Services

A new trend meeting with mixed results is to outsource all of your firewall management and monitoring. These managed security service companies pipe all of your firewall data to their secure network and monitor it for you 24/7. They are not in the business of building secure networks for you, but are like 24-hour-a-day security guards to watch all your fences. They notify you when there is a breach or attempted breach in your security and act to further safeguard your system.

This is wonderful at removing the tedium of network monitoring out of your hands. You also don't have to worry about staffing as they have the staff and the expertise (hopefully!) to be able to protect your systems. They use sophisticated log analyzers that can read through tens of megabytes of logs very quickly. They also keep abreast of the latest attack methods and scenarios and can probably recognize an attack much quicker than you.

The key to this relationship is in your contract with them. You have to be very clear what they are allowed to do and not allowed to do. What are their guidelines and restraints? If they have multiple clients experiencing attacks at the same time, how do they decide priorities? Who is responsible if you lose data or sustain damage from an attack that manages to get past them? And where will you be if they go out of business? These are just a few of the questions you need to ask before employing one of these firms. I'm not saying they are bad; I'm just saying be careful.

Choosing the Size of Your Chain Link Fence

I'm comparing the rules on your firewall to the width between links in your chain link fence of security. Why? Because if your attackers are the size of snakes, you definitely need smaller links to keep them out. The tighter and more restrictive your rules are, the smaller the links are going to be.

How are you going to decide on your firewall rules? Go back to your security policies that I talk about in Chapter 4. Take some of those policies and convert them into firewall policies that tell you how to set the rules. For example, if your company disallows Web browsing by policy, then the extrapolated rule would be to deny any HTTP/port 80 traffic. A majority of the policies and rules will be based upon how you want your Internet connection to be used by your employees and what business you need to conduct. You'll work on the principle of *least privilege* — give the users only what they really need and no more.

One example of least privilege is streaming audio. Many employees enjoy listening to Internet radio stations on their workstations, but firewalls have a very difficult time dealing with streaming content. This is because some of the streaming content needs to have a huge range of multiple ports opened for it to be able to work. In some cases, all the firewall can do is let the traffic pass with no examination, which isn't at all secure. If your company's security policy says, "No streaming audio on the desktop," then no one in the company will have the privilege of using it. It's all or nothing.

Another example of least privilege is the use of FTP. Let's say that you have only two people in the company who have a real need to download and upload files via FTP. Maybe they have to transfer reports to the home office. Because those people are the only ones who need FTP, have the firewall restrict that service to just to their computers. Because no one else needs it, they don't get the privilege of using it.

You're also going to have to look at all the applications you use that connect to the Internet. The applications tell you which ports and services to allow or deny. For example, if you use e-mail, you have to allow SMTP (Simple Mail Transfer Protocol) and/or POP3 (Post Office Protocol). If you allow Web browsing, you have to allow HTTP (Hyper Text Transfer Protocol). All of these protocols have associated port numbers, which you'll use in setting up your rules. If you are unfamiliar with which port numbers are associated with which services and applications, you can find them at www.iana.org/assignments/port-numbers.

Auditing the Logs

When your firewall detects a possible intrusion or attack, it's not going to let off bells and whistles and scream "Danger!" at the top of its lungs. It's probably going to very quietly send out an e-mail to an administrator and write the event to a log — and that's only if you have set it up that way. That's why so many hacker intrusions are not caught — no one was looking at the logs or reading the alerts. In some cases, administrators have even turned off the alerts because they found them to be so irritating. They are interruptions in the daily flow of events that most people find to be annoying at best. They think, "The firewall is configured for security, so it's probably keeping all the bad guys out." The key word here is "probably."

Yes, many of the alerts are false-positives, but you have to read them anyway. I know of many companies who have been hacked whose firewalls had been logging alerts for months before the attack was noticed. Don't put yourself in that position.

Logs can be difficult to decipher. They are long lines of text with lots of numbers and strange phrases. In many cases you need some training to be able to read the logs and make any sense out of them. Here's an example of an actual firewall log:

```
14:17:38 Supervisor Unused port blocking has blocked
         communications. Details:
Inbound TCP connection
Remote address,local service is (12.146.49.110,6347)
2/11/2002 14:17:32 Supervisor Unused port blocking has
         blocked communications. Details:
Inbound TCP connection
Remote address,local service is (12.146.49.110,6347)
2/11/2002 14:17:29 Supervisor Unused port blocking has
         blocked communications. Details:
Inbound TCP connection
Remote address,local service is (12.146.49.110,6347)
2/11/2002 10:27:55 Supervisor Rule "Block Port 80 From
         Internet." blocked (loki-
         i1(17.35.31.120),http(80)). Details:
Inbound TCP connection
```

Now imagine that you have hundreds of pages of such stuff to read — believe me, that's a mind-numbing exercise!

You can buy log analyzers to help you decipher the logs. Some firewalls have analyzers built-in while most are third-party installations. The simplest ones read through the logs and give you a report from most common log entries to the least common. These analyzers do no interpretation of the logs; they just give you lists of entries. There are more sophisticated analyzers that compare the log entries to a database of known attack methods and attempt to interpret what's happening. Many also analyze bandwidth usage and let you know when something out of the ordinary happens. You have to read through the vendors' technical details of the products to figure out which way a particular product works before you make a purchase.

Responding to Danger

A firewall attempts to block attacks; it can't attempt to attack the attacker. Therefore, when a firewall lets you know that something bad is happening, it is up to you to respond. Hopefully, you already have an emergency response plan as outlined in Chapter 19. If you don't, well, be prepared for a couple of crazy, sleepless nights!

One thing that is difficult to discern from firewall logs is whether or not you are experiencing an attack or if what you are seeing is just some other problem with the network. I've seen what looked to be attacks turn out to be a couple of routers that got confused or misconfigured somehow. It really is difficult to tell the difference at first glance. Experience is the best teacher in this case.

However, we'll assume that you have discovered an intrusion. Someone has actually breached the firewall and gained entry to your system. Now you're going to have to figure out if the intruder is still snooping around and if he has caused any damage. Here are some of the steps you need to take immediately:

- **Change all root passwords immediately.**

  All users must change their passwords, too, but it's more important that you change the administrative passwords first to prevent any further intrusions.

- **Don't arbitrarily turn systems off or power down.**

  You could inadvertently lose data that could be used in a forensic investigation. (See Chapter 22 for more information.)

- **Identify any unexpected, unusual, or suspicious changes to files and directories and their possible implications.**

  Hackers often change files and install programs to hide their tracks. You may have to remove drives and install verifiably clean systems.

- **Document everything you do, every step of the way.**

  You may need this later if the intrusion becomes a criminal case. This also keeps the staff from spinning their wheels on something that's already been done.

- **You may need to keep the contaminated disks for further forensic investigation (see Chapter 22).**

- **Come up with a plan for cleaning up your systems.**

  This may mean taking the network offline for a while. It all depends on your situation.

- **Take measures to make sure this can't happen again.**

  Learn from your mistakes and improve your security.

Chapter 10

Intrusion Detection Systems

● ●

● ●

*I*ntrusion detection sounds like something they'd use in a movie. You know — the bank heist type where there are motion detectors, lasers, heat sensors, and floors sensitive to additional weight. Intrusion detection is an effective way of letting security know when the bad guys have gotten into the vault. Intrusion detection systems (otherwise known as *IDS*) are the relative newcomers to the security mechanism front. They add another layer of security and can catch possible exploits that a firewall may not be able to detect.

A common misunderstanding is that a firewall can recognize attacks and block them. This is not true. A firewall is simply a pass/no-pass gateway. It either lets traffic through or turns it away. An IDS is better able to recognize attacks or misuse because they further examine the traffic that has been allowed through and is moving around your network.

Intrusion detection is like having little spies running around your network. They snoop around, gather information, analyze it, and then give you a report of what's going on. IDSs monitor logs from your systems, watch network traffic, and attempt to identify patterns that look like an attack or misuse. They also look at the programs and processing happening in a system to let you know when someone or something is trying to do something they shouldn't. Intrusion detection can tell you almost everything that is happening in your network. What it can't tell you, however, is the *significance* of everything that is happening.

It's All in the Analysis

An IDS analyzes logs and activity and sends reports when it thinks it has found something suspicious or of interest. There are no standards for the various IDSs, and each vendor has its own method of implementing analysis techniques. However, on a very basic level, and IDS uses two different methods for analysis:

✓ Pattern matching

✓ Anomaly detection

Pattern matching

Pattern matching works similar to the way that anti-virus software does. The IDS contains a large database of known attacks and creates a *signature* of these attacks. When data is captured the IDS looks for patterns in that data. There is a database within the IDS that contains patterns of known attacks. When the captured data has been checked for patterns of behavior, the IDS compares these patterns to see if there is a match.

The signature databases in an IDS consist of hundreds of known attacks. The attacks are sorted into different types or classes to better assist in matching a pattern. Sometimes a previously unknown attack will appear but, because it fits into the same class as other attacks, it may be detected. As with anti-virus software, an IDS signature database needs to be updated often. However, new attack methods don't appear as often as new viruses do, so the updates are required far less frequently.

Anomaly detection

Anomaly detection is like the heuristics used in anti-virus software. Anomaly detection uses algorithms to create a sense of "logic" of what it sees happening. Because pattern matching can be defeated by completely new and previously unrecorded attacks, anomaly detection is added in response to that problem.

When an IDS is first installed, the anomaly detection portion starts to gather data to establish a *baseline* of behavior. After it has gathered network traffic for quite a period of time, it sets that baseline and says that this is the norm for a particular network. After the IDS has its baseline, it compares all traffic against it to see when anything unusual is happening. Anything that deviates from the norm is further evaluated to see if it could possibly be an attack or misuse.

The baseline includes a huge number of variables, which is why it takes a period of time for the baseline to be established. Included in the baseline are such things as the average number of logged-in users, the average length of an FTP session, or the type and number of files that a particular user accesses on a daily basis. If the system detects a large deviation from the normal behavior, it signals an alarm. The magnitude of a large deviation is defined as a threshold set by the IDS or the administrator.

Each vendor uses its own set of algorithms for anomaly detection, and these are closely guarded secrets. A lot of bad press is given to this method of intrusion detection because it's susceptible to "false-positives." When the IDS sends an alert that an attack has been noticed, security must respond to see if the attack is real. If the attack has been falsely reported, then time has been wasted attending to this emergency. This is akin to Chicken Little shouting, "The sky is falling!" However, in most cases, there has not been a false-positive reported, but a "false alert." The difference is that the algorithm worked correctly and identified a situation as a possible attack, but the attack turned out to be some misconfiguration on the network that was causing the alert. It's difficult for anomaly detection to tell the difference. It sees an anomaly, so it sends out an alert.

Events are happening

An IDS also looks at the sequence in which traffic or data appears. This sequence is used in both the signature database and the detection of anomalies. You know how sometimes people say bad things happen in threes? Well, sometimes the same can be said for intrusion attempts or methods of intrusion. An IDS looks at events three ways:

- A single event
- A sequence of events
- A threshold of events

A single event can be data sent out over a specific port; a sequence of events can be the issuance of a distinct series of commands, and a threshold of event is simply a way of saying "enough is enough." One example of a threshold of events can be too many ping requests coming from different sources all at the same time. This is a type of *denial of service* (DoS) attack in which all the resources of a system are tied up trying to answer all of these requests and it is unable to respond to normal requests, thus denying the service of the system. Ping is simply a command that checks to see if another network is there. It's sort of like a "knock knock" on the door of the network. If the other network is available, it answers "hello, I'm here." Imagine you are in a room full of doors. A DoS attack is like thousands of knocks on all of the doors at once, all coming from different directions, and the network goes into overload trying to answer them all.

Network-Based IDS

Network traffic is broadcasted loudly across a network and is received by the network cards installed in each computer. These cards can be set to listen only for traffic destined for the particular segment of the network on which it resides, or they can be set to *promiscuous mode* so they listen to all traffic sent to all segments. To ease traffic congestion and increase efficiency, most cards are set to listen only for their own traffic. A network-based IDS is a specific machine (or machines) with its network card usually set to promiscuous mode. The IDS captures all the traffic traveling along the wire, regardless of its destination. The capturing mechanism is basically the same packet sniffers or scanners that hackers use to gain information about your system. After the IDS has captured traffic, it sets about to analyze what it has found.

A network-based system is simply concerned with the protocols and packets on the network and can't examine the individual processes happening on each machine. Therefore, there are some attacks or forms of misuse that a network-based system can't see. Here are some of the attacks that this sort of system can recognize:

- A daemon program reading data from a file and dumping it into a buffer. (A daemon is a service that runs in the background and a buffer is an area of memory used for remembering things in the short term.)
- Copying buffered data into a number of smaller buffers
- Port scanning from a particular IP address
- Spoofed IP packets

Of course, with any system, there are benefits and drawbacks, and an IDS is no exception. The benefits of a network-based IDS are

- **Relatively low cost of ownership.**

  Because there are usually a limited number of IDSs deployed, hardware and software costs can be controlled.
- **No impact on network performance.**

  A network-based IDS is just collecting the traffic that is there — not adding to the traffic.
- **Real-time reporting.**

  The IDS analyses traffic as it happens, so you know immediately when attack conditions are present.

✔ **Operating system independent.**

It doesn't matter if you have a mix of operating systems on your network because they all communicate with the same set of network protocols.

The drawbacks of a network-based IDS are

✔ **It can't read encrypted traffic.**

Because most encrypted traffic is decrypted when it reaches the host, it looks like garbage to the network-based IDS.

✔ **The network can be flooded with traffic.**

The IDS can become overwhelmed and miss important packets.

✔ **The IDS can reassemble packets incorrectly.**

This causes a fragmentation attack to be allowed through.

✔ **It doesn't understand protocols that are specific to some applications.**

Complex applications such as an Oracle database often have proprietary protocols that use unusual ports for communication.

✔ **It can't understand outdated/obsolete network protocols.**

Some IDSs won't understand the older versions of Post Office Protocol (POP) or an obsolete protocol that were used in early Novell networks.

✔ **It won't work on switched networks.**

IDSs need to have routed traffic to work and they have trouble with switched networks. This is because switched networks work at a different level from what routed networks do. If you have a switched network, you will need to install a monitor port for your network-based IDS to work.

Host-Based IDS

Where a network-based IDS looks at traffic indiscriminately on the network, a host-based system has sensors placed on one or more hosts (individual computers) on the network. Instead of capturing all traffic, this system gathers information from logs that are stored on specific hosts and does some analysis of traffic. The logs are generated by the network operating system and some applications and contain records of activities. These activities include such things as individual log-ins, reading, writing and deleting files, and using applications.

The host-based system analyses the logs in much the same way that a network-based system does. It uses a signature database that is customized by rules and uses anomaly detection. A host-based system is more concerned with who has permission to do what and how often. Because of this, these system are normally used to monitor the conditions on the internal network rather than traffic coming through the firewall.

Before setting up a host-based system, you have to decide which events are going to be logged. It's common for some first time users to log everything and have their IDS report everything. What they don't realize is that the volume of data contained in logs is enormous! They quickly learn to be more discriminate in what they want logged and what gets reported. This is where the rules-based signature comes in. Using the IDS interface, a rule is made to read X log and send an alert when Y happens.

Here are some of the things that a host-based IDS will detect and report:

- A number of failed password attempts
- A user tries to read a file for which he has no privileges
- A user's privileges have been increased
- A program deletes too many files in succession

As with a network-based IDS, a host-based system is not without its pluses and minuses. These are to be considered when choosing a system for yourself. The advantages of a host-based system are

- **It requires no additional hardware.**

  The software is installed on specific machines you want to protect.
- **It can detect whether an attack succeeded or failed.**

  This is based on the entries stored in the logs.
- **It can operate with encryption.**

  Because decryption usually happens on the host machine, the IDS sees the data after it has been decrypted.
- **It can monitor specific activities such as file and user access.**

The good goes along with the bad, so here is the bad news for a host-based IDS:

- **It cannot see network scans or attacks that target the entire network.**
- **It's harder to manage.**

  Each host must be individually configured and managed because each host is different.
- **Reports are in near real-time and not as the event happens.**

  Events are written to the logs first and then the events are analyzed.

✔ **The amount of information stored can become enormous.**

Logs quickly fill up tons of space, and you may need additional storage.

✔ **Performance can suffer.**

Because the host is writing to logs, analyzing the logs, and processing as normal, the amount of processing needed for analysis can have an adverse effect.

✔ **Subversion is easier.**

A host machine can succumb to an attack not seen and the logs can be changed or deleted.

The IDS Monitor

Of course, if you are going to have an alert system, you have to have a way to watch what is going on. Like an office with security cameras, someone has to look at the monitors and/or view the tapes. Usually, all the monitors feed into a central location. You could have separate monitors for each IDS, but then you'd have to constantly be on the run checking what's on the monitors. A more effective way to manage IDS messages and management is via a central console. The console can then display all alerts from all IDS machines, thus giving the administrator a clearer picture of what is going on. With a clearer picture, he or she can then respond more appropriately.

Many large networks have network management systems such as OpenView or Tivoli installed to help them with the day-to-day network operations — recognizing a new computer that has come online, that a server has rebooted, routing problems, or that a particular system has failed, for example. Some of the IDS systems can send their alerts directly into this management systems while others have their own management systems that are held completely separate.

The data is sent to the monitor via an *SNMP trap*. SNMP stands for Simple Network Management Protocol, and a trap is a section of data that is like a snapshot in time. In order for this to work, the IDS machines must have SNMP *agents,* which are little programs to send data to the monitor. The monitor continually polls the agents to see if they have any data to send. In other words, traps are messages that are sent to a message manager. When the administrator receives an alert via the monitor, he can usually respond a number of ways directly from the monitor. Some IDS can even change the firewall and router rules via the monitor. This can be used to temporarily block certain traffic. Most monitors are also able to reset sessions, so an attack can be interrupted.

All of this is valuable information for the IDS administrator. Unfortunately, it can also be very helpful to the intruder. An intruder can possibly intercept these traps and read them for himself. He could possibly delete the data so that it never reaches the monitor, or he can change it to skew the results. Even if the data isn't changed or deleted, an intruder who knows he's being tracked can change his tactics to try to prevent further detection.

For this reason, it's important that IDS monitors either encrypt the traffic or send the traffic via a different route. Some IDS monitors are put on a separate network dedicated for the intrusion detection sensors and monitors. This is not the same network on which the IDS machines reside. Another solution is what is called an *out-of-band* network. This is a separate network that typically uses serial ports or modems to transfer the data. Check with vendors to see which options they offer and then decide which is best for you.

Defeating an IDS

Uh, oh. I've just described the perfect machine and now I'm going to rain on your parade by telling you the downsides. Yes, sorry, IDSs are prone to failures and defeats, too. Unfortunately, these methods are well known in the hacker community and the IDS vendors haven't found ways to overcome them all — yet.

Here, then, is Table 10-1, which is all you want to know and more about defeating an IDS.

Table 10-1	Common Ways to Defeat an IDS
Method	*Results*
Bombardment	You render the IDS "blind" by giving it too much to do. You bombard it with so much traffic that it can't look at all of it and some traffic passes through without examination.
URL Encoding	You're probably aware that URLs and Web browsers have special codes for most characters. An attacker can send a request using a URL format instead of a normal text string. Thus, cgi-bin/test.cgi becomes /cg%69-b%69n/t%65st.cg%69
Slow Scans	An IDS expects traffic to come through at a certain pace. It only has a limited amount of memory, so it occasionally dumps what it sees. If a scan comes in slowly, there's a chance that the IDS dumped the first part of the scan and then doesn't associate it with the second part.
Extraneous Characters	You simply insert some special characters into the request. Similar to URL Encoding

Method	Results
Tabs instead of Spaces	Not all systems interpret spaces the same way. A malicious request could pass through undetected.
Reverse Attack	If an attack is usually sent like "Step 1, Step 2, Step 3", you can reverse the order and send it like "Step 3, Step 2, Step 1".
Multiple Sessions	Like the preceding, only log out and log back on between steps. This creates multiple sessions and the IDS won't get the connection.
Multiple Sites	Log in from multiple sites (different IP addresses) and send a portion of the attack from each site. Because the IDS sees the requests coming from different sources, it won't been recognized as an attack.

These are just a few of the ways that an IDS can be fooled. If you check around on the Web, you'll find a number of parodies of "50 Ways to Leave Your Lover," in which attack methods are detailed. One of the best is done by Fred Cohen and can be found at `www.all.net/journal/netsec/9712.html`.

Where to Place the IDS

Where is the best place to put intrusion detection on your network? The answer to that depends. It depends on what you are protecting and what you are protecting against. A network-based system is used to detect attacks on an entire network while a host-based system is used to detect attacks on a specific machine. The specific machine is usually mission-critical and needs more protection than others. The type and placement of system also depends on whether or not your network is switched and whether or not encryption is used.

In order to help you decide, I've come up with some simple scenarios and examples of where and what type of IDS can be deployed.

Scenario one

The internal network is connected to the Internet with a filtering router and a firewall. The internal network is small and there are no subnets. There is no encryption used and all packets are routed, not switched.

The proper type and placement is a network-based IDS inserted between the firewall and the internal network (see Figure 10-1). You could put the IDS in front of the firewall, but then it would work on analyzing traffic that may not make it past the firewall. It's more effective to put it on the inside of the firewall after certain traffic has already been blocked. An alert may mean that the firewall has failed or has been breached.

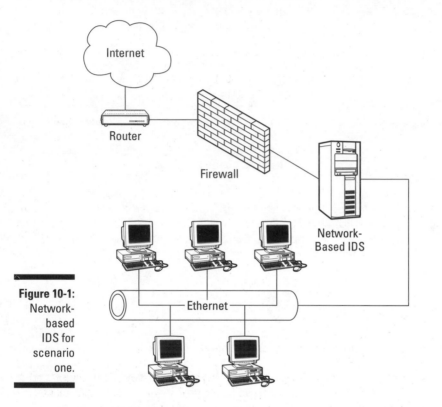

Figure 10-1:
Network-
based
IDS for
scenario
one.

Scenario two

The internal network is connected to the Internet with a filtering router and a firewall. There are two internal networks. There is no encryption used and all packets are routed, not switched.

As with scenario one, a network-based IDS is placed inside the firewall to detect any attacks coming from the Internet, as shown in Figure 10-2. Additionally, another network-based IDS is placed between the Accounting and Operations network to detect an insider attack originating from either one of those networks to the other.

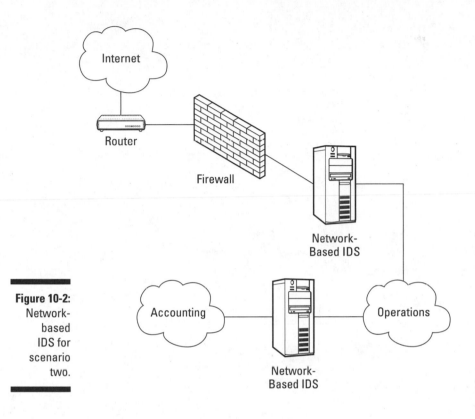

Figure 10-2:
Network-
based
IDS for
scenario
two.

Scenario three

The internal network is connected to the Internet with a filtering router and a firewall. The internal network is small and there are no subnets, but one machine on the internal network is mission-critical and needs more protection than the others.

In this case, a network-based IDS is placed inside the firewall to detect attacks coming from the Internet (see Figure 10-3). Additionally, a host-based IDS is placed on the mission-critical machine. This detects any attacks on the operating system or programs on this machine.

Scenario four

The internal network is connected to the Internet with a filtering router and a firewall with an encryption tunnel running through the firewall. One or more machines on the internal network are mission-critical.

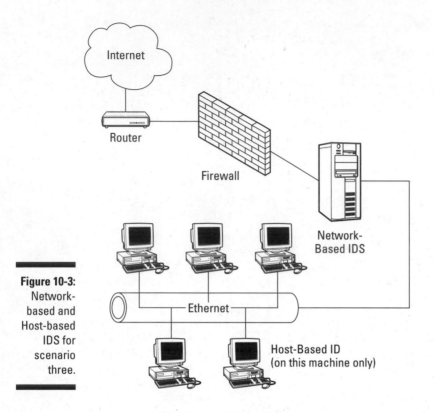

Figure 10-3:
Network-
based and
Host-based
IDS for
scenario
three.

There is no network-based IDS inside the firewall in this installation because the IDS would not be able to understand the encrypted traffic. Because the encryption happens when it reaches the host machines on the internal network, the only thing you can do is to place host-based IDS on all the machines considered to be mission-critical (see Figure 10-4).

Figure 10-4:
Host-based
and Host-
based
IDS for
scenario
four.

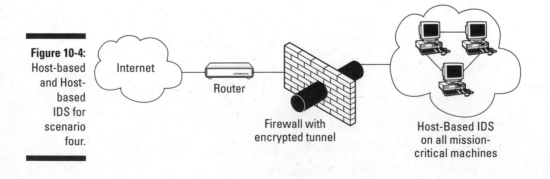

Chapter 11

Access Controls/Privileges

*W*hen you think about it, controlling access to your computers and your information is the cornerstone of network security. Almost every security mechanism you install has some type of access control included in its architecture. The purpose of access control is to protect your assets, and the means to this end is to:

- ✔ **Identify** — know who you are giving access to
- ✔ **Authenticate** — verify that's who they really are
- ✔ **Authorize** — let them do only what you want them to do

It's like when you go into a bank. You identify yourself to the teller with your checkbook, and he or she asks for a driver's license to authenticate your identity. When that is established, the bank authorizes you to withdraw only from your account — you aren't authorized to withdraw from others' accounts, nor are you authorized to go behind the counter and count out the money yourself. The bank has exercised a form of access control. (I was once in a bank when a man streaked through the lobby naked. I'm not sure if he was attempting to identify or authenticate himself, but he certainly wasn't authorized to do that!)

In the computer world, the process is not all that different. Your login name or UserID is your identity, and your password is the authentication. When you are logged on, you are authorized to do only certain things on the network. You aren't authorized to erase all the drives on the servers, for example. You need special privileges to be able to do that. Generally speaking, the more trusted you are, the higher your authorization is.

Permissions and Levels of Access

Your identity on a network is the UserID that was created for you when you joined the company. The UserID is also your logon name and is usually descriptive of you in some way, for example, your last name and first initial. It is also the label for your user account on the system. You authenticate yourself to your account by entering the password associated with the account. When the account was created, you were given certain authorizations on the system to enable you to do your job. These authorizations are also called *permissions*, and they allow you to do certain things and prevent you from doing others. You use the permissions in an operating system or application program to set the *levels of access*. This is a type of access control.

You aren't given access and permissions on a network based on whims. Basically, there are three standard ways of forming the type of access you should be given on the network. For one, you could be given access based on the role you play in the company. Two, your access could be given based on the group you work with, and three, you could be given access based on the type of transactions you will need to engage in on a daily basis. Chances are, when you were hired, your manager or someone in authority gave the IT department a set of access criteria based on one of these three models.

✔ The criteria may be based on the *role* that you're playing in the company. The role identifies the level of trust you were given and your need-to-know to be able to access resources on the network. If your role is that of a database administrator, you need permission to access more of the components of the database than a general user needs. When the IT department created your account, they told the system that you need permission to get on to the network and a higher level of permission to the database.

✔ Another way of identifying your level of access is through an association with a *group*. Normally, this is a group of people whose levels of access and activity are the same. If you have more than one person needing a given level of access, these people can be identified as part of a group on the network. Group-controlled access lists mean you have to describe the access levels only once and then people can be added or deleted from a group, according to your role.

✔ A third way of setting up permissions is to identify the types of *transactions* that you perform on a daily basis. The database administrator, for example, can build, repair, and maintain a database, but not be allowed to view confidential records contained within the database. Transaction-based access can limit the types of applications you can use and your ability to change files.

The reason that roles, groups, and transactions are used is that administering access control on a network can be a huge pain in the tookus. Imagine that you have over 500 users on a network. Individual accounts have to be created for every person, and giving permissions to servers, drives, files, and applications would take forever if you had to manually enter every permission. By creating "templates" like roles, groups, and transactions, an administrator can give permissions with fewer commands. In addition, people often change duties in a job, which may change the permissions and levels of access. It is much easier for an administrator to move your account to another group than it is to go through all the permissions one by one and make the necessary changes.

Removing inactive accounts and old accounts from a system is very important. This is a very common way that hackers gain entry to a system — they guess or discover an account, guess or crack the password, and then use that to log on to the system. Because the system still shows that account as active and valid, no red flags are sent up to indicate an intruder.

Always remove or disable any account with the name of "guest." This account almost always comes as a default on new systems, and it frequently doesn't require a password to use, which is an open invitation to hackers. Hackers will always check to see if a guest account exists.

Types of permissions

Generally, permissions are given for files and directories on workstations and servers. A good security practice is to set the permissions according to who needs to see and use the files and directories; otherwise, you are allowing everyone to see everything. You don't want the general populace of a company to be able to see and change the departmental budgets, and you are required by law to protect the personal information that is kept by the human resources department. Directory permissions are used to restrict access to everything within that directory. File permissions are more granular and allow you to further restrict access. For example, the permissions set on a directory called "Accounting" can be set so everyone within the accounting department can access all the files within that directory. But if you have a file in that directory called "Pay Scales," you can set the permissions on that file so only the accounting manager can open it. Everyone who has permission to look in the Accounting directory is able to see that file, but only the manager is allowed by the system to actually open it.

In Table 11-1, I've listed the types of permissions seen on most systems. The access name may vary between operating systems, but the concept is still the same.

Table 11-1	Common Access Permissions	
Access	*Access Symbol*	*Access Rights*
Read	(R)	The contents of the file or directory can be opened and read but no modifications can be made.
Write	(W)	Changes can be made to the file or directory. The contents of the file can be altered and new directories can be made.
Execute	(X)	A file with this attribute will be a program or script and the user will be allowed to start the program or run the script. A directory with this attribute means that a user can change subdirectories within the directory.
Delete	(D)	Files and directories can be deleted.

These permissions are set by using the operating system's commands. Only people with the highest level of permissions — administrators — have the permission to use these commands. In the next section, I take a look at the way three different operating systems handle the setting of permissions.

Unix permissions

To the uninitiated, the Unix operating system's views and commands look like total gobbledigoop. However, most of the Internet is run on servers running Unix because it's extremely stable and powerful. Most hackers cut their eye-teeth on this operating system. Now I'm not going to try to teach you Unix in this section because that is a whole other book in itself. (There is a *Unix For Dummies* you may want to check into!) However, I want to give you a general idea how that system handles permissions.

Figure 11-1 shows a screen shot of the directory listing of a Unix system

Note that the first column in the listing is a series of letters and some dashes (-). Let's break it apart to decipher its meaning (see Figure 11-2).

I've marked the separate areas of the permissions to assist with the explanation. First of all, I need to explain that Unix users can be given both individual and group permissions. There is also a set of permissions for All, which everybody inherits. Usually the permissions for All are quite restrictive. Unix also defines the creator of files and directories as *owners*. There are individual owners and group owners.

```
ls -la /

total 6087
drwxr-xr-x  16 root  wheel      512 Aug   9 11:36 .
drwxr-xr-x  16 root  wheel      512 Aug   9 11:36 ..
-rw-r--r--   1 root  wheel      658 Jul 26 23:14 .cshrc
-rw-r--r--   2 root  wheel      251 Jul 26 23:14 .profile
-r--r--r--   1 root  wheel     4735 Jul 26 23:14 COPYRIGHT
drwxr-xr-x   2 root  wheel     1024 Aug   9 07:45 bin
drwxr-xr-x   3 root  wheel      512 Aug   8 17:14 boot
drwxr-xr-x   2 root  wheel      512 Aug   8 13:03 cdrom
lrwxr-xr-x   1 root  wheel       11 Aug   8 17:14 compat -> /usr/compat
drwxr-xr-x   3 root  wheel    12800 Aug  13 10:03 dev
drwxr-xr-x  15 root  wheel     2048 Aug  12 19:21 etc
lrwxrwxrwx   1 root  wheel        9 Aug   8 17:15 home -> /usr/home
-r-xr-xr-x   1 root  wheel  3087410 Jul 27 00:44 kernel
-r-xr-xr-x   1 root  wheel  3087410 Jul 27 00:44 kernel.GENERIC
drwxr-xr-x   2 root  wheel      512 Jul 26 23:00 mnt
drwxr-xr-x   2 root  wheel     2560 Aug   8 13:45 modules
dr-xr-xr-x   1 root  wheel      512 Aug  15 10:11 proc
drwxr-xr-x   3 root  wheel      512 Aug  14 10:21 root
drwxr-xr-x   2 root  wheel     2048 Aug   9 07:45 sbin
drwxr-xr-x   4 root  wheel     1024 Aug   8 13:03 stand
lrwxrwxrwx   1 root  wheel       11 Aug   8 17:06 sys -> usr/src/sys
drwxrwxrwt   3 root  wheel      512 Aug  15 09:24 tmp
drwxr-xr-x  18 root  wheel      512 Jul 27 01:09 usr
drwxr-xr-x  18 root  wheel      512 Jul 27 01:05 var
```

Figure 11-1: A typical Unix system file and directory listing.

The first letter in the listing indicates whether the listing is for a directory (d), file (-), or a symbolic link (l). The first row in my example is a directory as indicated by the "d" and the second row is a file as indicated by the dashes "-".

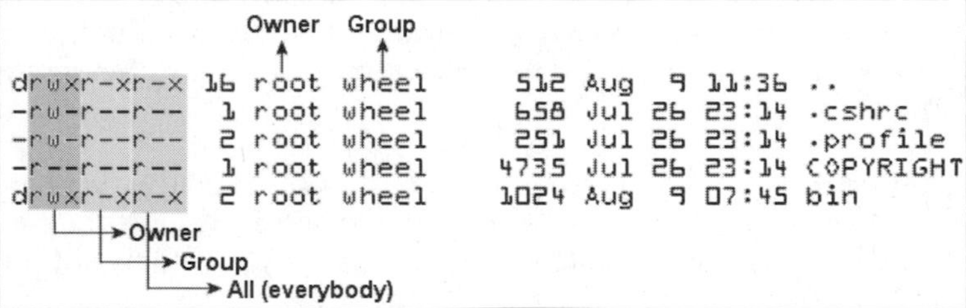

Figure 11-2: The Unix listing of file and directory permissions.

The next nine letters and dashes indicate the permissions for the Owner/User, the Group, and All, in that order. I've highlighted each set of three in Figure 11-2. You can perform one of three actions with a file or directory (three persons times three permissions equals the nine characters):

✔ You can read it (r)

✔ You can write to it or change it (w)

✔ You can execute it (x)

The read, write, and execute permissions are always set in that order and appear as "rwx" for a full set of permissions. If you are not allowed to read a file, a dash is placed in that position. If you are not allowed to write to a file, a dash is placed in that position, and the same goes for execute.

So, if I haven't totally confused you, what you are seeing in the pervious paragraph is that the owner of the first listing (a directory) has all three permissions, rwx. The group and all users can only read and execute the directory (r-x). The second line shows that the owner can read and write and the group and all can only read the file.

You'll also notice the words *root* and *wheel* in my example. Root is the name of the administrator account in Unix, and wheel is the default group for administrators. The root account is allowed to do everything and anything to a Unix system, and that is the account hackers try to use when hacking into a system. If they can log on as root, they can do anything they want.

In all operating systems, the number of administrator (or root) accounts must be kept to a minimum and, of course, they must have very strong passwords that are changed often.

Windows permissions

The operating system that most office workers are familiar with is MS Windows. There are numerous versions in operation now — Windows 95, Windows NT, Windows 98, Windows 2000, and Windows XP. They all can restrict access with individual accounts and passwords but the actual implementation of this feature is more secure with the later versions of Windows.

Windows permissions allow a user to read, write, and execute the same way a Unix system does, but the mechanics and semantics are quite a bit different. Table 11-2 lists the basic Windows permissions and what they mean.

Table 11-2	Windows Permissions
Permission	*Explanation*
Full Control	Everything and anything is allowed — full read, write, and execute permissions, which include changes and deletions.
Modify	You can change or delete a file or folder.
Read and Execute	You can read a file and run programs, but you can't change or delete.
List Folder Contents	You can only see what is in a folder. However, there may be other permissions set on the individual files within a folder that would allow you to read or alter them.
Read	You can only view the contents of a file; you can't make any changes.

Permission	Explanation
Write	You can create a new file and write data in an existing file, but you cannot read the file. In a folder, you can add new files to the folder, but you cannot see everything within the folder.

I find these choices somewhat confusing and I'm sure some administrators do, too. It's much easier to deal with the three basics of read, write, and execute, but Microsoft feels that these choices give an administrator better control. When setting the permissions on a file or folder, you explicitly "Allow" or "Deny" these privileges. By default, users and groups have Read & Execute, List Folder Contents, and Read permissions.

In addition to the set of permissions shown previously, Windows 2000 and Windows XP have an "advance" set of permissions, which expand on the basic permissions (see Table 11-3). As an example on how to get to these permissions (because they can be very difficult to find), right-click on My Computer and then choose Properties. Click the Security tab and then Advanced. Finally, click View/Edit.

Table 11-3	Advanced NTFS Permissions
Permission	Explanation
Traverse Folder/Execute File	This is a special set of permissions that allow you to move through a folder that you don't have List permission to. You can also run the application so you can open the file.
List Folder/Read Data	You can view the names of files in a folder and can read the data in a file, but you cannot make changes.
Read Attributes	You can view the Hidden, Read-Only, and System attributes of a file.
Read Extended Attributes	Some files have more attributes that are added by the application. This permission allows you to see those, too.
Create Files/Write Data	You can create new files inside a folder and you can make changes to existing files.
Create Folders/Append Data	You can create new subfolders and you can add data to the end of an existing file. You cannot delete or change what is already in the file.

(continued)

Table 11-3 *(continued)*

Permission	Explanation
Write Attributes	You can change the attributes of a file or folder.
Write Extended Attributes	You can change the extended attributes of a file or folder.
Delete Subfolders and Files	You can delete a subfolder and its files, but not a main folder. You can use this even if you haven't been given Delete permission on the main folder and each of the files within that folder.
Delete	You can delete a file.
Read Permissions	You can see what permissions are set on a file or folder. Even if you don't have permission to do anything, you can see who does have permission.
Change Permissions	You can change the permissions on a file or folder.
Take Ownership	You can take over as the owner of a file or folder. Usually, an owner has a full set of permissions.

As you can see, administering permissions on these systems can get pretty complex. But this is all in the name of security.

Unlike Unix views, when you list the contents of a drive or directory, Windows does not indicate the permissions associated with that file or folder in the window. In order to see the permissions associated with a file or folder, you need to check the Properties of it. You can right-click on any file or folder, and choose Properties to check out the permissions.

Mac permissions

Macs have always been viewed as the rogue or outsider of the mainstream operating systems. I have always loved the Mac and found it to be relatively secure, but I think that was security through obscurity rather than by design. There doesn't seem to be the same amount of interest in hacking Macs as there is in hacking Windows and Unix.

The newest version of the Mac operating system, OS X, has made a very interesting change. By default, it is still the same Mac that people know, but now the OS is based on a type of Unix called BSD. All the permissions used on a Mac are the basic read, write, and execute as mentioned for Unix, but you can use either the Mac interface or the Unix interface to view and set the permissions. By default, the Unix root account is disabled, but you can easily set it up. If you use the Terminal application in the Mac to view a folder and contents, you will see the same display you usually see on a Unix system with the series of r's, w's, and x's. If you use the Mac's Show Info command on a file or folder, you get a graphical representation of its permissions (see Figure 11-3).

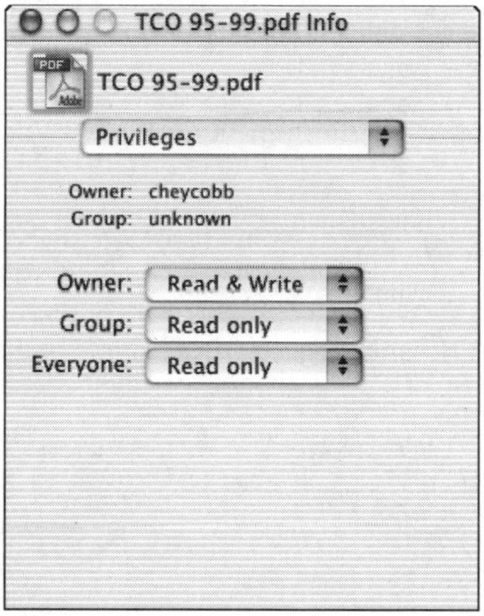

Figure 11-3:
Mac's
display of
permissions
on a file.

You have four choices of permissions in the Mac's view:

- Read & Write
- Read Only
- Write Only
- None

These are self-explanatory by now, I think. The permission "None" denies anyone except the root or administrator accounts from doing anything with a file or folder.

Identity and Authentication

In a network setting, your identity is your logon name or UserID, and your authentication is a password. This method of proving who you are is inherently weak and is the main way that hackers get into systems. Logon names are easy to discover, and most people use really bad passwords. Not only do they choose bad passwords, but then they tend to use the same ones for everything they do. But using the same password makes it easy for someone to steal everything you have if the password is guessed.

A better method of proving who you are is called *strong authentication*. It's based on the fact that using two proofs is better than one. The three different ways you can prove your identification are by providing:

- Something you know — like a password, a PIN, or your mother's maiden name
- Something you have — like a driver's license, ATM card, or ID card
- Something you are — biometrics — fingerprints, face recognition, retina scan, and so on.

Of the three, only the "something you are" is difficult to defeat on its own. The thing you know can be guessed and the thing you have could be stolen. However, when you require at least two out of the three proofs, then the possibility of counterfeit or subterfuge is lowered and the probability that the person is actually who he claims to be becomes stronger. That's way this method is called strong authentication.

Something you know

Although this is usually the weakest form of authentication, it's the only type of authentication that comes installed by default on almost every computer. That's because it costs nothing to include this feature and all the other methods of authentication require additional hardware and/or software.

So what if you can't afford the additional hardware and software to better authenticate your users? The only thing you can do is to educate your users on how to create good passwords and then use password checkers or password crackers to identify and weed-out the weak ones. Some of the operating systems allow you to set strict password policies that force the users to use long passwords and include special characters and numbers in the password. Password checkers and password crackers are very inexpensive and most are very easy to use. It may be worth the little bit of added expense to increase your security if you are only using passwords as authentication. Another option is to purchase a program that generates a password for the user. I generally don't like these because the users are more likely to forget one of these passwords than one they created for themselves.

So, what's the thinking nowadays on the creation of a strong password? I'll give you some tips:

- ✔ Never, never, never use a word that can be found in a dictionary as a password. This includes foreign dictionaries that can be easily loaded, like German, French, Italian, Portuguese, and so on.

- ✔ Never use a common word with some numbers at the beginning or end as a password. For example, "summer48" is not a good password.

- ✔ Make your password at least 8 characters long. Longer, if you can handle it!

- ✔ Include in your password both upper- and lowercase alphabet characters, numbers, and special characters.

- ✔ Use a cognitive phrase to help you create a password. For instance, the phrase, "I really, really hate my job here" becomes IRRHMJH. But, since that doesn't include upper- and lowercase or numbers or special characters, you could change it to: 1rRhmjh! (Use the number "1" instead of the letter "I" and end the phrase with an exclamation point for emphasis.)

- ✔ Use a book as a "key." Open the book to a page and take the first four letters of the word at the top of the left-side page and the last three letters of the word at the bottom of the right-side page. Now insert the number between the letters. You'll get something like "file24ehe". If you forget the password, just pull out the book at look at the page. (Hopefully you can at least remember the page number!)

Have too many passwords to remember? It's a big no-no to write down your passwords on paper, but there's nothing that says you can't write down a password hint or tip. Use your rolodex or address book to keep your hints organized.

There are still a couple of other things you can do to make passwords work better. One is to have your system expire passwords every three to six months so users are forced to change them. You can also "age" the passwords. The system will keep a list of the last few passwords used and will keep the user from using the same password again for a long time. And last, but not least, you should limit logon attempts. If someone gets the password wrong three times in a row, that person should be automatically locked out of the system. The person will have to contact the administrator in person to have the account unlocked.

Something you have

Okay, so you decided to go to something stronger to prove a user's identity. There are some other things you can do, but they are all going to cost money for hardware, software, and administration and maintenance. However, if you set up a strong authentication system based on two proofs, that is as good of a form of authentication as you can get.

Tokens

A token is a hand-held password generator. I'll bet you're asking, "If a password is something I know, how can it also be something I have?" That's a good question. In this case, you can't know the password ahead of time because the token creates it and you can't use the password unless you have the token. Additionally, tokens are usually set up so you have to enter two passwords. The first one is the one you created and know and then you have to enter the generated password. This creates the two proofs.

In order to use tokens, you have to purchase an authentication server and the individual tokens. The authentication server acts as a sort of security guard that asks for further identification. It's placed on the network to intercept any traffic destined for the internal network. Here's how it works:

1. You log on with your UserID and password.

2. Once the network operating system accepts you as a valid user, the authentication server issues you a challenge.

3. To satisfy the challenge, you enter the password given to you by your token.

4. The authentication server checks to see if that was a valid response.

5. The server says "OK" and lets you finish logging on.

There are some slight variations to this scenario, but the workings are basically the same. This is probably the least expensive authentication mechanism to set up and it's been around for a long time now. There are a lot of different vendors offering this solution and their implementation varies. This makes it hard to mix and match systems and you generally have to go with one vendor for everything. However, the only problems I've seen with tokens is that sometimes a time limit will expire before the user successfully enters the generated password and the authentication server rejects the logon. The other problem I've seen is that the tokens and the authentication server sometimes get out of synch with one another and have to be re-synced. While the systems are out of sync, users cannot log on.

There are a number of vendors of security tokens and the market is vast. The best place to check them out is at the Network Computing Buyers' Guide at http://ibg.networkcomputing.com/ibg/Chart?guide_id=3364. There are prices and links to all the vendors' Web sites.

Memory cards

This is like a credit card or an ATM card and has a magnetic strip on one side with information coded on the strip. The costs for this system can be expensive if you have a lot of computers because you need to add a card reader to every computer. You also have to buy the cards and the system that encodes the cards. Additional software is needed so the computers can read, transmit, and understand the information contained on the card. But, it's an easy solution. All a user has to do is to log on as usual with his UserID and password and then he passes the card through the reader to complete the logon process. These cards can also be used to lock a system quickly when you're going to be away for a while. Again, simple yet effective.

Smart cards

Smart cards are a slight step up from memory cards because they contain a microprocessor chip on the card itself. More information about the person using it can be stored on the card, but you have to have the programming software and hardware to be able to generate these cards. You need the software setup similar to what is needed for memory cards.

Generally, you have to enter a PIN to unlock the card before it will transmit its information and just running it through the reader is not enough. This works as an additional challenge to prove your identity. If someone has stolen the card but doesn't know the PIN — tough luck.

PKI

PKI is a catch phrase that stands for Public Key Infrastructure. The term "public key" refers to the use of algorithms and a pair of cryptographic keys. The keys are actually small encrypted text files that are generated by key creation programs One of the keys is used for encryption and the other is used for decryption of the encrypted message or object. One key is closely guarded and is called the *private key* while the other is freely available and is called the *public key*. Both keys are needed for a transaction and neither by itself is any good. There is more on PKI in Chapter 10.

PKI is a complicated and expensive investment in equipment. PKI uses a combination of software, encryption technologies, and services used to verify a person's ID. It makes extensive use of *digital certificates,* which are a type of online passport. It's not a real passport, but it acts as one to verify your online identity. Digital certificates are issued by Certificate Authorities (CAs), which are like the equivalent of digital passport offices. Again, they aren't real passport offices, but they work like passport offices to verify who you are before they will issue a certificate. CAs embed an individual's or an organization's public key along with other identifying information into each digital certificate and then cryptographically sign it as a tamper-proof seal, verifying the integrity of the data within it and validating its use. Whew! Sounds easy, doesn't it?

Setting up a PKI system to authenticate and validate users consists of many parts. These parts, in short, are

✔ A Certificate Authority (CA) that manages and signs certificates for an institution.

✔ Registration Authorities, operating under the auspices of the CA, that validate users as having been issued certificates.

✔ PKI management tools, including software to manage revocations, validations, and renewals.

✔ Directories to store certificates, public keys, and certificate management information.

✔ Databases and key-management software to store escrowed and archived keys.

✔ Applications that can make use of certificates and can seek validation of others' certificates.

Because PKI is such a generic term, how the technology is used varies. In its simplest form, users use the public/private key combination to encrypt and decrypt e-mail messages, for example. However, I'm talking about using PKI to provide strong authentication, and that is a different implementation of PKI.

To use PKI as authentication, the user typically uses a smart card to log on. The smart card had been programmed by the PKI administrators to include such things as a private key, a digital certificate, employee information, and a password cache. The smart card is inserted into a reader for that data to be able to be sent to the security software. After that data has been read, the user enters his password or PIN to finish logging on. As long as that smart card remains in the reader, the user remains logged on. Of course, the security of this device is defeated if the user leaves the card in the computer and goes to another area. A different user could sit down at the computer and the security system wouldn't know that anything has changed.

One big failing of the smart card system is that the card can be stolen and the user's password can be guessed. This is the same problem with ATM bank cards. In those cases, the transaction itself may be secure, but the identity of the user hasn't really been authenticated.

A company called Verisign was one of the pioneers of PKI and they have tons of information on their Web site to help you understand how to set up a PKI system for your network. Their PKI tour is located at `www.verisign.com/enterprise/tour/page1.html`. Each page on the tour has a list of links to explain concepts and implementations.

Digital certificates and signatures

This is part of a total *public key infrastructure* (PKI) and the infrastructure you need to set up is expensive and complex. This is not a solution for the weak at heart. PKI is generally used for encryption to keep things secret, but one small portion of the infrastructure can be used for authentication. I'll start out small and work my way up.

The first part of this mechanism is a set of *keys*. You create a *public key* and a *private key* with a software program like *PGP* (Pretty Good Privacy). This program uses random keystrokes and mouse movements to create a file that is the key itself. You then protect these keys with a *passphrase*. Your keys are used to encrypt and decrypt messages. The keys themselves are considered a form of authentication because only you know the passphrases to unlock them.

The second part of this mechanism is the *digital certificate*. This is a credential that contains your public key and is created by a *certificate authority* (CA). You have to request a digital certificate from a CA and the CA verifies your identity in some way, creates the certificate, digitally signs it, sends a copy back to you, and keeps the certificate in its database of certificates. If you send your public key to someone, he can contact the CA and they will check you up in their database and verify your identity. The certificate contains a serial number, version number, identity information, algorithm information, dates of the certificate, and the CA's digital signature.

The *digital signature* that the CA uses was created using their private key. You create your own digital signature by using another program that uses a *hashing algorithm* to create a small value like a string of characters. Then you use your private key to encrypt the string. This becomes your digital signature. You can attach this signature to a message, for example, and the recipient uses your public key to decrypt the string. If the string you sent matches the string they received, then your identity is verified.

Sounds confusing doesn't it? I'm not surprised because PKI is a whole other book in itself. If you decide you want to incorporate PKI into your system as a way of increasing your security, you are going to have to do a lot of research and will probably have to hire an expert to help you.

Kerberos

How many of you remember your Greek mythology from high school? If you were into that, you may remember that Kerberos (sometimes spelled as Cerberus) was a three-headed dog that guarded the gateway to Hades. In the computer world, however, Kerberos is an authentication protocol that has been around since the 1980s. Kerberos works by using secret keys exchanged between itself, users, applications, and services.

The main component of a Kerberos system is the *key distribution center* (KDC). The KDC holds all of the secret keys and issues a *ticket* whenever keys are exchanged to complete a transaction. For example, say you need to query the database for some information, this is how the transaction would work:

1. You start the query program for the database.

2. The Kerberos program on your computer asks for your UserID and password.

3. The Kerberos program sends the UserID and password to the KDC along with a request to let you use the query program.

4. The authentication service of the KDC checks to see if the UserID and password and the query program are in its database and if secret keys are available for both.

5. If the information in the KDC database checks out, it creates a separate, encrypted session key for the transaction.

6. The KDC issues a ticket that contains the session key and sends it back to your computer.

7. When the UserID and password have been verified, the Kerberos program on your computer sends the ticket to the query program and authenticates you as a trusted user.

The ticket has a time limit that has been configured by the administrators. Usually the ticket only lasts for one work day, so you would need to go through the process again tomorrow. However, if you quit the query program and then need to use it again, you will not have to go through this process again if the time has not expired.

This system meets the requirement of "something you have" because of the ticket created by Kerberos. If you cannot supply the "something you know" — your password — then Kerberos will not issue a ticket to be used.

Kerberos was first developed for the Unix operating system. Recently, Microsoft introduced of Kerberos into Windows2000 and included some secret programming code of their own in the program. Because of this, the two versions of Kerberos are not compatible. This may make it very difficult to implement Kerberos on your network if you have a mixture of systems.

RADIUS

RADIUS is an acronym that stands for Remote Authentication Dial-In User Service. Given its name, it's probably a bit obvious that this authentication method is used to protect networks that have a large number of users dialing in through a modem bank. RADIUS has been around for quite a while and is an Internet standard. The way the different vendors implement RADIUS might be slightly different, but the protocols and methods are all basically the same.

RADIUS works similar to Kerberos in that you need a RADIUS program (a *client*) on your computer and a RADIUS server on the network to do the authentication. You log on using the RADIUS program and are required to enter your *credentials*. The credentials often include the UserID, password (which is encrypted), the ID of the RADIUS client, the port number you are accessing, and a shared secret. All this is sent to the RADIUS server for verification. Sometimes the RADIUS server issues another challenge and you have to type in a passphrase or similar.

Once the RADIUS server has accepted the connection, you are usually restricted to only certain parts of the network. A session key isn't exchanged like it is for Kerberos, but the session is tracked and there is a time limit on the session.

TACACS

TACACS stands for Terminal Access Controller Access Control System. Huh? Seems they went in for a fair amount of redundancy in the name. This system has the same functionality of a RADIUS system, but it has many different types and no industry standard. You need to have both the TACACS client and the TACACS server on your system and there is an exchange of credentials between the client and the server. TACACS is more flexible in the type of credentials it will accept, however. It will accept Kerberos authentication, tokens, smart cards, and so on.

Something you are

The "something you are" really refers to something about you that cannot be changed such as your fingerprints, your voice, or the size of your hand. These and other methods are called *biometrics*, or the science of measuring biological features. These features do not change over your lifetime and are as individual as snowflakes. You've probably seen these in action more in movies than you have in person. I remember seeing hand scans used in the new version of "Planet of the Apes."

A biometric system added to your network involves the addition of hardware in the form of readers and the software needed to store and validate scans. To register your fingerprint, you first will press your finger on a small electronic pad so the system can take measurements of the characteristics of your fingerprint. After the initial measurement is made, the system will ask you to press your finger on the pad again to verify what it has stored. If you use another finger or if the measurements were skewed somehow, the process will repeat.

Once the measurement is complete, the system stores the fingerprint as a mathematical formula and is encrypted. It's not stored as a fingerprint like we know it. (Movies often get this part all wrong.) If someone were to gain access to the fingerprint database and sent your file to the printer, it wouldn't look like a fingerprint at all but a bunch of gobbledigook.

I've used fingerprint scans on systems that required a UserID, a password, and the fingerprint as authentication and found them to be very effective and easy to use. The systems can also be configured to lock and unlock your computer when you are going to be away from your desk for a while. (Which is always a good practice.)

The other biometrics use the same process to measure and store the patterns and characteristics of an individual's scan. However, some scanning methods are more prone to errors than others. Generally, palm and hand scans are the best, iris and retina scans are second, and fingerprints are third. Table 11-4 lists other scanning methods and the mechanics of each in the order of their effectiveness.

Table 11-4	Other Scanning Methods
Scanning Method	*Characteristics*
Palm scan	Measures the creases, ridges, grooves, and fingerprints of all the fingers.
Hand geometry	Measures the length and width of the hand and the length and width of each finger.
Iris scan	Measures the intricate patterns in the iris as well as the colors.
Retina scan	Measures the pattern of blood vessels at the back of the eye.
Fingerprint	Measures the ridges, grooves, and creases of one finger.
Voice recognition	Measures the variations of tone and emphasis of specific words. These variations are subtle and distinct.
Face recognition	Measures the geometry of the forehead, cheeks, and chin as well as the placement of nose, eyes, and mouth.
Signature recognition	Creates electrical impulses that measure the length, strokes, pressure, and so on of a person's signature.
Keystroke recognition	Measures the speed and pattern of a word or phrase typed on a keyboard.

Unfortunately, biometrics are viewed by many people as an invasion of privacy and for that reason, many companies have been hesitant to implement them. Of course, the initial start-up costs can be expensive for a large company and that may be another factor.

Gates and Fences

Another form of access control concerns the boundaries of your network and the devices that are used to define the boundaries. This is usually referred to as your perimeter defense. This perimeter can only be crossed (in theory, anyway) by those who are authorized. It's up to you to define who is authorized to access your network.

Routers

Routers tell the network traffic how to reach a certain point in the network. They are also used to set up boundaries by disallowing some types of traffic and allowing others. These boundaries are established by rules called *access control lists* (ACLs) and are key to good router security.

Routers are not aware of individual users. They can only track individual machines and the communication channels called *ports*. The individual machines (or groups of machines) are identified by their IP number(s) and subnet mask and the ports are identified by specific numbers which, in turn, identify the services that communicate on that port. By doing this, they can effectively hide your network from the Internet or other networks.

Router ACLs are simply a text-based file that is stored on the router. The ACLs are usually created using the command line interface of the router and will look something like this:

```
Access-list 33 ip permit 172.16.0.0 0.0.255.255 log
Access list 44 ip deny 172.16.13.7 0.0.0.0 log
Access-list 55 ip deny 172.16.64.0 any http
```

There is a real art to setting up router ACLs and each vendor's router will have slightly different syntax for the rules. It usually takes a fair amount of training to learn how to appropriately set rules. It's important to remember that the rules are numbered and will be followed in the order in which they are listed. So, if you allow someone in through a high numbered rule and then deny them access through a lower numbered rule, they will be allowed through.

The rules will be based on your security policies: who you want to allow to do what and what programs and services are allowed on what portions of the network. Since people generally use the same computer every day, you can restrict their access by identifying that IP address in the rules. Accordingly, you can restrict the ports that the particular IP is allowed to use, too. Of course, if the person uses another machine, these restrictions may be defeated.

Router ACLs can be set up on the router itself, remotely via a telnet session, or by uploading the ACLs from another computer to the router. The most secure way to do this is at the router console itself. This is a double-edged sword because you have better security but it's harder to get the rules correctly entered and in the right order when you are sitting at the router. Telnet is easier than sitting at the router, but it's easy to hack into routers that have telnet enabled. The best thing to do is to compose the ACLs on a separate machine, check them for errors, and then transfer them to the router.

Of course, you want to restrict physical access to the router by putting it in a locked room or other secure environment, too. It doesn't do you any good to have really good ACLs on your router if anyone can get to the router and change them!

Firewalls

Firewalls are seen as the ultimate access control devices. While they are very good at making sure that entrances and exits are controlled to your network, they are not in the position of actually verifying individuals. Like routers, they can only see IP addresses and port numbers and use rules to decide what traffic gets through and what doesn't.

Firewalls are more intelligent than routers, however, because they can look "inside" the traffic and verify its contents. It can look at an FTP connection and say, "Yes, this is following all the rules of an FTP connection" and let the traffic continue. A firewall can also be set up to run proxy services, which are like middle-men working in between two programs. This increases the access control because the program making the connection only has indirect access to the system.

For more information on firewalls, see Chapter 9.

VLANs

VLANs are short for *Virtual Local Area Network*. They work with switches as opposed to routers and are used to *virtually* split networks into segments. Before I can tell you how a VLAN works, I first want to make sure you understand how a switch works. A switch works by switching packets between two or more machines on a network. There are a lot of different types of switches, but I'm going to be talking about a LAN *(Local Area Network)* switch.

A LAN switch establishes a connection between two different segments on a network just long enough to send the current packet. Incoming packets are saved to a temporary memory area (buffer); the *Media Access Control (MAC)* address, contained in a special part of the packet, is read and then compared to a list of addresses maintained in the switch's lookup table. The MAC address is a unique number given to each network card. Although this sounds complicated, switching is much faster than routing in a network and is generally used on large networks that need the speed.

Normally, you would physically separate segments of a network by placing switches between the different segments. On a VLAN, however, the physical placement has nothing to do with which segment your computer is on. A VLAN uses a special protocol to add information to the packets that identify which segment the computer resides on. So, computers that are sitting right next to each other won't necessarily be on the same segment of the network. One could be on the Finance segment and the other could be on Operations. These computers can also be changed to another network segment with a simple command and physical cables and boxes don't have to be altered. The different network segments can also have different access requirements — it all depends on the set up and configuration of the VLAN.

Although I've just made VLANs sound very simple, they are actually quite sophisticated and require knowledge and experience to be able to set them up and configure them correctly. As I've stated before, different vendors have their own implementations and VLANs are no different. You usually have to go with one vendor for the entire solution as the different types aren't always interoperable. The outlay for the hardware can be expensive and there is certainly a lack of available talent in some areas of the country.

Part IV
Special Needs Networking

The 5th Wave   By Rich Tennant

"Our automated response policy to network security invasion is to notify management, back up existing data, and sell 90 percent of my shares in the company."

In this part . . .

Holey moley, partners! There are security holes in programs used on the network! You've got your anti-virus software and firewalls in place, but there's still more to protect. How are you going to keep up?

Don't despair! You're already well on your way to getting your network locked and loaded with security. The chapters in this section take an in-depth look at the systems and applications that may cause problems and, of course, what you need to do to fix them.

Chapter 12

When Patchwork Doesn't Mean Quilting: Unix Systems

- -

- -

Security geeks agree that the Holy Grail of the computing world is the truly secure computer. In fact, lots of people are searching for it (the truly secure computer, that is) and not finding it! If you look around on the Internet, you can find tons of tantalizing clues to this computer's existence, but no clear roadmap with a bright red *X* to mark its hiding spot. Regardless, you still do what you can to secure your networks. I guess the same can be said about a secure house. That is, no house is totally secure from break-ins, but I still lock my doors and windows just to be safe. Neither the house nor the computers may not be totally secure, but I take steps to make sure that break-ins aren't easy.

In this chapter, I cover the absolute minimums for securing Unix computers on your network. You have security holes — some big, some little — in almost every piece of software on your computer and this is especially true of operating systems. Unix is one of the oldest and most respected operating systems there is. Nonetheless, it still has holes. I'll tell you how to plug the big holes and describe some little ones you should watch for. Fixing these holes, a process known as *patching*, may seem technical and scary at first, but soon you'll be breezing through and patching like a true alpha-geek!

Finding Out about Patches and Where You Put Them

The general term for a security hole fix is a *patch*. A patch can take different forms, such as a small bit of software that you run on your computers or a change that you make in certain configuration files. Patches that require changes in configuration files generally involve turning off features and services you don't need so that they can't be used against you. The goal of all this messing about is to *harden* your computer's software — that is, to fortify it against hacking attempts or unauthorized use. (Later in this chapter I list most of the services that are most likely to cause security problems with your Unix system.) Believe me, when you mention that you've hardened your machines to security geeks, it makes them swoon with pleasure.

Following is a list of software components from a network system that commonly need patching:

- **Operating systems:** The operating system is the nerve center of the computers on your network, and it enables all other programs to operate by managing and allocating system resources. Leaving an operating system vulnerable to attack is one of the most common mistakes made by network administrators. (See Chapter 14 for Windows OSs and Chapter 15 for Mac vulnerabilities.)

- **Commonly used application programs:** Software programs that guide your everyday computing activities, such as e-mail, word processing, and spreadsheet programs, often contain security holes that hackers can use to wreak havoc on your computer. (See Chapter 15 about security patches for applications.)

- **Web servers:** If your network is connected to the Internet and you are using Web servers to display information on the World Wide Web, a common hacker can use the holes in the Web server software to possibly gain entrance to the rest of your network. Many of these holes allow said hacker to zip right through a firewall without even triggering an alert. (See Chapter 15 for Web security information.)

- **Databases:** Databases are often connected to Web servers to provide the flow of data to and from your Web browser. Also, they often hold very sensitive information such as credit card numbers, personal healthcare information, and even social security numbers. Some database software contains holes that allow a hacker to connect to your database and steal your data by using only a Web browser. (See Chapter 15 for information about securing databases.)

- **Common gateway interface (CGI):** CGIs are small programs created to allow disparate programs, like Web servers and databases, to communicate and share information. For example, a CGI is used to transfer the data from a form into the database. CGIs are often written in simple programming languages such as Perl or Tkl. A poorly written CGI can introduce security holes in an otherwise secure computer system. (See Chapter 15 for more information on CGI programs and how to secure them.)

Making Sure You Get the Patches You Need

After a vendor releases a new version of software, teams of anonymous people (most well-meaning, some not) examine the program to see whether it contains any holes. When they find holes, the good guys tell the software vendor and agencies such as *CERT* (Computer Emergency Response Team at Carnegie-Mellon University) about what they found. If the problem poses a real threat, the vendor or agency (or both) sends out an alert to the general public. Within hours of an alert's being posted by CERT, hackers the world over start looking for any computers that have exactly the same problem mentioned in the alert. They rely on the fact that most network administrators will not fix the security holes immediately, if at all. Once hackers find systems that are vulnerable, they tell other hackers of their find through chat rooms and newsgroups. If your system was found to be vulnerable, you could have many hackers knocking on your network door instead of just one.

The best place to obtain patches and information about patches is at the vendor's Web site. Another excellent source for information and links to patches is the CERT Coordination Center Vulnerability Database. You'll be amazed at how long the list is, but remember that not all the patches are going to apply to you. You have to consider your situation and what services you are running. Here's a list of some of the more popular Web sites for patches for various Unix systems and information about their vulnerabilities:

- Sun Microsystems: `http://sunsolve.sun.com/pub-cgi/show.pl?target=home`
- Red Hat Linux: `www.redhat.com/support/alerts/`
- Debian: `www.debian.org/security/`
- OpenBSD: `www.openbsd.com/security.html`
- Caldera: `www.caldera.com/support/download.html`
- CERT/CC Vulnerability Database: `www.kb.cert.org/vuls`
- Bugtraq (SecurityFocus): `http://online.securityfocus.com/archive/1`

Although patches are usually small programs that update existing software, they are still very powerful and can cause disruption on the network. For that reason, you should read the readme file that comes with any patch and have backups of your system available in case the worst should happen.

Holes That Need Fixing in the Unix Operating Systems

I know an old saying that goes like this: "The only way to make a computer secure is to turn if off, disconnect it from the network, put it in a safe, and throw away the combination." In other words, a completely secure computer is an impossibility. You can make no computer absolutely hack-proof, but you can many steps to plug the obvious, large holes and to make the smaller holes less noticeable.

The first stop on this hole-plugging journey is the Unix operating system. Because you need an operating system to even turn on the computer, it's the obvious starting point. Although you find hundreds of variations on operating systems, this section focuses on Unix. Why? Because a majority of computers that make up the Internet are, in fact, some type of Unix computer. (Windows and Macs are covered in Chapters 13 and 14.)

Plugging Holes in the Many UNIX Flavors

The original UNIX program was developed at Bell Labs in 1969. Since then, it has been poked, prodded, and changed to the point that there are almost as many types of UNIX as there are makers of cars. Like a car, however, no matter how many changes are made to UNIX, all variants still act and work pretty much the same way.

UNIX can be scary. Its command-line interface brings back horrid memories of DOS, and the UNIX commands sound like an alien language. So, if UNIX is so difficult, then why do people use it? Network administrators choose it because it's very stable, and its developers put forth a concerted effort to make it secure. The more popular forms of UNIX now have better interfaces and some are available at no cost! A free, secure operating system? Now, that's good news! Check out Open BSD at www.openbsd.org. Read on to find out where and how to start the process of hardening your UNIX operating system.

Starting your security efforts at the root

The administrative account in UNIX is called *root*. If you are logged on as root, you can make any change imaginable: install and run programs; move, copy, and delete files; change configurations; add and delete users; change permissions; and format disks. In hacker lingo, a person who has logged on as root is said to *own* the machine. In order to make any security changes or patches on a UNIX machine, you must be logged on as root.

The starting point for hardening the UNIX operating system is to turn off any unnecessary *services*. Services are like mini-programs that work within the system to take care of certain tasks on their own. Some services are also referred to as *daemons,* although they are not the same sort of demons who will haunt you if you don't harden your system! An example of an unnecessary service might be FTP. If you won't be adding and deleting files from a remote computer, then it's best to turn off FTP. Consider the following general points about finding and turning off the extra services that you don't need:

✔ You find many (but not all) services in a plain text file called *inetd.conf,* which lists the Internet related services that start every time the computer boots up. The inetd file is the configuration file for the daemons that control connection requests to start services across the network You turn off services in this file by commenting out the services you don't need or want. You can tell which services are commented out because their line in the file begins with the pound (#) sign.

✔ You can find other services and daemons listed in configuration files in the directories listed here. These are usually the startup files for your computer.

  • /etc/rc.conf

  • /etc/rc.conf.d/*

✔ You can usually disable services that run as standalone daemons by removing the file, changing the filename, or moving the file to another directory.

✔ You make all security changes to a UNIX machine in command-line mode, which means that there are no simple Windows-like dialog boxes with radio buttons or boxes to click. And you need to have is a basic knowledge of UNIX commands.

Follow these steps to turn off the unneeded services that you find listed in the inetd.conf file:

1. **Log on to your network's administrative account as root.**

   How to log on to your network's administrative account differs with how the network is set up.

2. **Type cd /etc at the UNIX command line to navigate to the /etc/ directory and find the inetd.conf file.**

   If you are already deep into another directory, it's best to go back to the root directory and start from there.

3. **Make a backup copy of the inetd.conf file.**

   You should never change a configuration file in UNIX without first saving a backup of the original and keeping another copy on a floppy disk. For security's sake, change the name of the backup file so that it is different from the original. Otherwise, a wily hacker can find the backup file and reinstall it.

4. **Open inetd.conf with a regular text editor such as vi or emacs.**

   When you open inetd.conf in a text editor such as vi, it looks something like the portion of the inetd.conf file I've included in Figure 12-1. Services that you see in this figure include *echo, discard, daytime,* and *time.* The inetd.conf file contains variations depending on the type of UNIX you are using, so don't expect your file to look exactly the same.

5. **To disable any service, type # at the beginning of the line containing the service you want to disable.**

   You'll notice that some of the lines in Figure 12-1 already begin with the pound symbol (#). These lines are *commented out,* which means that the services contained in the lines are ignored when the computer boots up. Services that aren't needed and should be commented out are *echo, discard, daytime,* and *time.* (Trust me on this; you really won't need these services!) In Figure 12-1, notice that discard has not been commented out.

6. **To finish the changes you would continue to place a "#" in front of all the services you want to disable.**

   Save the file with the text editor; do not change the name or location. The first step in securing your machine is nearly complete!

7. **Now that you have changed the inetd.conf file, you'll need to tell the computer to restart that file.**

   Different UNIX systems have slightly different commands to do this, but you'll need to find the *process id* number for inetd and then turn off or *kill* the process. Figure 12-2 gives an example of how this could be done in Red Hat Linux, which is a specific brand of Unix. Different brands of Unix will have slightly different commands from what I've shown here.

You should never do configuration work directly on computers that have important roles on a network, and you certainly should never reboot a server unless you know what you are doing. Other computers may be trying to communicate with the one you are working on, and making changes without warning could have huge repercussions across the network. When possible, take the computer you are working on offline or at least do your reconfiguration work when traffic on the network is very slow.

```
# /etc/inetd.conf:  see inetd(8) for further informations.
#
# Internet server configuration database
#
# Modified for Debian by Peter Tobias <tobias@et-inf.fho-emden.de>
#
# <service_name> <sock_type> <proto> <flags> <user> <server_path>
<args>
#
# Internal services
#
#echo            stream  tcp     nowait  root    internal
#echo            dgram   udp     wait    root    internal
discard          stream  tcp     nowait  root    internal
discard          dgram   udp     wait    root    internal
daytime          stream  tcp     nowait  root    internal
daytime          dgram   udp     wait    root    internal
#chargen         stream  tcp     nowait  root    internal
#chargen         dgram   udp     wait    root    internal
time             stream  tcp     nowait  root    internal
time             dgram   udp     wait    root    internal
#
# These are standard services.
#
telnet   stream  tcp     nowait  root    /usr/sbin/tcpd
         /usr/sbin/in.telnetd
ftp      stream  tcp     nowait  root    /usr/sbin/tcpd /usr/sbin/in.ftpd
#fsp      dgram   udp     wait    root    /usr/sbin/tcpd /usr/sbin/in.fspd
```

Figure 12-1:
The inetd.
conf file.

```
1. ps auxww | grep inetd [The command to find the inetd file.]
2. You will then see output similar to this:

root 187 0.0 1.7 932 404 ? S 09:32 0:00 inetd
root 494 0.0 1.5 1020 344 p0 S 09:34 0:00 grep inetd

3. After the word "root" in the first line is the number
   187. That is the process number. Notice the word "inetd"
   at the end of the first line. That identifies 187 as
   being the process number for inetd. Ignore the second
   line ending with the "grep inetd"; it's part of the
   command that you just issued.
4. kill -9 187 [This is the command to kill or stop inetd]
5. /usr/sbin/inetd [This is the command to have the system re-read the inetd
   file. The services that you have commented out are safely stopped from ever
   running.]
```

Figure 12-2:
The Red Hat
Linux way.

Deciding which services to turn off

In order to help you to decide which services to disable, I created Table 12-1. Although you find variations in the services run on different types of UNIX, some services that I consider dangerous can be found on most systems. The default installation of a UNIX operating system usually leaves these services on. Because these services are generally not needed anyway, I recommend turning them off so that they can't be used against you.

Table 12-1	Dangerous and Unneeded Services
File Name	*Reasons to Consider Disabling Service*
nfsd	Network File System Daemon. Controls the remote access of files across a network. You don't want just anyone to be able to access files. This is better handled by the permissions given to individual users.

(continued)

Table 12-1 *(continued)*

File Name	Reasons to Consider Disabling Service
lockd	Controls the file locks across a network. Again, you don't want just anyone locking you out of files.
mountd	Used to remotely mount disk drives across a network. Ditto as preceding.
statd	Provides network status after a crash or a reboot. Could give someone too much information.
rpc	Remote Procedure Call. Allows programs written in C to be run from external machines. Many hacking utilities need this to run. That's a good reason to disable it.
portmap	Changes remote procedure calls into TCP port numbers. Works with rpc. If you're not allowing rpc, then don't allow this service.
lpd	Line Printer Spooler Daemon. Looks for printers on the network and spools print jobs to them. If you don't share printers across the network, then you won't need this.
rsh	Remote Shell. Used to connect from remote machines and issue commands. Notoriously bad service to run. Most hackers will use this if it's there.
rlogin	Remote Login. Allows you to remotely log on to another machine on the network. (See previous.)
rexec	Remote Execute. Another command used to remotely connect to machines and issue commands. (See previous.)
telnetd	Terminal Emulation daemon. Allows a remote connection to your machine so commands can be issued. Very useful to a hacker as it gives access to the OS command line!
ftpd	File Transfer Protocol daemon. Allows someone to insert and delete files anonymously. Nothing anonymous should ever be allowed.
tftp	Trivial FTP. (See previous.)
rcp	Remote Copy. Used to copy files on a remote machine. This is better handled with user permissions.
echo	Displays on the computer screen what has been typed on the keyboard. Useful to a hacker to see what you are typing.
discard	Discards invalid characters. Arcane usage and not needed.
finger	Command used to display users and their names. This service gives out too much information to those who shouldn't know.

File Name	Reasons to Consider Disabling Service
daytime	Displays time in human readable format. Arcane and not in general use.
chargen	Character Generator. Could be used during a hack attack.
sendmail	Notoriously bad program to send e-mails. There are much better services to use than this one. If your machine is not the e-mail server, then you don't need this anyway.
nntp	Network News Transport Protocol. If you're not running newsgroups from your machine, then you don't need this.
uucp	Unix to Unix Copy Protocol. Can easily be used to put back doors and Trojans into your system.
pop-2	Post Office Protocol, version 2. If the machine is not your e-mail server, then you don't need this.
pop-3	Post Office Protocol version 3. If you need a pop server, there are better ones than this.
BIND	Berkeley Internet Name Domain. This is an implementation of the Domain Name Service (DNS) and it has had numerous holes discovered in it. Most operating systems have a proprietary version of DNS and you are better off running that one instead of BIND.
SSH	Secure SHell. Secure shell is a secure version of telnet. If you're not using telnet, then you don't need SSH, either. If you do use SSH, be sure to get the latest patch because there have been a lot of hacks made on this service recently.
WU-FTP	Washington University-File Transfer Protocol. A version of ftp developed by people at WU. If you don't need ftp, then you don't need this version, either. Many hacks have been associated with WU-FTP.
ntpd	Network Time Protocol daemon. This is only needed if you need to need to keep your servers sync'd in time with national time servers. There are many networks that need to have their times carefully sync'd but there have been hacks associated with this protocol. If you need it, be sure you have the security patches.
snmp	Simple Network Management Protocol. Used to gather information from the network and send the gathered messages to a central server so administrators can view what is going on with the network. Because so much data about your network is in these messages, you don't want the messages to fall into the wrong hands.
statd	Status daemon. Used to gather network status for monitoring. People have found hacks that cause this service to crash and then give a user root access.

Patching other UNIX holes

There are some services that can only be disabled by issuing directions in a *startup script*. The startup script is a small program written in shell code. Needless to say, programming and scripting is beyond the scope of this book and the differences between the versions of UNIX are so vast that it is best to refer to the vendor's specifications. If you can't find relief from the vendor's Web site, then posting a message to a UNIX newsgroup usually returns a wealth of information from users who have done it themselves.

Once you've gotten the changes in the configuration files done, you can move on to patches for your particular operating system. New patches appear daily. See the section "Making Sure You Get the Patches You Need" earlier in this chapter for information on vendors' Web sites about patches that are available for your flavor of UNIX. Again, there are so many differences between the different versions of UNIX that I couldn't possibly list them all here.

One of the most recent avenues of attacks on operating systems and applications has been the *buffer overflow*. You'll see that term a lot in security advisories and it's a popular attack method. The attack takes advantage of the fact that most services have been allotted a very small portion of memory in which to store buffered data. The hackers have discovered that if you overload the buffer, it can cause the machine to go a bit haywire and then let them have access to the command line as root. In the security industry, we have given this a highly technical phrase: the Barf-and-Puke-to-Root Technique.

Congratulations! Your UNIX operating system is now hardened and that's a big accomplishment. Studies have shown that about 90 percent of the major hacks that have occurred during the past few years could have been prevented if the systems had been hardened and patched.

Finding helpful programs to monitor UNIX services

After you make the necessary changes to inetd.conf, you may want to consider additional protection for this configuration file. The program *TCP Wrappers* is highly recommended and is available at `http://ciac.llnl.gov/ciac/ToolsUnixNetSec.html#Tcpwrappers`. The program monitors all incoming requests from external computers that attempt to start one of the services included in inetd. If the request is allowed, no problem. If the request isn't allowed, then the connection is denied and an entry is made to a log file on your machine.

Chapter 13

Boarding Up Your MS Windows

....

....

*P*robably the most controversial of all operating systems used on the Internet is the MS Windows family. Hackers have a love/hate relationship with Windows. They love it because it can be so easy to hack, and they hate it because it is so easy to hack. That's not to say that Windows is bad. Windows operating systems are easy to install and easy to use, and they are responsible for introducing personal computers to most of the world. However, if you are relying upon the built-in security of these operating systems, you're going to experience a lot of problems. Windows operating systems were not built to be secure; they were built to share as much as possible. And there's the rub: How do you combine the openness of sharing with the security policies of keeping things private? The answer is that you have to be rigorous in applying the security patches that Microsoft releases. And there are tons of them!

In this chapter, I focus on Windows NT, Windows 2000, and Windows XP. The Windows 95 and Windows 98 operating systems are more for home use than for use in a networked environment, and therefore, they do not employ the same security mechanisms. Some of the security measures are common sense, and others apply to a particular version. This chapter shows the main security components of Windows and what you should do to strengthen that security.

Windows Security

Since the inception of Windows, the emphasis of the operating system has been placed on the ability of different programs to swap and share information. This was a bold move because getting applications to work together without causing conflicts has always been difficult. This same interoperability has made hackers and virus writers jump for joy. With one set of programming tools, they could create viruses, worms, Trojans, and hacks that were almost guaranteed to work.

Microsoft began including security features in Windows NT 3.51. These features made it a better operating system to use in a network environment, using access controls in accounts and to shared drives as its main focus. However, the password encryption scheme in Windows NT 3.51 was very weak and easily broken. Since then, each successive version of Windows has included more security features in its architecture. Some features remained weak and others got stronger.

The main problem with the security in Windows and other operating systems is that the default installation is set for a minimal amount of security. Those relaxed settings are well-known and well-documented in the hacker world. Whenever hackers discover a network using Windows as its main operating system, they immediately check to see whether they can circumvent the security settings. If the default installation has been used on these systems, a hacker can very easily sneak in and do his dirty work. Imagine if we all had combination locks to the front doors of our homes and the default setting of those locks was "1234." It wouldn't take long to figure out that the setting would be easy pickings for a burglar, and we would probably change the combination very quickly.

Another problem with Windows security is the sheer amount of programming code that must be inspected for possible security holes. As near as I've been able to determine, Windows 2000 contains between 25 million and 30 million lines of programming code. Some of that code has been newly written, and other sections are very old. Some of the old code is to maintain backward compatibility, and other code is simply for menus and features that were never used or were never taken out for older versions. If you were to print out the entire Windows 2000 source code, you would get a stack of paper that would be taller than 48 volumes of *War and Peace*. (Actually, it would be taller than that, because *War and Peace* is approximately 600,000 words long and most lines of code contain more than one word. But, you get the idea!) Trying to find possible security holes in that brings to mind needles and haystacks!

Windows, because it is privately owned, has never been released to the public in its pure source code form. It has been held in-house by Microsoft for internal review of its security. Many forms of Unix, on the other hand, have been released as *open source* — meaning that the source code is available to the general public for use and review. Programmers have been examining Unix source code for decades to discover what works and what doesn't as far as security is concerned. Some groups have worked hard to plug the security holes in Unix and release them as *secure* forms of Unix. The fact that the source code for Unix runs between 4 million and 8 million lines of code has enabled people to discover, document, and plug the security holes much more easily.

Much of Windows security is dependent upon the proper installation and use of the security mechanisms. The current versions (2000 and XP) use a system called A*ctive Directory* to centralize the implementation and management of security policies. Active Directory relies upon relationships between segments of the network defined as *trusted* and the replication of the security policies among servers in the trusted domains. This replicated data includes account information such as logon hours, access rights, group memberships, and so on. If this system isn't set up and administered exactly correctly, the information can "leak" into the network or administrators can inadvertently overwrite security changes. Administrators can control changes to the Active Directory with scripts written in Visual Basic, ActiveX, JAVA, C, and C++. Needless to say, these scripts must be secure in themselves, and the changes they make must be secure. Care must be taken to verify that the scripts have come from a reliable source and that they are not a Trojan horse, which installs back doors for hackers. Be wary of any scripts you grab off the Internet. Do you really know who created the scripts?

Many of the Windows settings are also stored in a section of the software called the *registry*. The registry is actually a very large database that includes everything from the default font of the desktop to the minimum password length. Due to its size and complexity, the registry can become fragmented and corrupted. This can lead to huge problems in both the security and the operating of the software as a whole. I think we've all experienced strange goings-on with Windows, and the registry is usually to blame. If a hacker can get into the registry, he can make security changes that may not be noticed. Therefore, keeping recent back-ups of the registry so that it can be restored when problems arise is very important.

Patches, hotfixes, and service packs

Windows, like other operating systems, needs to be regularly maintained with fixes called *patches, hotfixes,* and *service packs.* When the general public discovers a problem, they alert Microsoft and expect it to respond to the problem found. (This is not specific to Microsoft; all the vendors work this way.) If the vendor deems a problem to be important enough, it creates a fix for the problem and releases the fix to the general public. All of Microsoft's fixes can be found at `www.microsoft.com/security/index.asp`. You can sign up for e-mail alerts of security problems and their fixes at `www.microsoft.com/technet/treeview/default.asp?url=/technet/security/bulletin/notify.asp`. Additionally, you can find alerts for all operating systems at `www.cert.org/nav/index_red.html`.

Many administrators become frustrated with Microsoft, because all fixes are not created equal. Often, you have to read through the security bulletins to figure out which fixes you need, and then apply them to your system, in a particular order, with a reboot required after you apply each fix. Sometimes you have difficulty discerning whether the available fixes are really needed on your system, and the fixes are tedious and time consuming to install.

To understand which fixes you need, you first need to understand Microsoft's terminology regarding fixes, shown on Table 13-1.

Table 13-1	Which Security Fix?
Patch Name	*Qualities*
QFE Patch	QFE refers to *quick fix engineering*. These patches are usually released to fix a bad bug in the program rather than a security hole, and they are an example of "quick and dirty" programming. These patches are not rigorously tested, and you have no guarantees that they won't affect other parts of your system. Be very careful with these patches, and only apply them if you're really sure that you need them.
Hotfix	A hotfix is a little bit more substantial than a QFE Patch because some testing (but not much) has been involved. A hotfix is not tested to see whether it is backwardly compatible, and also a hotfix can cause problems with the operating system or other applications. You can remove a hotfix if it is found to cause problems. Each hotfix has a Knowledge Base article associated with it at the Microsoft Web site. You have to read the article to see whether you need the hotfix.
Security Update/ Security Bulletin	An update or a bulletin is considered by Microsoft to be pretty important, and therefore, the associated patch is fully tested prior to its release. Because it has been tested, you can be fairly sure that you won't experience any problems with your system. Some updates/bulletins are not patches, however, but are instructions of changes you need to do manually to your system. Information on each update is on the Microsoft Web site, which includes instructions and the severity of the problem it fixes.
Security Roll-Up Patch	Every once in a while, Microsoft assembles a collection of security updates into one patch, called a *roll-up*. A roll-up includes all the patches released before a certain date, but it does not include any changes that still have to be made manually. You have to read the information about the roll-up to see what, if anything, is missing. You still have to apply any patches that were released after the date when the roll-up was created.

Patch Name	Qualities
Service Pack	A service pack is the granddaddy of all bug fixes and security patches, because it has been extensively beta-tested for problems. You can feel fairly comfortable that installing a service pack won't cause problems. However, you still have to check to see whether any security patches were released after the service pack was created, and you have to apply those separately.

I highly recommend that you sign up for the e-mail alerts sent out by Microsoft. New alerts appear almost daily. Also, remember that hackers are ready, willing, and able to check whether you've applied the necessary patches.

Microsoft Network Security Hotfix Checker

Whew! What a mouthful! The Microsoft Network Security Hotfix Checker is a command line tool called Hfnetchk.exe and is available at http://support. microsoft.com/directory/article.asp?ID=KB;EN-US;Q303215&sd= tech&. It's a freeware version of a more sophisticated program called HFNetChkPro. HFNetChkPro is available for purchase at www.shavlik.com/ security/prod_hf.asp.

You use Hfnetchk.exe to assess which patches you need for Windows NT 4.0, Windows 2000, and Windows XP, as well as hotfixes for IIS 4.0, IIS 5.0, SQL Server 7.0, and SQL Server 2000 (including MSDE), and Internet Explorer 5.01 or later. When you run Hfnetchk.exe, it first examines the computer to determine whether the registry key that is associated with the patch exists. If the registry key does not exist, the patch is considered not installed. If the registry key is not found, the program searches for other files related to the patch and compares the file version and checksum from the file in the program to the file version and checksum of the files on the computer. If any of the file tests are not successful, the patch is listed as "not found." When the program is finished running, it gives you a list of patches that are *best* for your computer, but these are not necessarily all the patches that are available. The program tries to take into account that not all patches are security patches.

Microsoft Baseline Security Analyzer (MBSA)

The Microsoft Baseline Security Analyzer program, also known as MBSA, is a recent release by Microsoft and is a more complete security scanner than the Hfnetchk program. It uses some of the same features as Hfnetchk, but it also includes searches for common security best practices, such as strong pass-words. In addition to checking the operating system, MBSA scans servers running IIS and SQL Server for security misconfigurations, and it checks the security zone settings in Microsoft Office, Outlook, and Internet Explorer. You must be an administrator to run either Hfnetchk or MBSA, and you can check all the computers on your network from one centralized workstation. You can get this tool at `www.microsoft.com/technet/treeview/default.asp?url=/technet/security/tools/Tools/MBSAhome.asp`.

Because this is a recent release (April 2002) and is only version 1.0 of the program, it is sure to have some minor problems. Therefore, don't rely upon it totally. Do some of your own checking to see that all the fixes it suggests are all that you need. MBSA and Hfnetchk are both freeware, so you might as well check them out.

Microsoft also offers another security checker for its IIS Web server, which I cover in Chapter 15.

Hardening the Installation

Although the newer versions of Windows offer more security than the older versions, you still need to make some changes to the default installations of NT, 2000, and XP in order to harden your system. *Hardening* is the act of making changes in order to make the system harder to attack. It tightens up the installation to make the security better. One of the number one rules in security is to never accept a default installation!

Where applicable in this section, I note whether the changes to be made are for NT, 2000, or XP. In some cases, a change works for all three versions; in other cases, the change doesn't work or isn't needed. Be sure to check the changes against the version you are installing. I divide the changes into two different types: system changes that are done with the normal administrative tools, and changes to the registry that must be made with the registry editor.

You will probably use a policy editor to change some of the settings. In Windows NT/2000 servers, you have a program called Policy Editor ("poledit.exe"), and in Windows 2000 Pro/Server there is a program called Local Policy Administrator. These programs are usually found under Administrative Tools in the Default User Properties dialog box (see Figure 13-1). When you open the Policy Editor, you see that most of the check boxes are grayed out. Here's what that means:

✔ White box: The policy setting will not be applied; or, if it has previously been applied, it will no longer apply.

✔ Grey box: The policy will not be applied; or, if it has previously been applied, it will be left as is.

✔ Checked box: The policy will be applied, no matter what the previous setting was.

System changes

I've mentioned before that you should change many of the default settings that are created when Windows is installed. Well, just what changes do you need to make? There are many and to help you out I've created Table 13-2 to help you decide which changes should be made on your system.

Table 13-2	Changing the Defaults	
Action	*Reasons*	*NT, 2000, or XP*
Rename or disable the built-in Administrator account	Every hacker in the world knows that Windows comes with a built-in account called "Administrator," and they spend large amounts of time trying to crack that account. If you rename the account, don't make the name something obvious. If you disable the account, you need to give administrator level privileges to a user — and place that user in the Administrator's group. Be sure to use your best and strongest passwords on this account.	NT, 2000, and XP

(continued)

Table 13-2 *(continued)*

Action	Reasons	NT, 2000, or XP
Rename or disable the built-in Guest account	The previous advice applies here, also. If you rename it, name it something distinctive (like Whoops). Then, if it shows up in an audit log, you'll be sure to catch it.	NT, 2000, and XP
Password protect screen savers.	This is a nifty little feature that keeps co-workers honest. Enable the "Password Protect" option of the screen saver and set a time limit of between 10 and 15 minutes for it to activate. When your computer is inactive for that defined time period, the screen saver comes on and you need your password to unlock it. This can be irritating, but it's very effective.	NT, 2000, and XP
Enforce strong passwords	Install Passfilt.dll into your Winnt\System 32 directory.	NT only
Enforce strong passwords	Use the Policy Editor (poledit.exe) to change the following policies: • Enforce password history (set to 6 or more) • Maximum password age (set to 60) • Minimum password age (set to 15) • Minimum password length (set to 8) • Password must meet complexity requirements (set to Enable) • Store password using reversible encryption for all users in the domain (set to Disable)	2000 and XP
Set account lockout policies	Using the Policy Editor, set the following policies: • Account lockout duration (set to 30) • Account lockout threshold (set to 5) • Reset account lockout counter after (leave at 0)	NT, 2000, and XP
Hide default shares	Place a dollar sign ($) after the following shares to hide them from the general users: • Admin • C, D, and so on (drives) • IPC	NT, 2000, and XP

Action	Reasons	NT, 2000, or XP
	• Print • Repl • SYSVOL	
Set audit policies	Turn on and set the following audits: • Logon and Logoff (failure) • File and Object Access (failure) • Use of User Rights (failure) • User and Group Management (success and failure) • Security Policy Changes (success and failure) • Restart Shutdown and System (failure) • Process Tracking (failure)	NT only
Set audit policies	Turn on and set the following audits: • Audit account logon events (success and failure) • Audit account management (success and failure) • Audit directory service access (disable) • Audit logon events (success and failure) • Audit object access (failure) • Audit policy change (success and failure) • Audit privilege use (success and failure) • Audit process tracking (success and failure) • Audit system events (success and failure)	2000 and XP
Disable task scheduler	If you don't need to schedule tasks on workstations, disable this service.	NT, 2000, and XP
Disable the Server service	The Server service is only needed on workstations that will be sharing their local hard drives and folders. Because this is usually not needed, disable this service.	NT, 2000, and XP
Disable NetMeeting desktop sharing	This can be used to remotely control a desktop and should not be used by users. Disable this service if you are not using NetMeeting.	NT, 2000, and XP

(continued)

Table 13-2 *(continued)*

Action	Reasons	NT, 2000, or XP
Disable routing and remote access	Disable this service on workstations, so that no one can direct dial in to the system. You also don't want a workstation to do the work of routing.	2000 and XP
Disable SNMP	This protocol gives out a lot of information about the network. If you are not using a centralized management system (such as Tivoli) that uses this service, disable it.	NT, 2000, and XP
Disable NetBIOS	Unbind the NetBIOS interface from the WINS Client (unless you have applications that require it).	NT, 2000, and XP
Disable Computer Browser on workstations	This is not absolutely essential on workstations, and it uses up CPU resources.	NT, 2000, and XP
Required services for workstations	These are the only services required on a workstation. If you need others, evaluate their impact to security before running. DNS Client EventLog Logical Disk Manager Plug & Play Protected Storage Remote Procedure Call Security Accounts Manager	2000 and XP
Remove the Everyone group from shared folders	By default, the Everyone group has Full Control access to shared folders. Either remove this group, or change the permissions.	NT, 2000, and XP
Disable Internet Connection Sharing on workstations	This is not needed for workstations on a network.	2000 and XP
Disable PWS and RAS on workstations	Personal Web Server (PWS) and Remote Access Service (RAS) are not needed on workstations and introduce security holes. Don't use them.	NT, 2000, and XP

Action	Reasons	NT, 2000, or XP
Remove OS/2 and POSIX subsystems	Delete the \winnt\system32\os2 directory and all of its subdirectories. Delete the OS2 and Posix keys from HKLM\System\CurrentControlSet\ Control\SessionManager\Subsystem. Delete all files that begin with "os2" and "posix" from the C:\Windows\ System32\dllcache.	NT, 2000, and XP
Disable dump file creation	This is the file created by the Blue Screen of Death (BSOD) and is only needed for programming debugging. A hacker can use this data, so disable it.	NT, 2000, and XP
Disable alternate booting	Disable the ability to boot from a floppy or CD on workstations.	NT, 2000, and XP
Enable the ICF	Enable the Internet Connection Firewall (ICF). It will monitor only incoming traffic.	XP only

Registry changes

The registry is a database used to store settings and options on Windows systems. Whenever you install new software, for example, new entries are made in various files in the registry to tell the system how and when the program was installed and what its settings are. Normally, users do not make any changes to the registry. That's an administrator's job. In order to make changes to the registry, you have to use a program called *regedit.exe*, shown in Figure 13-2, or with *regedt32.exe*. This program lets you navigate through the sections of the registry database and make changes.

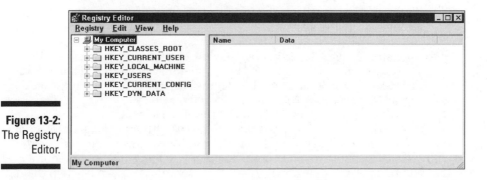

Figure 13-2:
The Registry
Editor.

There is a difference between *regedit.exe* and *regedt32.exe*. Of the two, regedt32. exe is more commonly associated with the Windows NT, 2000, and XP. Regedit. exe is the older of the two versions. When you make changes to Windows NT, 2000, and XP, you *must* use regedt32.exe or you can cause your system to become unstable. This is due to the fact that the older version can store the registry keys incorrectly and results in your system repeatedly crashing.

You need to understand the architecture of the registry before you can make any changes to it. Each folder icon is called a *hive*, and hives contain *keys*. Each key can contain other keys (sometimes referred to as *sub-keys*), as well as *values*. The values contain the actual information stored in the registry. The registry includes three types of values: *String*, *Binary*, and *DWORD*. The use of these depends upon the context. Figure 13-3 shows an example of a branch of a hive.

The registry has six main hive branches, and each one contains specific information stored in the registry. They are as follows:

- HKEY_CLASSES_ROOT: This branch contains all of your file associations, OLE information, Windows shortcuts, and core aspects of the Windows user interface.

- HKEY_CURRENT_USER: This branch links to the section of HKEY_USERS for the person currently logged on to the PC and contains information such as logon names, desktop settings, and Start menu settings.

- HKEY_LOCAL_MACHINE: This branch contains specific information about the type of hardware, software, and other preferences on your computer.

- HKEY_USERS: This branch contains individual preferences for each user and is represented by a SID (security identification) sub-key, located under the main branch.

- HKEY_CURRENT_CONFIG: This branch links to the section of HKEY_LOCAL_MACHINE for the current hardware configuration.

- HKEY_DYN_DATA: This branch points to the part of HKEY_LOCAL_MACHINE that is for use with the Plug-&-Play features of Windows. This section is dynamic and changes as devices are added and removed from the system.

In the registry changes listed in the following sections, you sometimes need to alter data that already exists, and you sometimes need to add a new key. To add a new key, click the Edit menu on the registry editor and then click Add Key or New (it's not the same on all systems).

You should NEVER make changes to the registry without saving a backup of the current registry set! Changes to the registry can cause major problems with your system if you don't know what you are doing and could require that you reinstall the operating system from scratch. You can back-up the registry by choosing the "Export Registry File" command. It will ask you where you want to store the file.

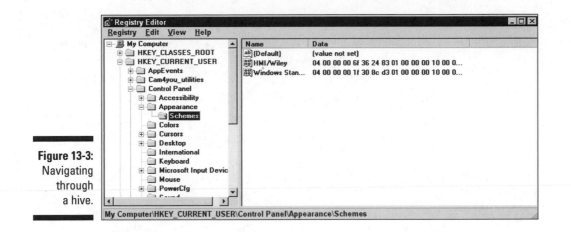

Figure 13-3:
Navigating
through
a hive.

Restrict access to the event logs (NT, 2000, and XP)

The event log contains sensitive data about applications, security, and system events. You don't want anyone other than Administrators to have access to the logs.

System Key: HKEY_LOCAL_MACHINE\SYSTEM\CurrentControlSet\Services\EventLog

Value Name: RestrictGuestAccess

Data Type: REG_WORD (DWORD Value)

Value: (0 = guest access, 1 = restricted access)

Restrict anonymous user access (NT, 2000, and XP)

Anonymous users can list the user names and the share names by default. Change the key to restrict access.

System Key: HKEY_LOCAL_MACHINE\SYSTEM\CurrentControlSet\Control\Lsa

Value Name: RestrictAnonymous

Data Type: REG_WORD (DWORD Value)

Value: (0 = none, 1 = do not allow enumeration of SAM accounts and names, 2 - no access without explicit anonymous permissions)

Change LAN Manager authentication (NT only)

NT has two types of authentication, and the LAN Manager type is extremely weak. The LAN Manager password can be cracked in a matter of seconds. Therefore, you should disable this authentication.

System Key: `HKEY_LOCAL_MACHINE\SYSTEM\CurrentControlSet\Control\Lsa`

Value Name: `LMCompatibilityLevel`

Data Type: `REG_DWORD (DWORD value)`

Value: `(4 = refuse Lan Manager responses)`

Hide the last user name (NT, 2000, and XP)

Normally, when you log on, the last user to use the machine has his user name shown in the logon box. To prevent unauthorized users from finding user names, disable this feature.

System Key: `HKEY_LOCAL_MACHINE\Software\Microsoft\Windows NT\CurrentVersion\WinLogon`

Value Name: `DontDisplayLastUserName`

Data Type: `REG_SZ (String value)`

Value: `(0 = display name, 1 = remove name)`

Secure access to floppy drives

If you don't want your users to be able to use their floppy drive to take data off their machine or to add data or programs to their machine, you can disable the floppy with this change. This may help to keep unauthorized software and viruses off your systems.

System Key: `HKEY_LOCAL_MACHINE\Software\Microsoft\Windows NT\CurrentVersion\WinLogon`

Value Name: `AllocateFloppies`

Data Type: `REG_SZ (String value)`

Value: `(0 = administrators and user can access floppies, 1 = only local user logged on can access floppies.)`

Secure access to CD ROM drives (NT, 2000, and XP)

This setting is similar to the previous one, but it is used to restrict access to the CD-ROM drive.

System Key: HKEY_LOCAL_MACHINE\Software\Microsoft\Windows
NT\CurrentVersion\WinLogon

Value Name: AllocateCDRoms

Data Type: REG_SZ (String value)

Value: (0 = administrators and user can access CD ROM, 1 = only
local user logged on can access ROM.)

Clear paging file at shutdown (NT, 2000, and XP)

The Page file is a temporary swap file that Windows uses to manage memory
and enhance the performance of Windows. The trouble is that some applications may store unencrypted passwords in this file. To clear it at shutdown,
change this key.

System Key: HKEY_LOCAL_MACHINE\System\CurrentControlSet\Control\
SessionManager\MemoryManagement

Value Name: ClearPageFileAtShutdown

Data Type: REG_SZ (String value)

Value: (0 = don't clear file, 1 = clear file)

Remove OS/2 and POSIX keys (NT, 2000)

After you have removed the directory and subdirectories for OS/2 and POSIX,
you should go ahead and remove the registry keys as well. The four of them
are as follows:

System Key: HKEY_LOCAL_MACHINE\Software\Microsoft\OS/2 Subsystem
for NT

(Delete all subkeys from this key)

System Key: HKEY_LOCAL_MACHINE\System\CurrentControlSet\
Control\Session Manager\Environment

Value Name: Os2LibPath

Value: (delete all the values)

System Key: HKEY_LOCAL_MACHINE\System\CurrentControlSet\Control\
Session Manager\SubSystems

Value Name: (optional)

Value: (delete all values)

System Key: `HKEY_LOCAL_MACHINE\System\CurrentControlSet\Control\ Session Manager\SubSystems`

Value Name: (delete both OS2 and POSIX)

After you make changes to the registry, you have to exit the registry editor and reboot for the changes to take effect.

Remember to make a new Emergency Repair Disk (ERD) after you make changes to the registry. The repair disk contains a compressed version of the registry, and you need it to restore a dead machine. Also, make a backup of the registry and store it in a secure location. The procedure for making an ERD varies according to which version of the system you are running. Use your Help feature and search for "Emergency Repair Disk" and you will receive instructions on how to make one for your machine.

Preventing Denial of Service (DoS) Attacks

Denial of Service (DoS) attacks have created havoc for a number of big name companies, such as Yahoo and EBay. The computer networks at these companies were unavailable for the major part of a day because they were experiencing a DoS attack. A simple explanation of a DoS attack is that someone floods the computer with so many requests that the system can't respond to anything anymore, similar to when you try to make a phone call on Mother's Day, and you get a busy tone most of the day because all of the phone lines are tied up. The TCP/IP stack is particularly vulnerable to this sort of attack. You have no way to completely prevent these sorts of attack from happening to your systems, but you can harden the TCP/IP stack to increase its resistance and (hopefully) make it stronger in an attack. The following information comes courtesy of Microsoft's TechNet site and can be found in its entirety at `http://www.microsoft.com/technet/treeview/ default.asp?url=/technet/security/prodtech/network/secdeny.asp`.

This is a major change in the registry and should be tested on a subnet of your network before you incorporate the changes everywhere. In some instances, this could cause some applications to go wonky, but you won't know that until you do the tests. Make a backup copy of the registry to fall back on, in case this does not work for you.

Make all of these changes to the following system key:

`HKEY_LOCAL_MACHINE\System\CurrentControlSet\Services\Tcpip\ Parameters`

Value Name: SynAttackProtect

Data Type: REG_DWORD

Value: 0, 1, 2 (0 = no synattack protection, 1 = reduced retransmission retries and delayed route cache entry creation if the TcpMaxHalfOpen and TcpMaxHalfOpenRetried settings are satisfied, 2 = in addition to 1 a delayed indication to Winsock is made.)

Recommendation: 2

Description: Synattack protection involves reducing the amount of retransmissions for the SYN-ACKS, which reduces the time for which resources have to remain allocated.

Value Name: TcpMaxHalfOpen

Data Type: REG_DWORD

Valid Range: 100 - 0xFFFF

Value: 100 (Professional, Server), 500 (advanced server)

Recommendation: 100

Description: This parameter controls the number of connections in the SYN-RCVD state allowed before SYN-ATTACK protection begins to operate.

Value Name: TcpMaxHalfOpenRetried

Value Type: REG_DWORD

Value: 80 (Professional, Server), 400 (Advanced Server)

Recommendation: 80

Description: This parameter controls the number of connections in the SYN-RCVD state for which at least one retransmission of the SYN has been sent, before SYN-ATTACK attack protection begins to operate.

Value Name: EnablePMTUDiscovery

Data Type: REG_DWORD

Valid Range: (0 = False, 1 = True)

Recommendation: 0

Description: When this parameter is set to 1 (True) TCP attempts to discover the Maximum Transmission Unit (MTU or largest packet size) over the path to a remote host.

Value Name: `EnableDeadGWDetect`

Data Type: `REG_DWORD`

Valid Range: (0 = False, 1 = True)

Recommendation: `0`

Description: When this parameter is 1, TCP is allowed to perform dead-gateway detection. With this feature enabled, TCP may ask IP to change to a backup gateway if a number of connections are experiencing difficulty.

Value Name: `KeepAliveTime`

Value Type: `REG_DWORD`

Valid Range: (1 - 7,200,000) (time in milliseconds)

Recommendation: `300,000`

Description: The parameter controls how often TCP attempts to verify that an idle connection is still intact by sending a keep-alive packet.

Value Name: `EnableICMPRedirects`

Data Type: `REG_DWORD`
Valid Range: (0 = False, 1 = True)

Recommendation: 0 (False)

Description: This parameter controls whether Windows 2000 alters its route table in response to ICMP redirect messages that are sent to it by network devices such as a routers.

The following registry key is found under `HKEY_LOCAL_MACHINE\System\CurrentControlSet\Services\Tcpip\Parameters\Interfaces`

Value Name: `PerformRouterDiscovery`

Value Type: `REG_DWORD`

Value Range: (0 = disabled, 1 = enabled, 2 = enable only if DHCP sends the router discover option)

Recommendation: 0

Description: This parameter controls whether Windows 2000 attempts to perform router discovery per RFC 1256 on a per-interface basis.

The following registry key is found under
`HKEY_LOCAL_MACHINE\System\CurrentControlSet\Services\Netbt\Parameters`

Value Name: `NoNameReleaseOnDemand`

Data Type: `REG_DWORD`

Valid Range: (0 = False, 1 = True)

Recommendation: 1

Description: This parameter determines whether the computer releases its NetBIOS name when it receives a name-release request from the network.

Chapter 14

Is Anything Eating Your Mac?

In This Chapter

▶ Learning about the vulnerabilities

▶ Hardening your Mac

There's good news, bad news, and good news for Mac security. The good news is that Macs have always had the most secure operating system. The bad news is that this has changed with the release of version OS X. The other good news is that OS X is not all that bad!

To get some perspective on this, realize that the original intended use of a Mac was for single users. Macs weren't originally designed for networks, and there was no way to remotely log on to a Mac. Apple assumed that the person who owned the Mac would be the only person using it. The built-in networking services were very limited, too.

Because Apple assumed that only the owner would be using the Mac, it also concluded that the owner would have no need for accessing the guts of the operating system — because most computer owners are not programmers. If you follow that logic, you understand why finding tools that would allow you to get to the Mac's command line was very hard. Even if you did get to the command line, the internal workings of the Mac's operating system weren't easy to understand. Therefore, hackers didn't spend a lot of time figuring out how to hack Macs. Sort of a "security through obscurity" technique: If you don't know how it works, you won't know how to break it.

But now all that has changed. The core of the Mac (no pun intended!) is now based on BSD (Berkeley Software Distribution) UNIX. Now, don't get me wrong. BSD is a wonderful operating system, and it is the one that DARPA chose to use on what eventually became the Internet. But, all versions of UNIX have their security flaws, and these flaws are extremely well-known in the hacker community. So, why did Apple intentionally decide to use something with known security flaws? They actually did it very carefully and, from what I've seen so far, they've created a very secure installation straight out of the box.

This chapter covers both the good and the bad, and it gives you some advice on how to make your Mac just a little bit better at handling security on your network.

Mac Insecurity

The World Wide Web Consortium (W3C) has been on the forefront of Web security since the early 90s. In their World Wide Web Security FAQ (`www.w3.org/Security/Faq/wwwsf1.html`), they state, "The safest Web site is a bare-bones Macintosh running a bare-bones Web server." That's pretty strong language, especially when you consider all of the operating systems and software security products! Granted, the W3C said the same thing prior to the release of Mac OS X. You have to make some changes to your Mac now to make it as secure as it used to be.

Logons and passwords

By default, OS X stores all users' passwords and logs them on automatically without requiring them to enter the password. Not a good move! To change this, you must go to the System Preferences and click on the Login icon. Under the Login Window panel, select the Name and Password entry fields and deselect Automatically log on. You also want to make sure that the users' names are not displayed to everyone by choosing the radio button to indicate that you want only the boxes for the user name and password to show. (See Figure 14-1 for an example.) You also want to lock this setting so that others can't change it.

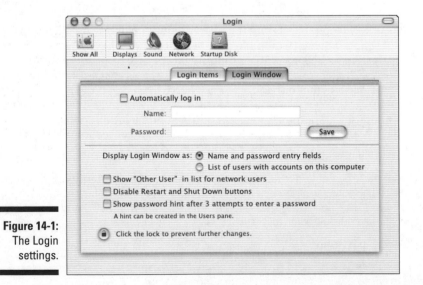

Figure 14-1:
The Login
settings.

Mac OS X is set up to dual-boot with both OS X and OS 9.x, which allows backwards compatibility with software that hasn't been upgraded to run on the newest version of the operating system. The problem with this is that

OS 9.x allowed a maximum of only eight characters for a password. OS X recognizes longer passwords, but older software may not accept that password. What's the solution? Well, for now, limit your passwords to eight characters, but make sure that they are really strong passwords. I'm sure that Apple will get around this limitation in future releases.

OS X also has a new "feature" for storing all the various passwords for programs, files, Web sites, and so on. It's called *Keychain*, and it stores all the passwords you tell it to in an encrypted file. When a program needs a password, the Keychain program pops up to the screen and asks whether you want Keychain to decrypt and release the password. By default, the password to open the Keychain is the same as your log on password. Whoops! If you're going to use the Keychain, you should change this password immediately. If someone guesses or cracks your log on password, that person also has access to ALL your passwords if you are using Keychain to store them. This comes under the "putting all your eggs in one basket" school of security. Although the Keychain is a real convenience — we all have too many passwords to easily remember all of them — keeping all your passwords together is generally not a good idea. Use this with caution and make sure that all your users have changed the default password.

Dual booting

The Mac OS X supports two different file systems: *HFS* and *UFS*. HFS stands for Hierarchical File System and has been the standard file system on Macs for years. The problem with HFS (and the newer version called HFS+) is that this file system has little to no local security. UFS stands for UNIX File System, and it supports the greater granularity of permissions usually found in UNIX systems. When you first set up your Mac, it creates one HFS partition, and both OS X and OS 9.x are installed on this one partition, which is like setting up a Windows NT machine on the same partition as Windows 9x. The result is that security is compromised because everything defaults to the lowest common denominator.

Apple includes both the older version of the operating system and the newest version, so that older programs will still run. Eventually, programs will catch up and be released for OS X. But, for now, if you have older programs, you need both operating systems on the same machine.

One possible solution is to format your hard drive with two different partitions: an HFS partition for OS 9.x and a UFS partition for OS X. This creates better security, but it has some big drawbacks, too. For example, your Airport wireless network card won't work on a computer that has a UFS partition. Your computers must be formatted with HFS partitions if you want to use wireless networking on your Macs. Apple has a very good technical article on the problems with UFS at Apple's Knowledge Base Web site. The complete URL is far too long to reproduce here, so go to `www.info.apple.com/` and enter #25316 in the search box. You're looking for the technical files entitled, "Mac OS X 10.0: Choosing UFS or Mac OS Extended (HFS Plus) Formatting."

The root account

The default installation of OS X includes three accounts: root, administrator, and regular users. The root account allows you to do everything, just like the UNIX root account. The administrator account in Macs is restricted and does not have a full set of privileges like the root account does. For example, you cannot delete the core system files as an administrator, but you can as root. Not that you would really want to erase these important files.

The root account in OS X is not enabled by default. You have to go through a number of steps to enable it and set up a password for it. For the most part, if you need to have greater administrative privileges on your Mac, you can use the `sudo` command (superuser do), which enables you to upgrade your privileges and do what you have to do and then exit from that enhanced status. The good thing about `sudo` is that, once you start the command, everything you do is logged to a file, which is great for tracking and tracing who did what and when.

If you find you must use the root account for your Mac, I've included the instructions for doing so next. Don't do this unless you find you absolutely have to — and be sure to change the name of the account from "root" to something else. This is because the operating system uses "root" internally for some of its processing, and trying to figure out which "root" is issuing commands can confuse the heck out of your Mac.

Instructions for enabling the root account:

1. **From the Finder, hit Command + Option + A to open the Applications folder.**

2. **Open the Utilities folder.**

3. **Open the NetInfo Manager application.**

4. **Choose Domain⇨Security⇨Authenticate.**

5. **Enter an administrator's name and password in the dialog and click on the OK button.**

6. **Choose Domain⇨Security⇨Enable Root User.**

7. **Enter a password for the root user.**

8. **Quit the NetInfo Manager application by choosing NetInfo Manager⇨Quit NetInfo Manager.**

Mac OS X allows you to use a blank password on the root account. Never allow this to happen on your systems. A blank password equals no password, which means that everyone can hack your machine.

One big "no-no" I've found with OS X is that you can easily boot the computer from the CD and reset the administrator or root password. This is fine for a home computer, but it is clearly not a good thing for a network. Normally, you could disable the ability to boot from a floppy or CD-ROM drive by setting the BIOS, but Apple has not provided any documentation on how to do this with a Mac. You have two ways to get around this, though. You can download a program called Open Firmware — available at www.firmworks.com/www/ products.htm. However, Open Firmware is an uncompiled program. You need to be able to compile and run programs to be able to use this. Be aware of the fact that Apple is not supporting Open Firmware at this time, and its use on your machine could void your warranty if the program causes any damage.

The other solution is a program called Startup Security (shown in Figure 14-2), which is a GUI-based program for the Mac. You can get Startup Security from www.digitalspecter.com/startupsecurity.html. I must say that Startup Security is much easier than Open Firmware to use. Some people may find Open Firmware's command line intimidating and confusing. Perhaps Apple will include its own BIOS password tool in the future.

Figure 14-2:
The Startup
Security
program to
control
BIOS boot
up settings.

Startup Security

Startup Security provides a greater level of protection for your Macintosh system. You must always enter the old password and a new password before changes take effect. This is to protect your system from others making unauthorized changes.

Security Settings

Mode:	Allow Boot Device Only
Old Password:	•••••••
New Password:	•••••••
Verify Password:	•••••••

☑ Ask For Password During Mac OS 9 Startup
☑ Don't Allow Shift Key To Disable Extensions
☑ Ask For Password During Mac OS 9 Wakeup

Cancel   Change

The inetd.conf file

One of the biggest security flaws in UNIX is due to the misconfiguration of the *inetd.conf* file, which tells the operating system which services to run. (See Chapter 12 for more information on inetd.conf.) Because OS X is based on BSD UNIX, the Mac also now has this file. However, unlike its UNIX relatives, the services that cause security flaws are turned off by default. No telnet, no httpd, no sendmail. In fact, they've even commented on insecure services in the comments in the file (as shown in Figure 14-3).

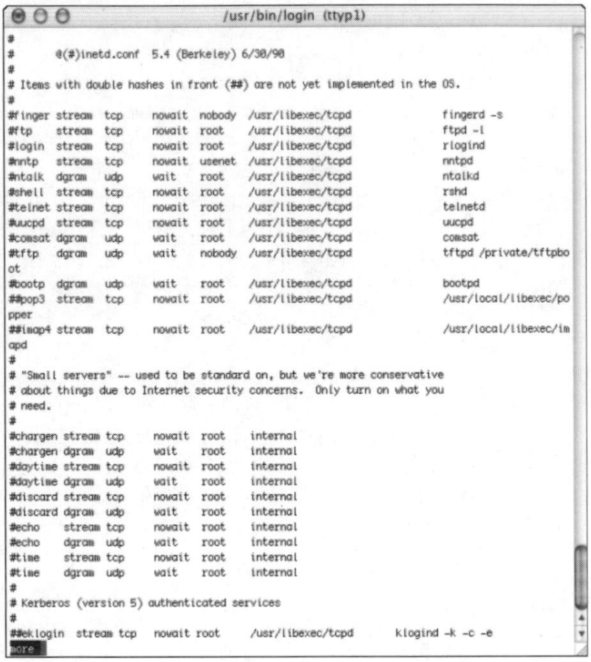

Figure 14-3:
The inetd.conf file in Mac OS X.

Because Mac OS X has already implemented security on this file, you don't need to change anything. However, if you decide that you do need some of the services started by this file, be sure to act carefully or you may expose your computer to undesirable vulnerabilities.

If you must use the Internet services in inetd, you may want to consider using xinetd instead. Xinetd is available at `www.xinetd.org/` and stands for eXtended InterNET services daemon. It is a more secure version of inetd. You have the ability to limit how and where the services are run, and it is more resistant to DoS attacks as well. You have to compile the source code on your machine to create the xinetd.conf file.

Groups

Only two user groups are set up when you first install OS X: admin and staff. The admin group has slightly less than root privileges and staff has minimal privileges. This is a good thing. However, you probably want to create some other groups so that you can more finely control the roles and permissions of people on your network. You have to use the command line to create groups and to set their privileges using the `newgrp` and `chgrp` commands. (The reasons for creating more groups are also discussed in the following sections on SUID and SGID.)

NetInfo

NetInfo is an account management program included with OS X. This program has been around for a long time and was also used in the NeXT operating system. One big problem with this program is causing some concern in the security community: NetInfo does a horrible job of protecting the passwords! All the password hashes are stored with permissions that allow all users to read them. Yes, the password is hashed and looks like garbage, but cracking a hashed password is very easy because quite a few good password cracking programs are available.

The only solution I can see to this problem is to change the permissions on the NetInfo program so that only Admins can use it. This isn't a total solution, but you could consider it as a stopgap until Apple makes changes to NetInfo and releases a patch for this security hole.

Security patches

With any operating systems, sometimes holes are discovered and they can be fixed only with a software patch created by the vendor. Macs are no different in this matter. OS X has a small program called Software Update (shown in Figure 14-4), which is included in the System Preferences. You can set the updater to look for updates daily, weekly, or monthly. Given that updates can be released at any time, I suggest that you set it to daily. If you set it to weekly, a patch could be released the day after you do an update and you won't get the patch until the next week. If the patch secured a particularly nasty hole, it could be too late after you wait a week to get it.

I haven't seen any programs that will search your system to see what patches have been installed, but you can view them by going to the directory /Library/Receipts/. All the software updates have a "pkg" file extension.

Of course, the Software Update program is going to look for software for only your operating system. You still have to look for patches for programs such as Internet Explorer or MS Word at the individual vendors' Web sites.

Figure 14-4:
The
Software
Update
program
for OS X.

Better Security

So far, not so bad. This section requires you to brush up on your UNIX commands so that you can take advantage of some further security enhancements. When you're finished with this, though, your Mac will be as hard as steel and very resistant to hacks.

Use the built-in firewall

OS X has a built-in IP firewall called *ipfw*. This program has been around for years and is still the core of many commercial firewall products. By default, the firewall is running, but no rules have been set. Therefore, it is running wide open and not doing any firewalling. Because this firewall program is old, you configure it from a command-line interface instead of a GUI. This configuration is not something that you want just anyone to do, and it is easy to misconfigure a firewall. You can read the built-in instructions on the manual page (*man ipfw* at the command line). However, a nice shareware program, called BrickHouse, gives you a GUI to use with ipfw. You can get BrickHouse from `http://personalpages.tds.net/~brian_hill/downloads.html` or at Apple's site at `www.apple.com/downloads/macosx/networking_security/brickhouse.html`. It's a good deal for just a little bit of money.

BrickHouse has a nice little monitor that lets you see what traffic is being filtered. It also includes several preloaded firewall filter sets for several situations, including a typical, secure set for the average home user, one that allows access to Web and FTP servers, and one that allows all access from computers on a home Ethernet network and no incoming access via the PPP/Internet connection.

Secure telnet

Sometimes you have to allow others to remotely log on to your computer and issue commands. Administrators love this capability because it means that they can remotely administer a machine without having to go down the hall and sit in the cold server room to work directly from the machine. Telnet is the program most commonly used for remote access, but it has some security problems. Apple has done a good job by including *SSH* (Secure SHell) in its default installation. SSH is a secure telnet program that encrypts the communications between machines.

How to start SSH is not exactly obvious in OS X, but it is really simple. Just open the System Preferences and click on Sharing. Then click on the Application tab and check the Allow remote login checkbox (as shown in Figure 14-5). That's all there is to it! The operating system automatically makes changes in the /etc/hostconfig file, which controls SSH. Of course, you could edit this file yourself, but letting the operating system do it for you is easier.

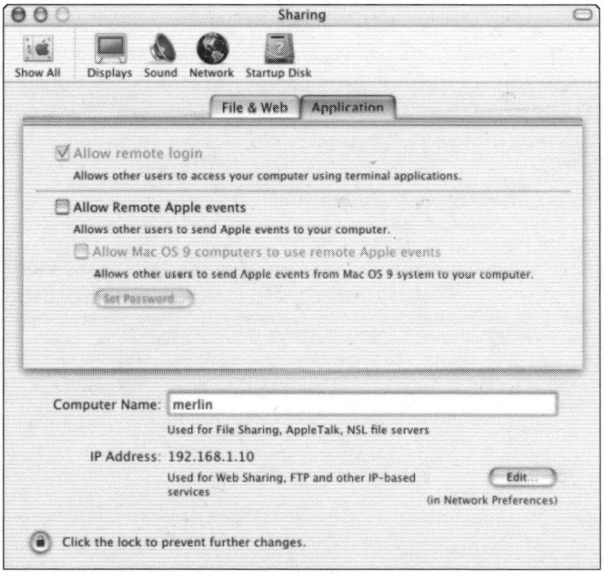

Figure 14-5:
Turning on SSH.

The SSH program used by OS X is a recent version of OpenSSH, which supports both the SSH1 and SSH2 protocols. You shouldn't have any problems connecting from other UNIX systems to your Mac.

Changing SUIDs and SGIDs

Normally, when a user runs a program, the program uses the user's permissions to accomplish whatever task it's being asked to perform. Sometimes, however, a program needs to have more permissions than the user has. We would all go crazy if a program suddenly halted and said, "You don't have permission to do that," so a method has been set up to temporarily give the program the permission it needs: You give the program a *SUID* (System User ID) or a *SGID* (System Group ID). The operating system automatically sets these permissions. The problem is that programs with these permissions can sometimes be tricked into doing naughty things — such as giving an intruder full access, which is frequently accomplished with buffer overflows.

You can change permissions using the `chmod` command from the command line. For example, to remove the SGID from a program called "whoops," use the command `chmod g-u whoops`. If you're not familiar with UNIX commands, especially changing permissions, you shouldn't bother with these changes. You could create more problems than you solve if you change permissions incorrectly.

A number of programs have SUID and SGID permissions in OS X. These programs should be deleted completely, or they should have their permissions changed so that they don't use a SUID or SGID to run. In other cases, you may want to create a special group for these programs and adjust the group's permissions accordingly. A lot of programs hold SUIDs and SGIDs in OS X, so Table 14-1 tells you how to make modifications.

Table 14-1	Unnecessary Programs and Services	
Path/Program	*Action*	*Reason*
/bin/rcp	Delete from system.	Any "r" programs are security risks and are generally not used.
/sbin/rdump	Delete from system.	See previous.
/sbin/rrestore	Delete from system.	See previous.
/usr/bin/rlogin	Delete from system.	See previous.
/usr/bin/rsh	Delete from system.	See previous.
/usr/sbin/sendmail	Delete from system.	If the computer is not a mail server, it doesn't need this program. If you need send mail, make sure you have a patched version.

Path/Program	Action	Reason
/usr/bin/chfn	Delete from system.	The "ch" programs let users make changes that are usually handled by administrators.
/usr/bin/chpass	Delete from system.	See previous.
/usr/bin/chsh	Delete from system.	See previous.
/usr/sbin/sliplogin	Delete from system.	This program is used only on systems needing "SLIP" connections. Because this is out dated and not generally used, it should be deleted.
/usr/sbin/netstat	Remove the SUID permission. Create a special group with admin permissions and change the SGID to execute.	This is an admin tool not needed by general users.
/sbin/ping	See above.	See previous.
/usr/sbin/traceroute	See above.	See previous.
/usr/bin/crontab	See above.	See previous.
/usr/bin/at	See above.	See previous.
/usr/bin/atq	See above.	See previous.
/usr/bin/atrm	See above.	See previous.
/usr/bin/batch	See above.	See previous.
/sbin/dump	See above.	This program is used by backup systems and is not needed by general users.
/sbin/restore	See above.	See previous.
/sbin/route	See above.	Admin only tool.
/sbin/wall	Remove the SGID.	Terminal sessions use this program. General users don't need to use it.
/usr/bin/write	See above.	See previous.

And that's it for hardening your Mac. If you are uncomfortable removing the files I've mentioned previously, your alternative is to rename the files and move them to another directory. If you find that you need them later on, you can always restore them to their original name and place. After you complete these changes, your Mac is about as secure as it can be.

If you are going to be using your Mac as a Web server or a database server, you also have to incorporate the security changes for those applications. That information is covered in detail in Chapter 15. Additionally, the normal desktop applications such as browsers, word processing, and spreadsheets have security considerations, which are covered in the same chapter.

Chapter 15

Application Software Patching

*U*nfortunately, we are lulled into a false sense of security with our firewalls, intrusion detection systems, anti-virus software, and so on. Because we have these mechanisms in place, we think we are totally protected and we feel confident that nothing can get inside and hurt us. But, what about the stuff that is already inside? We give our trust blindly to the applications we use on our networks because we don't see them as threats. They are our friends; they make our jobs easier. How can applications hurt us, you ask? Think about it. We trust these programs. We use them to store sensitive information. We connect these programs to the Internet. Yes, the programs are behind the firewall, but the firewall blocks only distrusted traffic. Because we trust these applications, we give them free access in and out of the network via their allowed path through the firewall. If someone figures out a way to follow that traffic back through the firewall, the firewall doesn't stop him because it sees him as trusted traffic.

This didn't happen often when programs stood alone and did not know how to talk to other programs. Nowadays, though, most programs contain vast libraries of information on how to talk to other programs, which enables us to move data from a word processing document to a spreadsheet and then change that spreadsheet into an HTML page. Then we can put that HTML in an e-mail and the e-mail program automatically opens the Web browser so that you can see the data. We enter URLs into the address line of our browser to go to a Web site, but did you know that you can just as easily enter a command in a URL and make the Web server do something it wasn't supposed to do? Don't forget that some programs regularly connect to the Internet without your instructions. These programs are sharing data about your computer with the software vendor. And we trust all this to happen. We leave the gates open through our security perimeters.

This chapter investigates some of the applications that we use on a daily basis that can also create holes in our security. In most cases, software patches are available to close the holes; in other cases, the onus is on you to fix the holes. Most of the patches are easily done. It's just up to you to find them and install them.

E-mail Vulnerabilities

In addition to the host of virus threats that come through e-mail messages, the e-mail program you use can be used to attack your machine in other ways. Most users know about .exe as an executable extension, but often they don't know that files with the extensions .scr, .pdf, .ppt, .xls, .rtf, .pif, .doc, and so on can also execute and carry an unwanted payload. In 2001, Microsoft released an alert about an attack via an ActiveX control in the Outlook 98 e-mail program that could potentially run anything on a user's computer. This attack launched as soon as the recipient opened the e-mail message; it required no clicking on attachments. Microsoft released a patch, but the problem got worse with newer releases of Outlook, and other patches had to be created to fix those holes.

Because virtually all e-mail is allowed past a firewall or intrusion detection system, increasing security by patching the e-mail programs used by your organization makes sense. There lies the paradox. In order to fix these holes, *every single computer on the network must be patched*. Imagine that you have thousands of computers spread geographically over a large area. How long do you think the IT department would take to install a patch on every machine? What if new patches are required every couple of months? It doesn't take a genius to figure out that the efforts of the IT department will probably be focused on more "pressing" problems.

You can configure most e-mail programs so that they don't use the questionable extra features that open security holes. You can manually turn off some of the features, such as mobile code execution and HTML formatting of e-mail. Sometimes, finding where to turn these features on and off requires navigating through a labyrinth of menus and buttons. For example, in Microsoft Outlook 2000, to disable the execution of ActiveX code in e-mails, you follow these steps:

1. **Choose Tools⇨Options.**

2. **Select the Security tab.**

3. **Click the Zone Settings button.**

4. **Click the Custom Level button.**

5. **You can manually go through the list to enable or disable the features, or you can click on the list at the bottom of the window and choose High settings (as shown in Figure 15-1).**

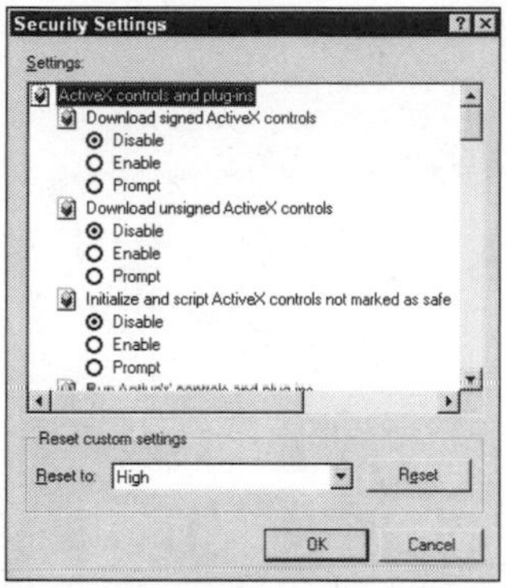

Figure 15-1:
Disabling
ActiveX
execution
in Outlook
2000.

Of course, Outlook isn't the only program that has these problems, but it is the e-mail application that most businesses commonly use. You have to check the vendor's Web site for updates and patches and watch the CERT alerts for new vulnerabilities, which takes some time and effort on your part. And you need to act as quickly as possible when you find new vulnerabilities. The damage done by the ILOVEYOU virus would not have been nearly as extensive if businesses had responded to the initial reports that appeared weeks before the large outbreak of the virus.

You could also switch to e-mail programs that are not as vulnerable to security holes as the popular Microsoft Office products are. I've used Eudora for more than 10 years now and have never (knock on wood) been infected by a virus or malicious code vulnerability. You can get Eudora at `www.eudora.com`. Home users can get a free version with limited features, and I have found it easier to use than most other e-mail applications. Netscape also has a pretty good e-mail program called Netscape Messenger that comes with the Netscape browser. To the best of my knowledge, the Netscape Messenger has not had any major security breaches. You can get it at `http://wp.netscape.com/computing/download/index.html?cp=hop05ft6`.

If you're not sure whether or not your e-mail program is properly configured or patched, I found a neat Web site that sends test e-mails to you to check your vulnerabilities. The Web site is the GFI E-mail Security Testing Zone, and you can find it at `www.gfi.com/emailsecuritytest/`. You check the vulnerabilities for which you want to be tested, and you fill in your e-mail address. GFI then sends the appropriate e-mails to your system, with a test of the vulnerability and an explanation of each one. The e-mail even has a note to the system administrators explaining the purpose of the e-mail, just in case the message was trapped and quarantined by the e-mail system. Figure 15-2 shows an example of one of these tests.

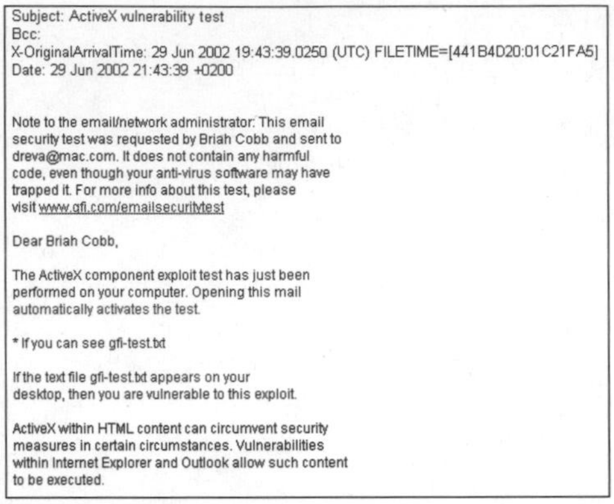

Figure 15-2:
Test e-mail
from GFI
E-mail
Security
Testing
Zone.

Subject: ActiveX vulnerability test
Bcc:
X-OriginalArrivalTime: 29 Jun 2002 19:43:39.0250 (UTC) FILETIME=[441B4D20:01C21FA5]
Date: 29 Jun 2002 21:43:39 +0200

Note to the email/network administrator: This email
security test was requested by Briah Cobb and sent to
dreva@mac.com. It does not contain any harmful
code, even though your anti-virus software may have
trapped it. For more info about this test, please
visit www.gfi.com/emailsecuritytest

Dear Briah Cobb,

The ActiveX component exploit test has just been
performed on your computer. Opening this mail
automatically activates the test.

* If you can see gfi-test.txt

If the text file gfi-test.txt appears on your
desktop, then you are vulnerable to this exploit.

ActiveX within HTML content can circumvent security
measures in certain circumstances. Vulnerabilities
within Internet Explorer and Outlook allow such content
to be executed.

If you find that your e-mail program is vulnerable to any of the tests, you can check the vendor's Web site to see whether the vendor has a manual fix or a patch for you to use. Remember that a patch will have to apply to all computers on your network — not just to the important servers.

The e-mail client (e-mail program) isn't the only part of an e-mail system that is vulnerable to security holes. The application and the protocol on the e-mail server are also potential sources for problems. E-mail servers frequently run a program such as *sendmail*, which uses protocols such as *SMTP* (Simple Mail Transfer Protocol), *POP3* (Post Office Protocol), and *IMAP* (Internet Message Access Protocol). Sendmail is notorious for being vulnerable to malicious exploits, and it requires almost regular updates to fix the holes. The protocols that sendmail uses have been found to fall prey to malicious use. In most cases, you don't fix the protocols themselves, but you fix the way the programs use the protocols.

The SMTP protocol is one of the biggest e-mail security problems. SMTP is inherently insecure because even fairly casual users can trick an SMTP server to create and send "spoofed" e-mail messages, which means a message is made to look like it's coming from someone other than who sent it. When I worked for the government, a couple of us techies had an argument with our boss about the insecurities of SMTP. In order to prove our point, one of my co-workers sent a message to our boss from the President Of The United States (POTUS), stating that he was giving us all the day off for being so good at securing networks! We didn't get the day off, but it sure impressed our boss!

Regardless of whether you use one of the large commercial mail servers (from vendors such as Novell, GroupWise, NetMail, Microsoft, or Netscape) or you use one of the lesser known products, you need to check with CERT for vulnerability alerts and check with the vendor for upgrades and patches. Some of the vendors have an e-mail service that alerts you when a patch is available. Firewalls or intrusion detection systems do not know when security has been breached, and they do not know whether patches are needed or have been applied. Antivirus software does nothing to stop these breaches, either.

Windows Office Application Problems

Although the integration of the MS Office suite of programs has made our business lives much easier, security problems have appeared in Word, Excel, Access, and even PowerPoint. Because these programs have become so large and complex, the security problems were not known before Office's release. The security problems come to light as industry experts begin playing around with the programs. If Microsoft deems the problem to be big enough, it releases an immediate fix. For the most part, however, Microsoft relies upon service pack releases to fix most of the problems.

Most of the security problems involve the fact that people can make the programs do things without the user's knowledge or consent. For example, you can open a Word template file with macros and have those macros immediately execute if you haven't set high security settings for the program. Even if you get a warning stating that macros are present in the file, you won't know whether they are good macros or bad macros until after you let them run. Last year, computer users discovered that macros could run in Word and Excel without the user's consent and that this vulnerability could be exploited by someone to do damage to a computer. Microsoft released a patch for this hole. Unless you really, really, really need macros, I suggest that you simply disable their use in MS Office products. In most of these programs, you click Tools⇨ Macro⇨Security to disable macros. The dialog box shown in Figure 15-3 appears. You can set the security level to high, medium, or low. If you set the level to high, no macros will run unless they are digitally signed by a trusted source. If you are developing macros in-house for company use, you can certainly implement this option.

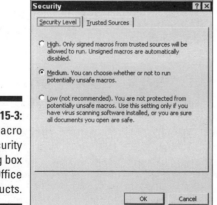

Figure 15-3: The macro security dialog box in MS Office products.

People discover new vulnerabilities every day within business productivity programs such as word processing programs, spreadsheets, and presentations. You might even see a proof-of-concept virus that imbeds the code in a graphics file. The only thing you can do to protect yourself is to keep up to date with the vulnerability alerts and to patch the applications as quickly as you can. Remember that you have to patch every computer that uses the affected program.

I've found a free, albeit limited, vulnerability database that you can use to check for alerts and patches. It's just a demo of a full product, but it may help you with your initial search for security holes. The database is called the Security Search VDB (Vulnerability DataBase), located at `www.security search.net/vdbdemo/vdb.cfm`. You can get the full version only by subscribing to the service, which costs a little over $1,000 per month. There is also another good, free vulnerability database that is managed by the Mitre Organization. You can check out their database at `http://cve.mitre.org/`.

You can also subscribe to a number of newsletters and e-mail alert forums. One forum that I like is SecurityFocus Online, which has dozens of lists that you can subscribe to. The complete list of their forums is at `http://online.securityfocus.com/cgi-bin/sfonline/forums.pl`. A good list of archived discussions and lists that you can join is located at `http://lists.insecure.org/` and is called Insecurity.org. Last, but not least, I recommend that you subscribe to the CERT advisories. Send a message to `majordomo@cert.org` and include the words `subscribe cert-advisories` in the body of the message.

Web Browser and Server Insecurity

If anything has become a hacker's friend in the past decade, it's been the Web browser and the Web server. Both of these applications were designed to explicitly share information with no thoughts of security. When designers first developed them, they had a Utopian view that this sharing would be used only for good and never for evil. Bwahh-ha-ha! Ve haf you in our power now!

But the Utopian dream didn't last, because in recent years, hackers have found their way into networks using only Web browsers. The browser and server vendors have tried to plug some of the bigger holes, and lots of data on the Internet explains how to make your Web servers more secure. However, the Web is still one of those applications that have new vulnerabilities found in them every week. Combine this with the fact that the Web offers huge advantages for companies wanting to share information or conduct e-business, and you see that the Web is considered a necessary evil by most companies.

A Web browser's address box is basically a command-line interface to the Web server. Hackers soon discovered this fact and found that they could imbed root-level commands in a URL to make the Web server give them access to the internal network or make the server give them data that they weren't supposed to have — such as credit card numbers from purchasers. One of the reasons that this particular hack is so easy to do is because the Web server does little to validate who is asking for the information. As far as a Web server is concerned, if you use the correct command to ask for information, it gives you the information.

The amount of information stored in a Web browser and the amount of information that can be pulled from your own machine via your browser is amazing. For a good demonstration of what I'm talking about, visit the BrowserSpy at `www.gemal.dk/browserspy/`, which includes a long list of simple tests for you to click to see what information leaks to the outside. There is also another, excellent and informative set of browser tests at Qualys' BrowserCheck Utility at `http://browsercheck.qualys.com`. There is a fix or workaround listed for each vulnerability found.

Securing the browser

The number of browser hacks and the way they work could fill a book in itself. Almost all browsers are susceptible, and not all the holes can be fixed via the browser. In some instances, you have to enforce stronger security on the Web server itself. The following are some of the most common browser exploits:

- Entering a directory path in the URL to view your local hard drives.
- Entering a file name in the URL to pull up the file in the browser.
- Using ActiveX to write files to your hard drives.
- Using a maliciously coded Web page to open applications on your machine.
- Inserting too many characters in a URL, causing the Web server to crash or deny the service to others (DoS attack).
- Using problems in *CGI scripts* (Common Gateway Interface) to gain access to the internal network or files on a local machine.
- Using a malicious script on a Web page to gain access to your internal network or to elevate access privileges.

In order to secure your Web browser, here are a few things you can do:

- Disable ActiveX and Java scripting. ActiveX is used by only MS Internet Explorer; Netscape 6.2 has Java disabled by default. Disabling these scripting features may cause some Web pages not to load correctly, but that is a small inconvenience for the added security. Because so many different types and versions of Web browsers exist, I can't go through the steps to change the scripting settings, but you can usually find them under Options or Preferences somewhere in the command menus.

✔ Install the security patches for the browsers or upgrade to a newer version. You have to check with the vendor to see which step is appropriate. Again, you have to patch or upgrade the browser on every computer on your network. Just doing it for a few of them doesn't do you any good. That would be like locking the windows in your house but leaving the doors unlocked.

✔ Take advantage of the Security settings available in the newer versions of most browsers. Most allow you to block cookies and encrypt sensitive data stored on your hard drive. Again, I can't go through the steps for accomplishing this on all the different browsers. You have to hunt and peck through the command menus to find all the different settings.

✔ Don't have the browser store your passwords. I know that remembering and typing in the passwords yourself is inconvenient, but I'd rather do that than give an intruder the password to my bank account!

Securing the Web server

Securing your Web servers is a more cumbersome task, which involves careful configuration of the Web server as well as applying patches to the server's application software. An excellent resource is Lincoln Stein's World Wide Web Security FAQ (www.w3.org/Security/Faq/), which has been up for nearly ten years and is updated fairly regularly. Although some of the specific instructions may be a bit outdated, the general advice is always right on the mark.

Table 15-1 shows some of the things you should do to configure your Web server correctly.

Table 15-1	Configuring Your Web Server for Better Security
Action	**Reason**
Restrict access to the cgi-bin/ directory.	Only administrators and HTML authors should be able to read and make changes in this directory, which is where the CGI scripts are held. You don't want the general public to be able to make changes here.
Restrict access to the urations.	Same as previous. This directory holds the server config-conf/directory.
Restrict access to the httpd file.	Same as previous. This file is the Web server daemon/ executable that makes the service work. (This file does not appear in all Web server applications.)
Restrict access to the htdocs/ directory.	This directory holds the files that are shown via Web browsers. You want only administrators and HTML writers to have access to this directory.

Action	Reason
Restrict access to the logs/ directory.	This directory holds the logs of connections to the Web server and should be accessed by administrators only.
Don't allow automatic directory listing.	Automatic directory listing allows all users with a Web browser to simply browse through all the files and directories on your Web server.
Don't use symbolic links.	Symbolic links are usually used to move to another machine in the network. Creating a symbolic link to the wrong machine and giving outsiders access is very easy to do.
Don't use server side includes.	You use server side includes to include static data on every page. The `exec` form of include contains a large security hole. Don't use includes if you don't really have to.
Don't allow individuals in your company to create their own CGI scripts.	Creating a CGI script with security holes in it is very easy. All scripts should be written and maintained only by knowledgeable staff.
Don't allow FTP service on a Web server.	A hacker can upload malicious programs onto your Web server using FTP. FTP programs also include security holes. If you need FTP, set it up on a separate server.
Don't put your database on your Web server.	If your database contains sensitive information, it should be on the inside of a firewall, and the Web server should be in the DMZ. This physical and logical separation makes hacking much harder. If both servers run on the same machine, a hacker can very easily wreck the database.

Every Web server application I researched seems to have security holes, too. Even the Apache Web server, which is accepted as the most secure, has had its share of problems recently. Because none of the Web servers seems to be immune, you are going to have to check the vendors' Web sites to check for patches and upgrades for their products.

Microsoft's IIS (Internet Information Server) Web server has been notorious for its security holes. Numerous patches and upgrades exist for this product and now Microsoft has a security tool called the IIS Lockdown Wizard, which runs through your server to turn off unnecessary services and set permissions on directories. You can download the executable file at `www.microsoft.com/downloads/release.asp?ReleaseID=33961&area=search&ordinal=2`. It's available to run on Windows NT and Windows 2000.

CGI script security

CGI stands for Common Gateway Interface and is a way for computers of different types to talk to one another. It's most often used to exchange data between Web servers and databases because a database doesn't understand HTML and a Web server doesn't understand database query languages (such as SQL). Therefore, you can think of a CGI script as an interpreter of sorts. It passes a request for data from the Web browser to the script, the script translates the request into something that the database can understand, and then the script reverses the process to send the data back to the Web browser. CGI scripts pass data entered into a form to an e-mail address, search for particular products in a catalog, and store chat room dialogs. Without CGIs, the Web would consist of only static data.

The problem with CGI scripts is that they are actually small programs that are telling the computer what to do. Because they are programs, they have the ability to do almost anything — including deleting and changing files. What's even worse is that most people don't know how to write CGI scripts themselves, so they copy ones they find on the Internet. Some of these public domain scripts have big security holes that are well known. The accepted rule is this: If you don't know what the script is doing, don't use it. This includes sample CGI scripts that may have come preinstalled with your Web server. Some of these scripts that are installed by default have security holes in them.

Most CGIs are written in simple shell languages such as Perl or Tkl. The scripts are actually plain text files that are interpreted as opposed to compiled. Because these are plain text files, a hacker can quite easily gain permission to the file and overwrite it. More and more scripts are also being written in Java and ActiveX. You can use compiled languages such as C or C++, which makes your scripts a bit safer because the source code can't be easily viewed. However, security holes can be contained in compiled code, too.

One of the main problems with scripts is that they allow special characters to be used in the URL, and those characters can be characters to execute other commands. Some of the special characters are [,], ;, <, >, and &. Some CGI scripts attempt to circumvent this problem by identifying those characters as invalid for use. However, this doesn't always work. A script called csPassword is used to manage passwords for Web access to restricted pages. By entering an invalid character in the URL, an intruder can actually obtain all the passwords.

Many of the Web-based e-mail programs have used various types of CGI scripts to send and display e-mail messages in Web browsers. Although this was really convenient for people who needed to access their e-mail while traveling, it also exposed the users to security risks. In some loudly publicized exploits, hackers were able to read people's e-mail and had full access to their e-mail accounts and passwords. Most of the Web-based e-mail programs have tightened their security, but they can never be totally secure because the Web wasn't designed to be that way.

Because CGI scripts are like Greek to a lot of people, a new industry of CGI "middleware" cropped up in the mid 1990s. These are applications that work like CGIs but enable you to write simple statements or queries in the HTML page itself rather than having to write a separate script. The middleware is run on the Web server, and it does the interpreting instead of the script. Cold Fusion by Macromedia and Front Page Extensions by Microsoft are good examples of what I am talking about.

Here are some tips for using CGI scripts and scripting middleware:

- Store all of your scripts in one directory with the correct permissions assigned. This is much better than having scripts scattered all over your Web server.

- Remove sample CGI scripts that are installed by default. Many of these scripts have been found to have big security holes.

- Make sure your scripts do not run with SUID privileges.

- Can you understand what the script is trying to accomplish? If you don't understand it, you shouldn't be using it.

- Don't hard code important stuff such as user names and passwords in scripts. (Don't laugh — it's been done!)

- If you have a public domain script, are any comments in the script about the security measures taken by the script?

- If you have to use public domain scripts, do a search on the Internet for any possible security holes introduced by the script. In this case, no news is probably good news.

- If you are using middleware, check with the vendor for patches and upgrades.

- Get the CERT advisories to check on security holes in scripts and middleware.

SSL security

SSL stands for Secure Sockets Layer, and it runs whenever you connect to a secure Web site. You know that a site is running SSL because the address changes to `https` instead of `http`. SSL directs the traffic to the Web server to port 443 and encrypts the data during the transmission. Many financial institutions and Web shopping sites use SSL for the pages that pass your credit card information to their Web servers. If you use SSL you'll have to remember to let your firewall allow this traffic through.

SSL has been a standard for quite a while now and is generally accepted as safe. However, recently some vulnerabilities have been discovered in the way that different Web server applications validate the SSL session, and some buffer overflows have been discovered.

The only way you can fix the problems with SSL is to obtain a patch from the vendor of the Web server software. A newer version of the software may have fixed the problem if you are running an older version. Although the problems found with SSL are not easily exploitable, I felt it was worth mentioning because so many companies rely upon SSL for securing data during transactions.

Hacking Databases

Databases are increasingly becoming an integrated component for Web servers and the unmanaged security vulnerabilities within the database can have a direct connection with downtime, system integrity, and consumer confidence. Many databases include default accounts and user roles, which can give unauthorized users privileges that they shouldn't have. For example, in Oracle, the CONNECT method allows a user the ability to do more than just connect to the database. In addition, the DBA role gives a user almost unlimited privileges, which should really be given only to developers.

This is all pretty amazing because databases are mature and sophisticated applications that rival the operating system in complexity. However, some of the basic security mechanisms that are standard in operating systems are not included in database systems. For example, most databases allow a blank password for the "sa" or "sys" accounts, which are basically the same as "root" accounts. A default installation of most databases includes accounts with well-known default passwords, and there is no method for forcing the password change. Additionally, there is usually no way to lock out the administrator accounts after bad password attempts, so a hacker can try a brute force dictionary attack on the password and no one will know.

Databases usually provide authentication, authorization, and auditing on a basic level. So, most of the databases do not ensure password robustness, and they are sometimes even stored as plain ASCII text. Some of these passwords can compromise the whole system — in some cases, allowing users to access the underlying operating system with system privileges. Because most database administrators have no training in security, it's no wonder that many databases contain serious security vulnerabilities and misconfigurations that are never noticed until it's too late.

Databases also transmit their data on specific ports. Sometimes people mistakenly open these ports through the firewall, thinking that the path must remain open in order for the database to work correctly. Bad move! Anyone with database query tools can connect directly to that port and completely bypass security mechanisms. Again, these ports are well-known and well-documented in the hacker world, and a simple port scan of your network tells a hacker whether you have left your database ports open to abuse.

As with operating systems, you have the option of installing additional services or packages on your database. Usually these services amount to nothing more than bells and whistles — things you don't really need. Some of them can lead to potential misuse and thus compromise any security you have in place. Let common sense be your guide. If you don't need the service or package, don't install it. If you find that you need it later on, you can easily install it then.

One database vendor sells its product as "unhackable." Of course, the vendor doesn't tell you that the product is not unhackable in the default installation. You have to make quite a few changes to the default installation in order to meet the unhackable status — and I'd question that even then.

As with other applications, security holes are often found after release and the vendor releases patches to fix the holes. Some databases are better at security than others. Do your homework before you buy. You can find a ton of data on the Internet about the relative security of database products.

The following is a list of things you can do to harden your database to make it more resistant to attack from unauthorized personnel:

- ✓ Install only what is needed. Don't rely upon a "typical" install. Read through the documentation, decide what you need, and do a custom install of the features and services you need.

- ✓ Change the passwords on every single account installed by default. In many cases, the password is the same as the account name. Remember that other applications (such as your Web server) need to use the passwords in order to access data, so keep track of the passwords.

- ✓ Use really strong passwords on all accounts. No plain dictionary words, please!

- ✓ Go through all the accounts in the database and manually lock out, expire, or disable accounts you don't need.

- ✓ Go through all the directories and make sure that they have the appropriate permissions. Don't allow any directories to be world readable and writeable.

✔ Disable the operating system back doors. SQL has extended stored procedures (which begin with the letters "xp") that can be used to run commands directly from the operating system. Oracle has packages (which begin with the letters "UTL") that do the same. Either restrict the privileges on the procedures and packages or remove them from the system. You have to experiment on a test machine to see which can be safely deleted.

✔ Disable mail capabilities. Leaving mail open makes it possible for an attacker to e-mail Trojans and hacking programs into the database. Mail can also be used to send important data back to a hacker.

✔ Enable logging and set for failed object access and logons. Read and review the logs regularly, too!

✔ Control the distribution of database query tools in your organization. Only database administrators should be able to use these tools.

✔ Put your database behind a firewall. Make sure the ports used by the database are closed on the firewall. If you can't put your firewall behind the firewall, be sure to harden the operating system and all applications.

✔ Never put a Web server on your database. Given the huge number of security holes contained in Web server applications, it's bad practice to incorporate the two on the same machine.

✔ Use encryption where possible. Encrypt the transmission of data between the outside and the inside of your network and encrypt the stored data. This is especially important when storing critical personal information such as credit card information, healthcare info, or bank account details.

✔ Harden the operating system that the database runs on. It doesn't matter if you're using Windows, Unix, or Mac. The base of your system must be strong and stable.

✔ Apply security patches and upgrades as soon as they are available. Watch the vendor site and CERT for announcements and alerts.

Other Programs with Holes

New applications for use on networks have allowed us to interact and communicate with others in ways that used to be seen as pure science fiction. You can stand on a street corner and send live video to a computer that is a block away — all without wires or fancy equipment. You can buy the stuff you need right off the shelf, ready to go. To make this interactivity possible, new applications have been developed to allow you talk to others, play music, and have virtual meetings. Unfortunately, some of these new programs have security holes that are easily exploited.

Windows Media Player

Windows Media Player allows you to play video and audio on your computer. Recently, holes have been discovered that would allow an outsider to run malicious code on your computer when you are running Media Player. These vulnerabilities have been fixed with a patches from Microsoft. Be sure you have the latest version of Media Player and watch the Microsoft and CERT alerts for new exploits.

mIRC Chat

This program allows users to have a text-based chat with other users on the same network channel. A flaw has been discovered that would allow someone to cause a buffer overflow by sending too much data in the nickname. This could cause the program to allow an outside user to remotely run programs on your computer or even install Trojan horses or hacking tools. Another exploit happens when an IRC server has been compromised and then users connect to it.

The newest version of mIRC has a list of 108 bugs that have been fixed since the last version, but no specific mention has been made about whether or not the security flaws have been fixed. If you don't really need mIRC, don't run it. If you must use it, make sure you have the latest version and watch the CERT alerts for new vulnerabilities.

NetMeeting

This program allows you to have virtual meetings across a network and even allows you to share data on your computer with others attending the meeting. It's a cool tool, but there's not much security built into the product. It's not bad if you are only going to have meetings on your internal network, but if you are using it across the Internet, you could be in for a shock.

Someone can join the meeting and convince a user to share information on their computer that really shouldn't be shared. That's just a simple case of "social engineering" — otherwise known as a con job. Be sure you know who you are letting connect to your system.

My main gripe with NetMeeting is that you have to blow a hole the size of a truck through your firewall to get all the features to work. For example, if you want to be able to hear and see others across the Internet, you have to allow 64,511 ports to be open in your firewall! That means that anything coming in through those ports will be allowed, even if it's not a NetMeeting broadcast!

Of course, you could close down those ports, but that means you can only hold text-based meetings. One possible solution is to run NetMeeting only on a VPN (Virtual Private Network), which encrypts all the traffic. Then you can specify ports on which to run the VPN for your meeting. This is not really an ideal solution but is more of a band-aid than anything else.

Because NetMeeting runs the way it's supposed to, the issue of the huge number of ports to allow is not seen as a security flaw by Microsoft. Hopefully, Microsoft will reconsider and release a version with some security built in to it. Until then, you have to watch the vendor site for new releases and patches and watch the CERT alerts for new vulnerabilities. Don't use NetMeeting across the Internet is my advice.

AOL Instant Messenger

This program is quite heavily used and is similar in a way to mIRC chat. It allows "buddies" to hold text-based chats across the Internet, and I know literally hundreds of students who use it to stay in touch with their folks. Again, it's easy and it's fun, but little to no security is built in. This program has been found to have holes that would allow an outsider to run commands on your computer, and the possibility is high that a worm can be introduced into your system.

In order to protect yourself, don't allow everyone to connect to you. Only allow people you know and trust to connect. Use the most current version of the program and keep an eye out for new security alerts.

ICQ

ICQ is a play on words — I Seek You — and is another text-based chat program. Numerous security holes have been found in the program, but the vendor has responded well by releasing patches and putting some security controls in the product. That doesn't make it immune from new attacks, though. ICQ has the same vulnerabilities as the other chat programs — for example, the potential for someone to access your hard drive and read your files. Here are some security measures that you should enable for ICQ:

- ✔ Restrict connections by requiring authorization for others to connect to you.
- ✔ Choose "Do not publish IP address" in the security settings. (See Figure 15-4.)
- ✔ Set security to "high" in the security settings.
- ✔ Don't have the program save your password for you. You have to type it in more often, but then it can't be as easily stolen.

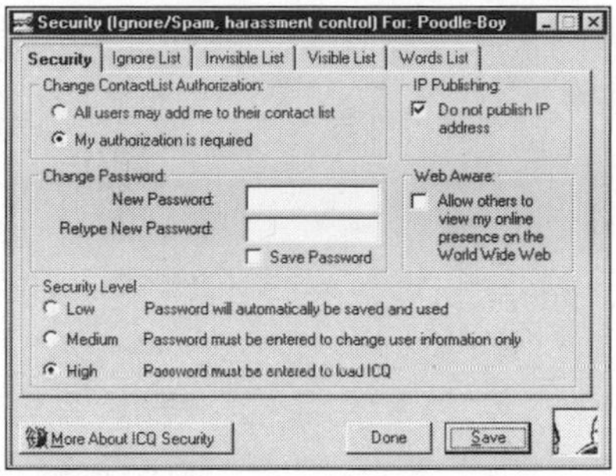

Figure 15-4:
ICQ's
security
settings.

Spyware

If you allow your employees to download and install programs that they find on the Internet, you may be inadvertently allowing *spyware* to be installed as well. Spyware is tracking software used by advertising agencies to follow what you do and when you do it. The software does this by storing data about your usage in a file and then it connects to the agency's server over the Internet and dumps your data to their machine. You won't even know this is happening! In most cases, the data that spyware collects is probably innocuous enough, but you should never let your computers do things that you haven't explicitly allowed.

There's no easy way to tell if you have spyware on your network. You have to install a utility that looks for spyware and deletes or disables it. A number of freeware and shareware products are available, and the big name anti-virus vendors are beginning to release products that search for spyware. There are some tests for spyware you can check out at www.grc.com. In addition, many of the newer personal firewalls will also block spyware.

PtoP

PtoP stands for Peer To Peer networking and includes products such as Napster and Gnutella. These are the programs that allow the sharing of music files across the Internet and have been the subject of some high-profile suits. Basically, peer-to-peer applications allow you to share whatever you have on your computer with anyone on the Internet who has the same software. I don't think I need to go on about how dangerous this could be. The safest bet is to simply not use these programs and don't allow their installation on your network. The risk is too high for abuse, and they are not really tools that increase productivity in the workplace.

Chapter 16

Very Precious Network Security

Chances are that if you are even remotely involved in network security you will have heard about *VPNs* — Virtual Private Networks. According to the Gartner Group, it's one of the fastest growing segments of the IT industry and is predicted to reach almost $6 billion in sales in 2006. That's pretty impressive when you think about how the markets have been doing lately.

VPNs were created to address two different problems: the high cost of dedicated leased lines needed for branch office communications and the need to allow employees a method of securely connecting to the headquarters' networks when they were on business out of town or working from home. VPNs succeed well in both areas.

In this chapter I'll discuss what constitutes a VPN and how it works. I'll also look at some of the different VPN technologies and how they might work for you.

Public versus Private Networks

Before VPNs, if a company wanted to have a secure network connection to an office in another geographic location, they only had one choice: a dedicated leased line. This was a physical phone line laid between the two offices and the only connections allowed on it were the two ends of the networks. No one could dial in to the network and you had to have physical access to the line to be able to connect. Leased lines had two major disadvantages — they were very expensive and they could be very slow. If a company had a lot of different offices to connect, the costs would soon reach astronomical levels.

When the Internet became available for public use, companies quickly discovered that they could use that network to connect to their various locations. But, the Internet is a public network, is not secure, and anyone can connect to it. Also, anyone who has the right kind of software can easily eavesdrop and capture as much traffic on the Internet as they want. While Internet connections are fast and cheap, that's not necessarily the best solution for most companies who want to share private data securely.

The other impetus for the development of VPNs came from the need for employees who work from home, or who are on the road, to securely access their company's network. They could direct-dial in to the network, but it was quite easy for hackers to discover these phone numbers and use them themselves. In other words, dial-ins were not very secure. These employees could possibly use the Internet to access their company's network but, again, that's not very secure.

So, you have the private networks that are expensive and slow and the public networks that are cheap and fast. Where was the happy medium? The answer was to use the public network — the Internet — but to hide the traffic so others on the Internet couldn't see it. This meant encryption. Encryption is the jumbling of data using specific mathematics — in other words, it's written in secret code. Of course, other users on the Internet can still see the encrypted traffic, they just can't tell what it is because it looks like garbage. No hacker in his right mind would go to the trouble to grab encrypted traffic, spend vast amounts of computing resources to decrypt it, to only discover he grabbed an e-mail that says, "Hi, Mom!" Problem solved. Well, not totally. . . .

What Makes a VPN?

A prototype of a VPN was Microsoft's first *RAS* (Remote Access Server) system. It was only used on NT-based systems and allowed remote users to dial in via modem. The difference from other dial-in systems was that RAS encrypted the session. It had its share of weaknesses, including a protocol that was not very secure, and the passwords could be easily cracked. Microsoft still offers RAS services on its servers, but it's not really considered to be a "true" VPN.

To be considered a "true" VPN nowadays, the service must support the following:

✔ **Data Protection** — the data traveling on the public network (Internet) must be unreadable by unauthorized users on the network.

✔ **User Authentication** — the VPN must be able to verify a user's identity and restrict access to only validated users. In addition, there must be a method of logging access.

✔ **Key Management** — the VPN must be able to generate shared, secret keys with the remote users.

✔ **Address Management** — the VPN must be able to keep the IP addresses of the internal network secret.

✔ **Multiprotocol Support** — the VPN must be able to handle multiple protocols so data of different types can be shared. This includes protocols like SMTP, HTTP, telnet, and so on.

From these requirements, three different types of VPNs have emerged:

✔ **Firewall-based VPNs:** All the VPN negotiations are handled by the firewall.

✔ **Hardware-based VPNs:** Generally, these are encrypting routers.

✔ **Software-based VPNs:** A complete package installed on a server dedicated to establishing and maintaining VPN connections.

So, how does a VPN work?

A VPN uses a special protocol to establish a virtual *channel* between two machines or two networks. Imagine if you could blow a soap bubble in the shape of a tube and only you and your friend could talk through it. The bubble is temporary and when you want to have another conversation, you would have to create another bubble. That's kinda like a VPN's channel. This channel is actually a temporary direct session. This is what is commonly referred to as *tunneling*.

Then the VPN also exchanges a set of shared secrets to create an encryption key. The traffic traveling along the established channel is *wrapped* with an encrypted package that has an address on the outside of the package, but the contents are hidden from view. It's sort of like a candy wrapper. You can see the candy, but you don't really know what the candy looks like on the inside. The same thing happens with the encrypted traffic. The original contents are hidden from view, but it has enough information to get it to its destination. Once the data reaches its destination, the wrapper is safely removed (see Figure 16-1).

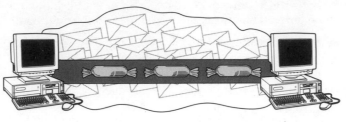

Figure 16-1:
A VPN
tunnel with
encryption-
wrapped
traffic.

There are generally two different protocols in use for VPNs: *IPSec* (Secure IP) and *L2TP* (Layer 2 Tunneling Protocol). The main difference between the two is that IPSec does not have a way to create security keys and L2TP does. IPSec must be combined with another protocol like *ISAKMP* (Internet Security Association and Key Management Protocol) or *IKE* (Internet Key Exchange). This is not a problem since most vendors include all the necessary components within their products for a complete solution.

Here are the basic steps that happen during a VPN session:

1. **The remote user requests a VPN connection.**

   This could be via a laptop with a dial-in through an ISP or via another computer connected to the Internet.

2. **The destination point receives the request and establishes a temporary tunnel.**

   The destination point is now beginning to set up the VPN.

3. **Both the remote computer and the destination share their keys and the destination network defines how the traffic will be encapsulated with encrypted wrappers.**

   Both of the keys had previously been created. They are encrypted and can't be understood by an eavesdropper.

4. **The destination point sends a challenge to the remote user to identify himself.**

   This is similar to the Army lookout shouting "Halt! Who goes there?"

5. **The remote user uses his UserID and password and whatever else is required (like a smart card or token) to authenticate himself to the destination network.**

   These steps will have been previously established when the VPN was first installed.

6. **The destination network verifies the remote user and assigns a temporary IP address to the remote computer.**

If the verification process is interrupted or if the remote user cannot be verified, the entire session is dropped and no more traffic is sent.

7. **The encrypted communication channel is established.**

   Data now starts traversing the VPN.

L2TP versus IPSec

When deciding on a VPN, it's important for you to know the differences between the two main protocols used, otherwise you could end up with a VPN that doesn't really suit your needs. These main protocols were developed for different types of traffic.

L2TP emerged from the original *PPP* (Point to Point Protocol) that was used for dial-up connections. This was very popular because it allowed the transmission of non-TCP/IP protocols like IPX, AppleTalk, and NetBEUI. L2TP works at Layer 2 of the *OSI* (Open Systems Interconnection) model, which is the Datalink layer. Since it works at Layer 2, it does not use *packets* to transmit data, it uses *frames* instead. A frame is a much simpler construct than a packet and it does not have as much information in it as a packet has. For example, a frame doesn't have any information on error control. You can think of a frame as a burst of data rather than a package of data.

IPSec, on the other hand, works at Layer 3 of the OSI model, which is the network layer. This is the layer we are more familiar with since it deals with IP packets that have all kinds of information in them. A packet has been likened to an envelope — on the outside of the envelope are the to/from addresses and a small description of the type of data enclosed. Since IPSec can only deal with packets, it is limited to transmitting TCP/IP traffic. IPSec couldn't handle AppleTalk or NetBEUI network protocols.

Therefore, L2TP is better suited for VPNs for dial-up connections or networks using a variety of networking technologies like Frame Relay or ATM (Asynchronous Transfer Mode). IPSec is better if you have a straightforward IP-based network. On the other hand, many users combine both Insect and L2TP on their VPNs for better security.

Setting Up a VPN

Not to oversimplify it, but there are two basic ways of setting up a VPN. The first way is normally used between networks and firewalls or encrypting routers to do the encrypting and decrypting of the traffic. In this setup there is no need for special software on the desktop or client computers. The second method is to have a firewall, encrypting router, or VPN server at the destination end and special VPN client software on the desktop or laptop computers. It all depends on whether the VPN is a two-way operation or a one-way operation.

You won't see the terms "one-way" or "two-way" in any of the vendors' technical data on VPNs. Those are my terms. In a two-way relationship you have two networks that want to work together and each has basically the same VPN setup as the other. The request to establish a VPN connection can come from either direction. No special software is needed on the desktop computers because all the encrypting and decrypting is done at the entry and exit points of the network. Both networks also have key management systems so they can both create secret keys for a VPN session. It's important that the two networks have compatible VPN components or they won't be successful in talking to one another.

In a one-way relationship, the destination network has the VPN setup and there is no agreement with another network to share. In that case, the computer wanting to make the connection with the network has to have VPN client software and the request can only be made in one direction — from the client to the network. The client software can request and authenticate itself, but the secret key making mechanisms are only on the network. The client computer will have a secret key stored on itself, but it cannot create new keys.

Generally, the one-way system is used for remote users who are dialing in from home or while they are traveling on the road. They dial up through their ISP and the mechanisms for establishing and maintaining VPN connections is all contained at the destination network. If someone with a laptop without the VPN client software tried to connect to the company's network, he wouldn't get too far because he wouldn't have the client software or a secret key. Additionally, the unauthorized user would not be listed on the VPN's database of authorized users. However, once someone dials in and is authenticated, their access is the same as if they were sitting in the same building as the destination network.

Inside or outside?

You can set up the VPN *endpoint* at various locations. The endpoint is where the VPN traffic comes into your network. In some cases the endpoint is also the firewall as many firewalls come with VPN capabilities nowadays. The endpoint can also be in front of the firewall, in a DMZ off one side to the firewall, or inside of the firewall. Each of these configurations has its pluses and minuses.

If you choose to put your VPN in front of the firewall, the mechanism does all of the encrypting and decrypting on its own. That means there is no need to allow an open VPN tunnel through your firewall. All of the traffic through the firewall will have been pre-filtered and formatted so the firewall can read it. However, if the VPN fails or is taken down, you'll be faced with a situation where all the traffic goes out unencrypted, or no traffic at all gets out. It depends on whether or not your VPN will fail in the open or closed position.

A VPN on the firewall would seem like a good solution because, again, you don't need to leave an open tunnel through the firewall. The firewall will handle all the encryption, decryption, and its regular job of the examination of traffic. This type of solution puts an enormous burden on the poor little firewall, though. You are asking this machine to do a hell of a lot of processing! Encryption and decryption is labor intensive for a computer, as is the examination of traffic and that could result in a bottleneck for traffic.

Another method is to put the VPN on the inside of the firewall. This relieves the firewall and/or the router of having to handle the encryption and decryption of the traffic, but you have to allow a VPN tunnel to pass through the firewall. A firewall cannot read encrypted traffic and it will allow that traffic to pass through unchallenged. Of course, the traffic will still be stopped by the VPN mechanism, but by that time it is already in the internal network.

Securing the client

Probably the easiest way to break a VPN's security is to get a hold of a laptop that is used to dial in for a VPN connection. I know of more than one person who has had a laptop stolen from a rental car within hours of arrival in a new city. The stolen laptop will have the VPN client software, the UserID, and the secret key all stored on one machine. A smart laptop owner will not have saved the password for the VPN tunnel on his computer. If he has, the thief has just gotten himself a free ticket to wander around in your network!

Users who use laptops to establish VPN connections with your network need to be given lessons in maintaining good security. They should have up-to-date anti-virus software installed and ensure that it runs every time they start their computer. Antivirus software is good at detecting Trojan horses that could be used to hijack or piggyback a VPN session. Additionally, the laptop should have personal firewall software set up. Some VPN clients already include personal firewalls, so you'll have to check with your vendor as to whether yours does or doesn't. The personal firewall can ensure that only the VPN client is making the connection and that it's not actually a

Trojan horse program masquerading as the VPN client. Another good precaution is to enable the BIOS password. That way, if the computer is stolen, it cannot even be started up without the password.

It's also a good idea to restrict remote VPN connections via laptop to those who really need it. You shouldn't be handing out this capability like candy to anyone who asks for it. Your employees should be able to present a good case for needing it or it just becomes another one of those bells and whistles that people like to have and brag about.

Some Terminology

You'll find that the term VPN means different things to different people — especially when it comes to vendors. However, the basic mechanisms that are generally agreed upon are encryption and authentication. Some vendors offer a "complete" solution and others only offer bits and pieces of the entire puzzle. You have to be determined and keep asking questions until you're sure you're satisfied with their answers. It's no disgrace to say you don't understand. In fact, if the vendor can't explain something to your satisfaction maybe he doesn't really understand it himself!

Table 16-1 lists some terms and expressions you may hear or read. Hope this helps you make a decision!

Table 16-1	Some Terms Used with VPNs
Term	**Meaning**
AES	Advanced Encryption Standard. The encryption algorithm used by the U.S. Government.
DES	Data Encryption Standard. One of the cryptographic algorithms used in encryption. A stronger version is known as 3DES (Triple DES).
Diffie-Hellman	Another cryptographic algorithm used in VPNs.
GRE	Generic Routing Encapsulation. A method for wrapping packets so that the original addresses are hidden.
IKE	Internet Key Exchange. The protocol used for exchanging secret keys in IPSec.

Term	Meaning
ISAKMP	Internet Security Association and Key Management Protocol. The forerunner of IKE. (See previous.)
LDAP	Lightweight Directory Access Protocol. A set of protocols for computers to obtain information from one another, based on the X500 standard. In VPNs it is used for secret key information.
MPLS	MultiProtocol Label Switching. Used to divert traffic when there are failures or bottlenecks in the network.
Oakley	A protocol used for exchanging secret keys.
PPTP	Point to Point Tunneling Protocol. A forerunner of L2TP.
QoS	Quality of Service. The amount of traffic a VPN can handle and how well it handles the traffic.
RADIUS	Remote Authentication Dial In User Service. An authorization system used to authenticate users.
RSA	Rivest-Shamir-Adleman. A cryptographic algorithm for key exchange.
SSH	Secure Shell. A secure form of telnet that encrypts the traffic.

Chapter 17

Securing Your Wireless Network

*W*ireless networking has become a hot technology — networks can be found almost everywhere. They are cheap and easy to set up, and many of the new laptops have wireless network cards included, something people are obviously excited about because it frees you from network cables and you can move about your home or office as you please.

The downside of the technology is that wireless networks are incredibly easy to hack into. One of the main reasons they are so easily hacked is that the default configurations of the networks employ the weakest security, if any at all. The manuals for the installation of the wireless base stations don't emphasize security, and most that I have seen are slightly less than stupid. My own manual suggests using the word "Home" as a password. But even when the stronger security features are employed in wireless networks, they are still quite vulnerable to unauthorized intrusion. Thus, wireless security has become somewhat of an oxymoron.

Not to despair, however. At least some security is better than nothing. In this chapter, I describe some of the technology used in wireless networking and detail the associated vulnerabilities. I also instruct you on setting up a more secure wireless network with tips and tricks on your configurations.

How Does Wireless Networking Work?

Wireless communications have been with us for some time and are used for cell phone and some ham radio transmissions. The difference between most wireless networks is the protocols, or sets of rules, that manage the transmission of data. In wireless networking, you are using the 802.11b set of protocols which confine the transmissions to the 2.4GHz (gigahertz) unlicensed radio band. The speed of these transmissions tops out at about 11MBits (megabits) of data per second. (That's a theoretical speed in any case. You'll find most networks work at a slightly slower speed.) Some cordless phone transmissions and microwave ovens also use this 2.4GHz frequency and can interrupt wireless network transmission.

The wireless network base station — also called an *access point* — sends its transmissions from radio antennas on the unit. Any computer that has a wireless network card can conceivably "see" the transmissions if it is in within range of the access point. The wireless network card will either be a built-in card or a PCMCIA card that has been inserted into the PCMCIA slot in the computer. Most transmissions are limited to about 1500 feet, line-of-sight, but weather conditions and reflections can alter this range. Some wireless network cards have stronger receiving antennas, too. I have picked up wireless transmissions that were as far as three floors and hundreds of yards away with just a standard wireless network card.

Each wireless network has a name, broadcast by the access point as a *Service Set IDentifier (SSID)*. Newer access points use an *Extended Service Set IDentifier (ESSID)*. In either case, this is the name that all wireless laptops or other clients use to connect to the network. Most access points use default SSIDs and you'll need to change it to something unique to help prevent unauthorized users from using your network. (This is just one security tip and there will be more, later on in this chapter.)

The wireless network access point typically sends out three or four different types of packets of information. This is important to remember because you need to understand this before you can secure your network. Even if you employ encryption, some of these packets are still sent in the clear. The different packet types are as follows:

- **Beacons:** These are continually broadcast by the access point with the SSID and the *Media Access Control (MAC) address*. These are sent so clients can find the network to join it. This data is NOT encrypted when encryption is enabled on the wireless network.

- **Probes:** Clients that want to join a wireless network will send a request for a probe packet from the access point. If the access point will allow the request, it responds with a probe packet. This data is not encrypted when encryption is enabled.

- **Data:** This is simply the data sent between computers. This is the only traffic that is encrypted when encryption is enabled.

- **Ad-hoc:** These are packets that allow the clients to speak to one another without having to go through the access point. These packets don't contain beacon data and are considered to be the same as data packets by the network.

Typically, in a commercial setting, there will be one or more access points located through the offices and/or buildings. The access points broadcast their packets to all computers within range that have the appropriate wireless network cards. Most systems are set up by default to accept "any" computers wanting to connect. When the connection is established, the wireless computers can communicate with any shared resources on the network just as if they were on a wired network.

You can add a small bit of security by telling your access point NOT to broadcast the SSID and to only allow connections from clients that request the connection by name. In that way, the client can't "see" the SSID and the client must know the SSID ahead of time to be able to request a connection. See Figure 17-1 for an example of what I mean.

Figure 17-1:
The difference between broadcasting and not broadcasting the SSID.

What Are the Vulnerabilities?

Because wireless networks are sending their packets of information via radio waves, it's very easy for anyone within the vicinity of your network to capture these packets and get information about your network. In fact there are many sites on the Internet that list all the "found" wireless networks in metropolitan areas that were discovered by people wandering around the streets with their laptops and sniffing for network traffic. These networks are usually corporate wireless broadcasts that have not been protected in any way. The companies in question simply installed a wireless access point to their network and neglected to enable any security that would limit who is allowed to connect to it. In effect, these networks are giving people free access to corporate networks and any Internet connections they may have because no login or other authorization is required to join the network. A new form of network has been created using these free connections and it is referred to as a *parasitic network*.

Because the network traffic is so easy to find and capture, wireless networks are vulnerable to all of the same attacks and hacks that plague wired networks. This includes unauthorized intrusion, denial of service (DoS) attacks, and the installation of malicious code such as Trojans.

Unauthorized access points

Like the unauthorized installation of modems on a corporate network, many companies are finding that employees have brought in wireless access points from home and installed them on the company's corporate network. While this may give the employee the freedom of walking around the offices with a wireless enabled laptop to do his work, an access point with no security can also allow outsiders to connect to the network *without anyone's knowledge*. If companies are going to allow their employees to install these access points, they need to establish a policy that requires not only written permission to install the access point, but a process to test the security of these installations.

Using default SSIDs

As I mentioned before, by default, wireless networks are set up with little or no security enabled. What little security is enabled often employs the use of default network names (SSIDs), passwords, and encryption keys. Not only are these defaults well known, they are publicly distributed on the Internet. For example, here are some of the default SSIDs used by leading access point vendors:

- **tsunami** — used by Cisco Aironet
- **linksys** — used by Linksys products
- **comcomcom** — used by 3com products
- **Compaq** — used by Compaq products
- **wireless** — used by Netgear products
- **AirPort Network** — used by Apple AirPorts

What this means is, that if you have turned off the *broadcasting* of the SSID, unauthorized users can still connect by simply typing in the default SSID.

There are other ways to protect against this, which I will describe a bit later in the chapter.

Using default encryption keys

There is an inefficient form of encryption available for wireless networks called *Wired Equivalent Privacy (WEP)*. There are two main problems with WEP - the first one is that the encryption keys used by default are well known and the second is that only the data is encrypted. The SSID and MAC addresses are still broadcast in the clear. This said, using WEP is much better than not using it. I'll tell you how to set up WEP later in this chapter but for now, here is a list of the common default encryption keys:

- 10 11 12 13 14
- 20 21 22 23 24
- 30 31 32 33 34
- 40 41 42 43 44

The danger is that if you have enabled WEP but are using the default keys, an attacker can capture your wireless traffic and easily decrypt it because he has they keys.

Default SNMP configurations

Many of the wireless access points use *Simple Network Management Protocol (SNMP)* to collect data to troubleshoot problems on the network. Using SNMP is bad enough because it can give an outsider valuable information about the internal workings of your network. However, the default configuration of the SNMP interface for most access points uses simple passwords that are documented on the Internet and well known by hackers. Most manuals I've seen don't even mention that you should change SNMP setup password to something hard to guess. If a hacker knows the password, he can gather vast amounts of network data and can also change configurations for your access point.

Web and telnet access

All access points will need to be configured at some point using administrative privileges and most will allow you to use your browser or telnet to connect.

Additionally, since most wireless networks will be set up as internal networks, they will be using an IP address in the private range of 10.x.x.x, 172.16.x.x, or 192.168.x.x. In fact, most manuals *recommend* that you use these default IP addresses. This means that you only have to type in the IP address in your Web browser to receive the configuration pages for the access point. Again, default passwords or blank passwords are the norm for these pages. All I'd have to do is sit outside your building, type in the IP address in my browser, and I can connect to your wireless access point and set it up any way I want to. Be sure to change the default IP address (if your system will allow it) and change the administrative password to something strong and unguessable.

Wireless sniffers

There are a number of programs called *wireless sniffers* that search the airwaves for network traffic and capture the packets of that traffic. The attacker does not have to install anything on the target network, he only has to be within range of the broadcast. Most of the sniffer tools will capture those packets that contain the SSID of the network and the user name and password (if required). Once the attacker has that information, he can log on as a seemingly legitimate user.

You won't know if anyone is using a sniffer on your wireless network because there are no physical connections and no sniffing software needs to be installed on your network for it to work. Check out the web site for a program called AirSnort (http://airsnort.shmoo.com) to see just how vulnerable wireless networks are to this threat.

In addition to being able to sniff the information needed to connect to your wireless network, an attacker with a sniffer can also capture such traffic as email messages, Web pages, FTP, and telnet sessions. Imagine if all the e-mail traffic on Wall Street could be captured and read — the stock market would go crazy.

Evil twin intercepts

No, this isn't a person but is an access point with a very strong signal placed in close proximity to an existing access point with a weaker signal. What's the harm in that? Your users' wireless clients could be fooled into thinking that they were joining the company's network when, in fact, they are joining a hacker's network. Once they have joined that network, the hacker can collect user names and passwords quite easily. Of course, your users would soon notice that they are not connected to the company's network because they won't be able to find their usual resources. They could log off and try again, but the damage will already have been done. The hacker has enough information to log on to your network now as a legitimate user.

Spoofing

There are a number of different methods of *spoofing* or masquerading as a legitimate computer on your network. These include IP spoofing, MAC spoofing, and *Address Resolution Protocol (ARP)* spoofing. This is a more sophisticated attack, but free tools such as *DSniff* allow intruders to forge these packets to fool the network to let them join. Once the intruder has joined the network, he is actually *hijacking* traffic from the network. He can hijack just about anything that is using TCP/IP to transmit data. This includes *Secure Sockets Layer (SSL)* and *Secure Shell (SSH)* sessions that are transmitting sensitive data such as credit card numbers.

Denial of service attacks

Since wireless networks are limited to the 2.4GHz range, conceivably any other transmissions within that range have the possibility of jamming your signal or at least bumping you off the network. Cell phones sometimes leak into this range and can sometimes be the culprit of unstable connections. This means that your wireless client has to send signals to try to reconnect. If the frequency is consistently jammed, this can prevent people from using the network.

Fixing the Vulnerabilities

First you have to accept that wireless networking is not going to be completely secure and you have to take that into consideration when deciding to set one up. If your network is not used to transmit ultra sensitive data, it is probably okay to use wireless networking. I would not suggest you using wireless networking if your domain name is "pentagon.mil" for example.

You can set up encryption using WEP, secure your routers, use personal firewalls on your client computers, and other means to secure wireless networks. Here are some of the specifics on what you should do.

Don't accept "any" SSID

Some access points will allow a client to connect no matter what they have entered as the SSID name. Follow your manual's instructions to turn this feature off.

Change the default SSID or ESSID

As I mentioned before, most systems use a default SSID like "wireless" as the name of the wireless network. DO NOT use these default names. Change it to something unique but not so obvious that it can be guessed by an outsider. I've seen cases where the legal department set up their wireless network SSID to "Legal Dept" and I've also seen where companies have used their own company name for the SSID. Keep it simple, but not stupid.

Disable SSID broadcasting

Different vendors put this option in different areas of their configuration set ups and some don't offer it at all. You'll need to refer to your user guide or manual to see how to accomplish this. This will require all clients to specify your network by SSID in order to join.

Enable WEP

You'll have to go back to the vendor's manual to set this up as each vendor has different steps and instructions. Most access points allow you to set up WEP for either encryption only or encryption and authentication. Encryption and authentication is stronger.

Be aware that, even with WEP enabled, only the data carried across your network will be encrypted. The SSID, the MAC address, and the encryption keys will still be sent in the clear. WEP is far from perfect, but it's better than no encryption at all.

Which level of encryption?

You'll need to decide the level of encryption for your network. Typically you can choose between 40 bit, 64 bit, or 128 bit encryption. There is usually a pull-down list in the security panel to do this. Of course the wireless network cards in your clients will also have to have encryption enabled. You

CAN mix the levels of encryption between the access point and the network cards, but it can cause some problems and you're better off keeping the levels of encryption the same.

Encryption passphrase or string

Some access points want you to enter a *passphrase* while others want you to enter a *string* — they are not the same. If your system wants a passphrase, you can use up to 32 alpha-numeric characters. This phrase is used to generate a hexadecimal secret key.

If your system asks for a string, you will need to create an alpha-numeric word or phrase that *matches the encryption length*. This is tricky, so here are some tips:

- ✔ 40 or 64 bit encryption – ASCII string = 5 alpha-numeric characters
- ✔ 40 or 64 bit encryption – HEX string = 10 numbers 0-9 + letters a-f
- ✔ 128 bit encryption – ASCII string = 13 alpha-numeric characters
- ✔ 128 bit encryption – HEX string = 26 numbers 0-9 + letters a-f

I know this is confusing, but you MUST match the length of the string to the level of encryption or you will not be able to connect to your network.

Which authentication method?

First of all you'll need to decide if you are going to use the *Open System* or *Shared Key* form of authentication. In simple terms the Open System simply checks that a encryption key is present and accepts the connection. The Shared Key authentication issues a challenge-response session before the connection is allowed. You'll need to refer to your manual to see how to set these up for your system. Each vendor does things slightly differently.

Whenever you make changes to WEP, all the clients on your network will lose access until they are reconfigured, too. Since the wireless connection will be lost, you will need to reconfigure each laptop or computer individually. In some cases you will also need to reboot for the changes to take effect.

Change administrative passwords

No matter how many passwords your system comes with, you need to change them to something unique. You never know if hackers know the default passwords that come stored on your system. If you need tips on creating strong passwords, have a look at the Cheat Sheet in the front of this book or check out Chapter 11.

Changing the administrative passwords keeps intruders from being able to change the configuration of your wireless network.

Turn off file and printer sharing

If you don't need to share files and printers in Windows, there's no need to have this feature turned on. Even if someone manages to connect to your wireless network to use your Internet connection, by turning off file sharing he won't be able to get to your sensitive files.

If you have to use file and printer sharing, be sure that you use strong passwords to access the resources and share only what you absolutely have to.

Use a MAC address access control list

Many systems allow you to limit the clients connecting to your network to only those whose MAC addresses have been entered in the configuration. This limits the connection to only those machines that are listed and no others. Unlike IP addresses, MAC addresses are static and never change. They are unique to each computer. You can find out the MAC address of your computers by using the *winipcfg* command in Windows 95/98 or *ipconfig* in Windows NT/2000 and Unix machines.

MAC addresses can be "spoofed" by a hacker who has the right utilities, so remember that this security method is not foolproof. Like most of the security measures for wireless networks, it's much better than having nothing at all.

Check with your user's manual to see how to enter the MAC addresses in your wireless access point configuration. Typically, you'll type up the addresses in a plain text file and import them into the access point's administration program.

Use personal firewalls on client computers

This can be done easily and quite cheaply, too. A basic personal firewall like Zone Alarm is free. You can tell the firewall to only accept certain connections and to deny others. This may not protect your entire wireless network, but it will protect your client machines from possible attack or hack.

Use a VPN

The ultimate wireless protection is a *Virtual Private Network (VPN)*. Granted, this may be costly to implement but if you are really concerned about protecting your connections and your sensitive data, this may be the way to go. There is more information on VPNs in Chapter 16.

Be smart when using wireless

Given that wireless networks are notoriously hard to secure, be sure that you are not endangering the security of your internal network simply for the sake of convenience. Do you really need wireless or is it one of those bells and whistles that are plain neat to have? Even though I use wireless at home, I have secured my home network just as I have described here. I have secured it to keep rogue users from sitting at the end of my driveway to get free Internet access. Securing my network also gives me peace of mind that my Dummies chapters won't suddenly disappear, either.

Chapter 18

E-Commerce Special Needs

Christmas of 1999 was both boon and bust for e-commerce sites. These sites, selling everything from apples to xylophones, were delighted to see the interest that had developed for ordering gifts and services online. They were less than delighted when many realized that their e-commerce servers were crashing under the extreme loads. Those that recovered soon became aware that there was no way they could deliver all the orders by Christmas. This spelled the demise of many online retailers such as Toys.Com.

Overselling isn't the only problem that has plagued e-commerce sites. Tales of hacks and frauds abound. In March of 2000 a hacker by the name of Curador lifted 2,000 records, including credit card numbers and other personal information from SalesGate. SalesGate was a New York-based marketplace "developed to help small and large businesses sell online in a way that guarantees the protection of the user's personal information." Obviously, they didn't do too well when it came to protecting that information. Almost exactly one year later the National Infrastructure Protection Center (NIPC.gov) issued a series of warnings about hacking tools and vulnerabilities that targeted e-commerce servers and databases. The incidents of the stealth of information from e-commerce sites skyrocketed. In August of 2001 a Web-based gift certificate service called Flooz filed bankruptcy because stolen credit cards were used to purchase the certificates. The company lost somewhere between $200,000 and $300,000 in bogus sales. The auction site eBay continues to have problems with identity theft of its sellers and just recently Singapore's DBS Bank confirmed that a computer hacker siphoned money from 21 online bank accounts.

E-Commerce woes are real and are not liable to go away soon. Conducting business on the Internet with Web-based products is like reading a sales ad in the newspaper and then sending your next-door neighbor's ten-year-old boy to the address with a box full of money. You've taped the box securely so people can't see the contents, but you don't know the seller or the boy. You are operating on blind trust. The sale could be a scam and you lose your money and never get the goods. Someone could intercept the boy and steal the money. The boy could be fooled into giving the money to someone else. Or, with luck, the boy comes back with the product you purchased. So much can go wrong but, remarkably, it usually goes alright.

In this chapter, I look at some of the special considerations needed for secure e-commerce. Many of the security measures have already been discussed in previous chapters, but others are new and are specific to e-commerce. Hopefully, after reading this chapter, you'll have what you need to run your cyber-business securely and successfully.

Protecting the C.I.A.

You'll have three goals in conducting e-commerce. These goals apply to all data that needs to be protected, but since you are dealing mainly with data that belongs to others and not yourself, it's even more important that the subject is dealt with here. I'm talking about Confidentiality, Integrity, and Availability — the CIA of network security.

- ✔ **Confidentiality** — You need to protect the confidentiality of your data. You may be collecting credit card numbers, names, and addresses of your customers. Your customers let you have this data with the implied agreement that you will protect this data and their confidentiality. If you are dealing with medical prescriptions, there are new laws that put teeth behind the confidentiality requirements. The confidentiality of your own data needs to be protected, as well. You don't want people to know how you process your data and how you pass this data to storage. If you suffer a breach of confidentiality, you will lose more than your customers' confidence — you could be subject to legal proceedings, too.

- ✔ **Integrity** — You and your customers need to be confident that the data you collect is not altered in any way, either in transit or at rest. If you don't protect the integrity of your data, how will you know that your orders are correct? Additionally, how will you know that you're not being defrauded by intruders or scam artists? A bank's reputation is based largely on its integrity. You may remember the Savings & Loans scandals of the 1980s. Many of these institutions went out of business because they could no longer ensure the integrity of the money deposited with them.

- ✔ **Availability** — The goods and services have to be available for you to have any customers. Banks protect the availability of your money by placing numerous locations and ATMs around the community. Customers are secure in the feeling that their money is readily available and they don't need to panic if they need money outside of normal business hours. Likewise, e-commerce sites need to be available when the consumers want to use them, which can be any time of the day or night. They have to anticipate times of high volume, too. For instance, a site that sells flowers had better be available in the days leading up to and including Mother's Day. If you're not there when the customers want you, they will simply go elsewhere.

Let's face it. You don't start an e-commerce site to ensure world peace. You do it for the money. More than any other type of Web site, e-commerce is there to make a profit. And, like a typical "bricks-and-mortar" business, your responsibility to your customers goes beyond ringing up the correct amount and collecting the money at the till. You can have the best e-commerce site in the world, but if the customer isn't comfortable with how you conduct business, you lose.

Protecting confidentiality

In June of 2001 the Eli Lilly company sent out a mass e-mailing to people who had subscribed to a service that had been sending out individual reminders to recipients to take their daily dose of the anti-depressant, Prozac. The company had decided to discontinue this service and wanted to tell everyone at once instead of having to send one e-mail at a time to each person signed up for the program. A well-meaning employee of Eli Lilly wrote a small script to gather all the e-mail addresses of the subscribers and send out the message to all of them. When the recipients got the e-mail, they discovered that they could see the e-mail addresses of ALL the recipients. The Eli Lilly employee had not properly set up the blind copy address field for the e-mails and, thus, all the e-mail addresses were released to everyone on the list. Subscribers felt this was a huge breach of confidentiality. The Federal Trade Commission (FTC) began an investigation and Eli Lilly was eventually fined. The FTC found that Eli Lilly was guilty of deceptive practices that were not in keeping with their own privacy policies.

Imagine that someone had posted signs on your house that said, "Paid too much for his car!" or "Has seen his doctor about Viagra!" That is essentially what is at stake when you undertake to keep data private. It's a big responsibility and one you should take seriously.

There are four ways that confidentiality can be breached:

 ✔ **Accidental Release** — Like the Eli Lilly Company, the release of data was not intentional. Accidental release usually happens through inadequate procedures, sloppy management, or employee ignorance. In this case, it's important to set policies and educate all involved on the procedures on how to collect and release data.

✔ **Malicious Release** — This could be from a hack where someone intentionally broke in to release incriminating or embarrassing data. Sometimes this is the result of a disgruntled employee wanting to cause harm to his employer's reputation. Whichever the case, this represents a breach of security and the systems and policies need to be examined to make sure it doesn't happen again. In this case you should exercise "need to know" and set access controls appropriately.

✔ **Statistical Release** — This is what is also known as "traffic analysis" and is intentional in nature. The perpetrator is looking for patterns or unique occurrences. Cookies used in tracking visits to Web sites can be used for this purpose and Web advertisers frequently seek this sort of data. Many e-commerce sites use cookies to track the buying habits of customers so they can build statistical profiles of customers. In 1999 a new book on secret satellites was released. The military claimed that the book contained no secrets, but online booksellers noticed that a large number of orders were coming through ".mil" sites. The key to protecting yourself from statistical release is to encrypt data in transit and in storage. Patterns are much harder to find if the data can't be seen by outsiders.

✔ **Compulsory Release** — A court order could compel you to release data. This is of particular interest in criminal proceedings. This is a potential ethic quagmire. If you feel the data is too sensitive to release or you feel that the ordering authority won't give the data adequate protection, your only recourse is to refuse to comply. This could result in penalties and/or jail time. If you must release sensitive data to the authorities, you must have a protection agreement with them before the data is released.

As noted in the preceding examples, not all inadvertent data release is due to security breaches but, by establishing strong policies and procedures, you gain some control. Access control is important as is the final storage of the data.

In a good security architecture, your Web server will be either outside the firewall or inside a DMZ. Your database will be separate from your Web server and an excellent idea is to place another firewall between the Web server and the database and the internal network. In any case, the database should not be easy for outsiders to get to (see Figure 18-1). Your firewall policies should be very restrictive and only allow the specific ports/protocols available to transmit what's absolutely necessary. Of course, it's always important to monitor those logs so you can recognize a breach if and when it occurs. Otherwise, these things can slip by without your noticing it.

Another method of preventing inadvertent release is through the use of content filtering software. This system is placed inside of the firewall and it examines the outgoing traffic for key words and phrases. If the system discovers an e-mail with specific words, for example, the system would prevent that e-mail from being released until it has been reviewed. The administrators configure the content filtering software by adding the words and phrases that you identify as being indicators of possible restricted data. There is more information on content filters in Chapter 9.

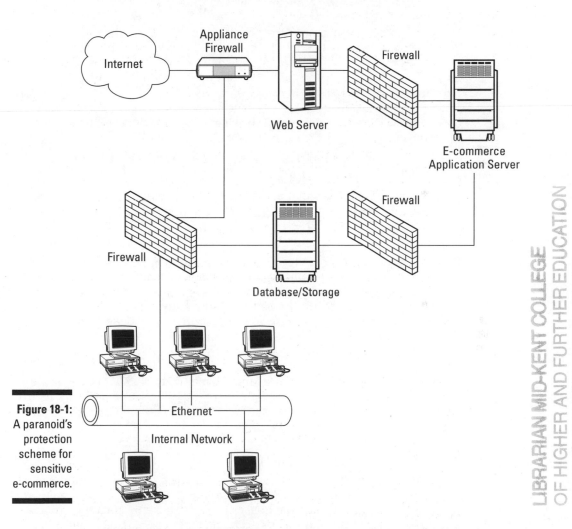

Figure 18-1:
A paranoid's protection scheme for sensitive e-commerce.

Data should be encrypted while in transit and while being stored. You can use SSL to encrypt the traffic between your Web server and the public and you should use encrypted cookies to prevent unauthorized leakage of data. (See the information about cookies later in this chapter.) Additionally, you can make the cookies *non-persistent*, meaning that they don't hold the connection open when data is not being sent. This will help prevent the use of traffic analysis tools.

Good back-ups of your data should be kept and the back-up tapes should be kept securely locked up. It won't do you any good to put dozens of firewalls in front of your database if someone on the inside can simply walk off with the tapes and the data. Maintain good access controls for the tapes and encrypt them if you have that capability.

There is another problem with the protection of confidentiality of records. How do you decide what should be considered confidential information? There are new products coming onto the market that address just those issues. One is by a company called IDcide and its product is PrivacyWall. This product claims to do four things:

✔ Shows all the personal questions used to collect information via your Web site.

✔ Warns about configurations in the Web server that cause leakage of sensitive personal information.

✔ Discovers Web pages that accidentally publicize personal information.

✔ Detects Web sites that are operated without management's approval or knowledge.

This last item is a potential biggie. When I was working for the government, one of the intelligence agencies found thousands of unauthorized Web servers running on individual workstations. In many cases the Web sites contained confidential and secret information that allowed anyone outside the organization to access it. Some of these Web sites were even indexed by a popular Internet search engine.

You can get more information on IDcide at `www.idcide.com` and PrivacyWall information is available at `www.idcide.com/pages/emp_intro_prod.htm`.

Protecting integrity

You know who you are but, on the Web, it's difficult to really know who your customers are. There is no universal ID Card that we all can use and the onus is upon you to verify who has placed an order and that the payment method is valid. For years online auction houses like eBay have been having trouble with people "stealing" valid seller's accounts and/or setting up "shill" accounts.

The integrity of the auction house's reputation is at stake when someone steals a valid seller's account and then sets up a sale for non-existent goods. The fraudulent seller gets the money for the goods and both the auction house and the real seller suffer the consequences. It's easy to set up fictitious e-mail accounts with false information and have auction bids inflated by ringers. In these cases, the auction houses are at fault for not making the sellers and buyers prove who they are. If the process of proving identity were onerous, however, that would decrease the popularity of these auctions. Some auction houses try to get around this problem by having the buyers and sellers independently rate one other. People with good ratings would appear to be worthy of trust — until their identity is stolen.

Many e-commerce sites attempt to identify their customers by having them create their own accounts. This is flawed because the e-commerce sites do nothing to verify that the data given by the customer is correct. Most e-commerce sites won't allow you to buy something with a credit card unless the shipping address and the billing address are the same, but this was instituted by the banks and not the e-commerce sites. The banks found they were losing too much money to people using stolen credit cards and having the goods delivered to a drop box.

Protecting the integrity of your own data is important, too. Imagine the chaos that would be created if one-tenth of all of your online orders were altered. Or, what if your inventories were changed to show that you had more goods than you really had? Not only would that alter your profit and loss, but it could ruin your credibility with your customers.

As far as verifying who your customers are, you can't do much about that unless you're willing go to the expense of implementing strong authentication and use something like smart cards or tokens. Not many consumers would be willing to wait for their credentials to come through the mail before being able to place an order. Most of them would simply go to another e-commerce site that doesn't have the same restrictions.

Your financial institution will work out a method of validating credit cards with you and they may impose restrictions like only being able to send to the same address as the billing address. Some credit card companies have special applications that will create a unique credit card number for every online transaction. MBNA has such a program called *ShopSafe*. The user has an application on his computer that requires a special user name and password to use. The user launches the program and defines the dollar amount and the length of time that the credit card number is good for. The application then creates a unique number for use with the online order. In this case you can be fairly sure that only the authorized user is using the account because of the additional verification process.

The integrity of incoming data and data in storage can be maintained with a combination of access controls and *integrity checkers*. Integrity checkers are programs that take a "snapshot" of the data, stores that snapshot, and then uses it to compare to all subsequent examinations of the data. It's like using a set of scales to make sure that the weight of packages is consistent. There are numerous integrity checking programs, but probably the most popular is

Tripwire. It gives you the ability to monitor files to see if they have been modified, added, or deleted, or somehow tampered with. When the program notices that something has changed, it sends a notice to the administrator of the change. Intrusion detection systems (IDS) can be used in the same manner and large e-commerce sites will probably want to implement them at the host level, which means installing IDS on the individual computers.

Firewalls will do well in protecting the integrity of your systems by attempting to stop intrusions. An intruder could potentially alter all your data or surreptitiously collect data, which would be a breach of confidentiality as well. Placement of your firewalls and intrusion detections is important as is the monitoring of the output of the logs they create. Back-ups should be done regularly and safely stored to bring your system back to an original state if a breach of security has compromised your data. You'll also need to protect the integrity of your system by hardening the operating system against attack and applying security patches to the operating system and applications.

Protecting availability

The goods or services you are selling must be available to your e-commerce customers 24 hours a day. If your network or systems are not available to them, they will lose confidence and possibly go elsewhere. Availability spells dependability. That means you are placing heavy dependence on your network being up and running and all applications working as they should be. This sort of system is commonly referred to as *mission critical* because it is critical to the mission of the company that it's available 99% of the time.

Denial of Service (DoS) attacks have become more prevalent in recent years as the tools required to launch such an attack are easy to come by and many people don't realize that their computers are unwitting accomplices in these attacks. A *distributed denial of service* (DDoS) attack is where numerous machines begin swamping one network with requests so that legitimate requests can't be processed. The individual machines participating in the attack have become infected with a Trojan horse that launches the attack. Anti-virus software is good at recognizing and removing these programs from your machines.

It's difficult to prevent a DoS or DDoS attack but there are some things you can do to ensure that you are less vulnerable to such problems:

  ✔ Ensure that your routers and firewalls will forward only IP packets if those packets have the correct source IP Address for your network. The source IP Address is the one that has been legally assigned to your network.

✔ Configure all of your systems (routers, workstations, servers, and so on) so that they do not receive or forward Directed Broadcast traffic. Set "no ip directed-broadcast" on each interface on the router that has an ip address. Many routers forward this traffic by default.

✔ Install software patches as soon as they become available. Some vendors have released patches that make their applications less susceptible to DoS attacks.

✔ Examine your own systems to make sure that DoS utilities have not been installed on your systems. You could be the source of DoS attacks and not even be aware of it.

Situations other than a DoS attack can bring your network to its knees. Abnormally high traffic, possibly due to a national promotion, can also flood your network with so many requests for data that the network cannot respond. It's like getting a "trunk busy" signal on the phone when you try to call your mother on Mother's Day. Outages often occur when a router has been misconfigured or routing tables get corrupted. In those cases the network ends up acting like a bird that has inadvertently flown into your house — the traffic flits around crazily, bumping into all sorts of things, trying to find its way back out again. There's not much you can do about the Internet having routing problems, but you can ensure that your own routers are correctly configured and maintained.

You can also help ensure availability by incorporating three things:

✔ Redundancy

✔ Redundancy

✔ Redundancy

Did I mention redundancy?

Redundant systems ensure availability by taking over the work when one or more systems fail. Some redundant systems rely upon *caching* in which each mechanism constantly keeps track of its "sister" systems and can take up where the sisters left off if and when they fail. The other type of redundant system maintains a *heartbeat* in which it constantly monitors whether or not the sister systems are online. If and when the other system fails, the backup takes over. The main difference between the two is that the first type is essentially a mirror and it runs in tandem with the sisters. The second type is essentially asleep until it needs to take over and will have to reinitiate recent transactions and requests.

The systems you should consider for redundancy are as follows (see Figure 18-2):

- ✔ Routers
- ✔ Firewalls
- ✔ Web servers
- ✔ Application servers
- ✔ Databases

Figure 18-2:
An example
of a totally
redundant
e-commerce
system.

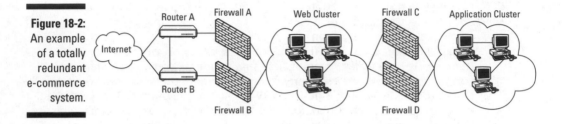

Obtaining Client Data

The Web is a funny creature because it is *stateless*. That doesn't mean it doesn't belong to a country and can't get a passport, but it means that the connections between a browser and a Web server are made without opening a consistent, constant connection between the two. Each bit of text and all of the graphics come to the browser through individual requests and connections. The Web server doesn't recognize, or care, that all the requests are coming from the same place. Therefore, in the logs of the Web server, one connection may look like many. A connection that maintains *state* is like a telephone call — it remains open and connected until one side or the other terminates the connection. The state of the connection also logs the locations of each end.

Cookies

One method to get a Web server to maintain state with an individual browser is by setting *cookies*. A cookie is simply a small text file stored in the browser's cache. The file contains the name of the Web site that wants to maintain state and a series of numbers that works as a type of identification number. When the browser makes a request of the Web server, the Web server will first look to see if it has left a cookie on the browser during a previous visit. If it finds one, it updates it and uses it again. If the Web server does not find a cookie, then it attempts to place one in the cache.

So, why this discussion of cookies in the e-commerce section? Simply put, if someone is placing an order through a Web site, the Web server has to recognize that all the page requests are coming from the same place. If there are no cookies, an ordering process could not be tracked. The cookie contains information like a session number and a temporary listing of the contents of a shopping cart. Cookies can also be used to hold names, addresses, phone numbers, and credit card numbers. That, however, is not considered a good practice.

If you must use a cookie to track a customer and intend to store confidential information in the cookie, it's best to use *encrypted non-persistent* cookies. An encrypted cookie can only be read by the Web server that contains the decryption algorithm. The file that is stored in the browser contains no data that can be considered "readable" by anyone who opens the cookie to have a look. A persistent cookie remains in the browser cache for a long time while a non-persistent cookie is deleted as soon as the session is completed. If the user is not allowing his browser to use cookies, the data is stored in the URL as a search query, which goes away when the user is finished with the session. In any regard, the cookie data is temporary and not recognizable as useable data by an intruder.

SSL

Another consideration on obtaining data from a client is that all the data sent and received is clear text. That is not something you want to be doing if your customers are sending you confidential information such as credit card numbers, social security numbers, or bank account information. In that case you will probably want to implement *SSL* or Secure Sockets Layer protocol. SSL makes it easy to encrypt data and pass it between Web browsers and Web servers because it has become a standard in almost all products.

SSL moves the traffic from port 80, which is used for http, to port 443 for https. It exchanges a set of keys for encryption and authentication and encrypts all traffic on that port until the session ends. You'll notice the change when you connect to a site using SSL because the URL will change from "http://" to "https://" and a lock or key will appear in the bottom of your browser window. This indicates that the session is being securely transmitted. You can also force a secure session to begin in the cookie by using the "setSecure( )" attribute in the cookie. If you set the attribute with *mySessionCookie*.setSecure(true), the session cookie is only transmitted if the connection is secure. If the session is not secure, the cookie is not sent and the session does not continue.

SSL adds some overhead to the processing of Web pages because it is encrypting and decrypting the pages as they are transferred. Customers will frequently notice the slow-down and think that the connection has been interrupted or stopped, which creates problems in the ordering process. It's important that your Web servers have more than enough processing power and memory to handle SSL or you will find that your customers frequently just give up and go elsewhere.

Secure forms

In order to get the data from the Web browser to the Web server, the customer is usually going to have to fill in some sort of form and then send the data back to the Web server. These forms are also used to store the details of the ensuing sale by storing the parameters that include the item's name, weight, quantity, product ID, and price Many times the Web forms have been designed to use *hidden forms,* which hide the information from the user. There is a known vulnerability in using these forms and it is known as the *hidden form field vulnerability*. What happens is that a person stores the ordering page to their hard drive, goes into the source code of the page, and changes the prices (or other important data), and then sends the page back to the Web server. As far as the Web server knows, everything is OK and the order is processed, especially if the credit card number is processed in real time because there is no time to verify the product cost.

The easiest way to prevent this sort of abuse is not to use hidden forms in your pages. If this is not possible, then you must validate all the data that is sent via a form. You should do this anyway, just to double-check that the data is correct. Another method is to encrypt all the hidden form fields and encrypt the CGI program information contained in the HTML code. Most of the newer shopping cart programs have implemented fixes for the hidden form field vulnerability, but many of the older ones (circa 1998) are still susceptible.

In either case, you'll need to have a CGI program to interpret the data from the forms and convert it from html to something that a database can read and understand. As mentioned in Chapter 15, CGI programs are prone to abuse and misuse. Here are some rules for creating CGI programs:

- **Know your code.** If you haven't written the code yourself, you should be able to recognize all the behaviors of the code. Put comments in your code so others know what you are trying to accomplish.

- **Check all the values provided by the user.** This is done by checking all the arguments. Not only will this help prevent malicious use of the CGI program, it will help catch errors in the user's input.

- **Check all arguments that you pass to the system.** Don't allow an argument unless you know what it is doing. For example, you don't want the program to open up files that it shouldn't.

✔ **Restrict the variables.** If a variable string like a zip code should only have numbers, then make sure that only numbers will be accepted. This also helps with errors from user input.

✔ **Test your program.** Be sure to test it in conditions that are as close as possible to real-life.

✔ **Don't allow your program to do a core dump.** Not only can core dumps quickly fill up a file system, they can leak confidential data to an intruder.

✔ **Put time-outs in your scripts.** If the session hangs or if there is some sort of interruption, make the script expire.

✔ **Avoid having your program run as a superuser or root.** It's better to create a special user and group for your programs to run under.

Secure Storage

Many e-commerce sites have gone to the trouble of making sure that the data transfer between the Web browser and the Web server is secure by using SSL or other encryption mechanisms. What is disturbing is that many of these same sites do nothing to make sure that the data is secure once it gets to them. In my work as a consultant I have found databases stored in the open that anyone in the company has access to. You don't have to worry about a hacker in that case — the data is just there for the taking. The employees of the company knew that this database contained personal information including credit cards and bank accounts and the only thing keeping them from stealing this data was their own sense of honesty. Unfortunately, we need to do more than that to help employees and former employees remain honest. Your security shouldn't stop once the data reaches your doors.

First of all, all databases or stored data should be kept in a locked, secure room. This doesn't mean controlling a door with a cipher lock in which everyone knows the code, either. I mean really secure with limited access. Once someone has physical access to the database or stored data, you also have to make sure that the person can't make copies of the data and walk out the door with floppies or a writeable CD. It's also a good idea to make sure that employees aren't allowed to take handbags, backpacks, and so on in and out of the room. If personal belongings are allowed in, they must be searched when the employee comes out.

Ideally, secure storage means putting it behind a firewall and encrypting the data. The firewall will help to ensure that only legitimate users are allowed access via the network and the encrypting makes sure that the data isn't easily read. This is such a simple solution but it's still one of the largest problems with e-commerce. At least monthly I get an alert about an employee or former employee has accessed a credit card database and walked away with tens of thousands of card numbers. If it's this easy for employees to get in, then it isn't that much harder for a hacker to get in either.

This goes back to the issue of confidentiality. You need to protect the confidentiality of your customers and that of your own data. Customers are getting fed up with inadvertent releases of data and you don't want to be on the wrong end of a lawsuit if you haven't done enough to ensure security.

Configuration Control

This is a big buzz phrase that will be familiar to any of you involved in government contracting. It means establishing a configuration baseline and then controlling any and all changes to the baseline. Usually, only certain people are allowed to make changes and they have to have permission from a change committee before they are allowed to make any changes. It certainly makes good sense to incorporate this sort of control in e-commerce.

You have many components involved in your e-commerce system: Web servers, application servers, databases, and programming scripts. Changes to any one of these parts can affect the whole. Therefore, it's important to document everything you have and how it was created to develop your baseline. Once you have your baseline established, and this can take a long time, then you need to control who can make changes, how they can make them, when and where. If you have a change team and a change committee, they all need to have rules and policies with which to work under. Just giving someone arbitrary control defeats the entire purpose.

The documentation should be maintained for every step. This is particularly important for when you make changes that don't work. You need to know what you did so you can undo it. This also includes documenting the steps you took for reversing changes you have made (called *backing out)*. Changes don't always go as planned and it's easy to forget what you did during the heat of the moment. Then, when you get ready to make the change again, you can make sure you don't make the same mistakes.

All changes need to be controlled. This includes everything from a new hard drive installation to a security patch being applied. Not only will this help you to maintain a secure system, it also helps identify problems when things do go wrong.

Part V
Dealing with the Unthinkable

The 5th Wave   By Rich Tennant

Now maybe these folks got a decent disaster recovery plan and maybe they don't...

DANGER
WILD RHINOCEROS

In this part . . .

In spite of the best-laid plans, stuff happens — we're human and mistakes *will* happen. We can't possibly control everything, no matter how much we try. But if the unfortunate occurs, it's not the end of the world. Just remember that bad things have happened to other companies' networks, and they have recovered and moved on.

In this section, you discover how to plan for the inevitable to make it a little less horrible. With proper plans of action, a disaster doesn't have to mean total disaster for your network. You'll read about the tried-and-true measures for controlling bad situations and about how to discover who did the bad deeds.

Chapter 19

Emergency! Incident Response

· ·

· ·

*N*o matter how careful you are and no matter how secure your systems are, bad things happen. Electronic components fail. Software can be found to be buggy. People make mistakes. And, just sometimes, people make mischief with intent to do harm to the network. Nature can affect whether your network works or not, too. All of these situations require that you respond to the emergency at hand quickly and efficiently. This is not the time to be running around like headless chickens. You must be prepared. The best way to be prepared is to have a Computer Emergency Response Team — also known as a CERT — ready to take action. A well prepared CERT is able to handle any emergency, whether the situation is man-made or not.

Take one look at the statistics in Table 19-1 and you'll think a mistake must have been made. Here is just a snippet of reported incidents from CERT at Carnegie Mellon University. These statistics reflect the increases in man-made computer incidents that involved security.

Table 19-1	Computer Emergency Statistics
Year	*Number of Computer Incidents Reported*
1989	132
1991	406
1995	2,412
1998	3,734

(continued)

Table 19-1 *(continued)*	
Year	*Number of Computer Incidents Reported*
1999	9,859
2000	21,756
2001	52,658
2002 (1st and 2nd qtrs only)	43,136

Amazing, isn't it? I would have expected the number of attacks to have started leveling off by now, but the reverse seems to be true. The number of attacks seem to be doubling or tripling every year.

The increase in numbers isn't due only to the number of attacks. Yes, it's easier to hack some systems now, and more people have the tools to launch attacks, but there are other reasons for this increase in numbers. For one, more companies are taking security seriously and reporting incidents that they would have otherwise ignored. Many companies were afraid to report past abuses for fear of adverse publicity. Now they realize that by reporting incidents, they do a service to the business community to get the word out. Another reason for the increase in numbers is that more system administrators know what to look for and can recognize an attack. To be honest, it's very difficult to know at first glance if you are seeing an attack or some sort of network anomaly. Of all the incidents I've responded to, probably 85 percent to 90 percent were actually problems of network failures and misconfigurations and not actual attacks.

In this chapter, I look at the steps to take during a suspected attack, the tools you need to discover an attack, and what is expected of a response team. You'll need to do a lot of planning and testing to prepare yourself for this eventuality, and this chapter can help take the sting out of getting burned.

What Is a CERT?

CERT stands for Computer Emergency Response Team and is sometimes also referred to as a *CIRT* — Computer Incident Response Team. Whichever way you spell it, these are the Ghostbusters of computer networks. They find the bad stuff and root it out. Not to totally confuse you, the CERT I'm talking about in this chapter is not the CERT at Carnegie Mellon University. The CERT I'm referring to is one that you will set up to handle emergencies within your own organization.

Contrary to popular belief, the CERT at Carnegie Mellon University in Pennsylvania does not actually *respond* to computer emergencies. It is simply a non-profit, educational organization that collects reports of computer abuse and gives advice. In my opinion, the team members all deserve medals of honor for the good work they do. They are under-paid and over-worked but dedicated to helping us get through computer crisis. I can't think of a better place to educate yourself than by regularly perusing their Web site at www.cert.org/nav/index.html.

The business model of a Computer Emergency Response Team is to *respond* to the emergencies much the same way firefighters and police do. They respond, identify the situation, isolate the area, and go to work. And because no one ever knows how long it will take to contain an emergency situation, they frequently work long, hard hours under tremendous stress. Frequently a team will sit around for long periods making busy work before they have the opportunity to respond to action. It's like six weeks of sitting around followed by six days of sheer adrenaline.

CERTs consist of highly skilled people who vary in their areas of expertise but are cross-trained to cover any eventuality. They need to have an in-depth understanding of networking, operating systems, and applications so they can recognize when something is awry. They need to be able to identify viruses and eradication techniques. They need to know hacking techniques, system vulnerabilities, and how to use many cross-platform network tools. Some of these tools are actually hacking tools and others are used to discover system intrusions. CERT members need to be able to work as a team and be cool under pressure. They also need to be able to communicate with others who don't have as high a level of understanding as they do. This is important to be able to give status reports and to recommend changes in security to prevent further occurrences.

Because CERT team members are so highly skilled, a company can't afford to hire a CERT team just to sit around for months on end doing nothing. The team members usually have full-time jobs doing something other than emergency response, for example, security officers, system administrators, and network technicians. Rarely do they ever hold more than supervisory or middle-management positions. However, when they are responding to a critical situation, they need to have the authority and autonomy to make executive level decisions. The life of your business may depend upon quick decisions.

You should have a section in your security policies and procedures document that spells out your company's arrangements for a CERT, regardless if it is in-house or outsourced. The roles and responsibilities should be clearly stated as well as who should call the team to action and when they should be called. For more information on security policies and procedures, refer to Chapter 4.

Responding Responsibly

Your network has been acting funny lately or you've seen some strange things that make you believe an intruder is in your network. The first item on the agenda is **Don't Panic**! Call in your CERT as soon as you can. Chances are that the intruder has been in there for some time, but this is just the first time you've noticed. Intruders are like roach infestations — they don't just happen overnight. Running around wildly is not going to get rid of the pest as he's probably watching what you do and getting ready to run. The CERT will take their time and work systematically to get rid of the nuisance. And unless they notice that files on your servers are being destroyed at an alarming rate, they will not shut down your network. Take some deep Yoga breaths, release the bad feelings, and let them get to work.

There are some basic steps you need to do before the CERT comes in and starts to work. These steps may vary slightly in order, depending on the situation. For example, in some cases you may call in the CERT before you notify company executives because it's more important to get the team working first. In any case, do all the following steps and don't omit anything. First and foremost, however — **Don't turn off or reboot any systems.** This could hamper the recovery process.

1. **Start taking notes.**

   Don't start typing commands like crazy trying to find the intruder. Let the CERT do that. It's more important at this point that you get a new notebook and write down everything you've noticed and what you did. It's very important that you record the time and date of *everything*. This notebook may become crucial evidence in legal proceedings later.

2. **Notify upper management.**

   Do not send e-mail messages as they could tip off the intruder. Hopefully you had prepared a call-sheet ahead of time with the names and phone numbers of those who need to know. The most effective way of handling the notification is for you to call two people and then have them call the rest of the list. Otherwise, you could spend hours on the phone explaining the situation over and over to dozens of people. Time is precious and should be spent on the emergency — not on hand-holding.

3. **Call in your CERT.**

   Do this quietly and without fanfare. You don't want the entire company's work to come to a standstill because you've called a general alarm. When the CERT gets there, brief them and then leave them alone to do their jobs.

4. **Enforce a "need-to-know" policy.**

   Don't tell employees something is up unless they really need to know. The intruder may have an inside accomplice, or it could be a false alarm and not an intrusion. You don't want idle gossip getting outside the office to your customers, the press, or your competitors. You can always say that the company is experiencing "network problems" as most people will accept that explanation without further questions.

5. **Someone in the company should be the point person in case word gets made public.**

   If you have a PR department, that's their job. You don't want a media storm on hand, so only the appointed person or persons are allowed to talk to the press and customers. Sometimes an incident isn't an incident at all but a misconfiguration in the network. Remind the press and the public that things aren't always as they seem.

6. **Give support to your CERT.**

   They probably work long hard hours without breaks. Make sure they get meals and refreshments sent into them. (This may mean more than just Cokes and candy bars.) If relief team members are needed, put them on alert and set up a shift schedule. Enforce the schedule, too. Many team members will be reluctant to give up their posts, but they can easily burn out after a day or two. If the team is in need of more equipment such as spare disk drives and network devices, get them quickly.

7. **Contact your legal department.**

   Let them know the situation. They can decide if any laws have been broken. If they advise you to contact law enforcement, do so.

8. **Conduct briefings and meetings after the clean-up.**

   Tell everyone what happened and why and what you can/have/will do to make sure it doesn't happen again. Don't point fingers; learn from your mistakes.

Make no mistake that this will be a stressful affair for many and that tempers can and will flare. Don't fall into the trap of getting so caught up in the moment that you forget what you're supposed to be doing. Remember, when you're up to your behind in alligators, you're first objective is to drain the swamp!

Advance Preparation

Hopefully you've anticipated that an intrusion may happen and you already have an CERT identified, rules of engagement established, and ammunition ready to do combat. If you haven't done this in advance, then your job is just going to be more stressful and take a little longer.

If you haven't already done so, install Tripwire on all of your systems that can support it. This program takes a "snapshot" of all important files and programs and stores them as a binary value. When changes are made to the files or programs, their values change. If you need to see if a file or program has been changed, you can compare the Tripwire value against the present value. If the two values are not the same, then something has been altered. (Tripwire can be configured to alert you when something has changed.)

The most important part of the advance planning is to prepare master copies of all operating software, application software, customized programs, and a tool kit to help you root out the changes that have been made to your system and where the compromise occurred. Why is this important? Because the modus operandi of hackers is that, after they've gained entry, to immediately change key parts of the operating system to allow them to roam through the system and collect data as they go.

When a system is compromised, hackers usually install Trojan horse programs to replace common commands. These Trojans look and act just like the real programs that they replace, and they are the sometimes the same programs that the CERT needs to use to track the intrusion and lock it out. Therefore it's extremely important that the tool kit contains verifiably clean command programs. Some of the most commonly compromised command programs are as follows:

- ✔ telnet
- ✔ login
- ✔ su
- ✔ ftp
- ✔ ls
- ✔ ps
- ✔ netstat
- ✔ ifconfig
- ✔ find
- ✔ du
- ✔ df
- ✔ libc
- ✔ sync

Many directories and files will have been changed as well, but I'll get to that later on.

Notice that the commands I've listed previously are Unix commands, although some of these commands are available on Windows machines, too.

Although most intruders initially obtain entry through a hole in an unpatched Windows operating system or application, many large networks still contain a core of Unix machines working as servers. The attacker goes straight to those machines. Windows-based Trojan horses make many of the same changes that a Unix Trojan does but need to be detected and removed with other tools.

Using a recent back-up to restore the system isn't a good idea because you don't know how long your system has been compromised. If you use a backup, you may simply replace the Trojanized programs with the same Trojans, which is why it's so very important to have CDs in your toolkit with verifiably clean programs. When you re-install these programs, you effectively remove the back doors that the intruder has left and lock him out again — at least temporarily.

You need software tools in your incident kit to help track what's going on in the network and what's being changed. Many of these tools are Unix-based, and for that reason it's usually a good idea to have a couple of laptops handy that are running a version of Unix so the CERT can plug these into the network to do their work. There are literally tons of tools, but Table 19-2 shows a list of programs that should be included in the CERT tool kit. Most of these programs are freeware and shareware, and all have good reputations.

Table 19-2	Incident Response Tool Kit
Tool	*Use*
Autopsy	An HTML interface to TASK (see following) that automates forensic analysis.
Byte Back	Disk imaging tool for Windows.
Chkrootkit	Checks for root kits installed on your systems.
Cpm	Program to check for possible network sniffers by looking for promiscuous interfaces.
Cryptcat	Encryption enabled netcat utility. (See netcat, following.)
Dd	Disk to Disk Dump utility copies data block by block. Used to make back-ups.
ddos-scan dds	Program to scan for distributed denial of service (DDoS) tools.
dnsiff	A collection of network auditing and penetration testing tools
EtherApe	Network traffic visualization tool.
Ethereal	A Windows or Unix tool for analyzing protocols.
Ettercap	A sniffer, interceptor, and logger of network traffic.

(continued)

Table 19-2 *(continued)*

Tool	Use
Firewalk	Checks for rules and access control lists (ACLs) on network devices.
Hexedit	A hex editor reader that allows you to read hex dumps in ASCII format.
Ifstatus	Program to check for possible network sniffers by looking for promiscuous interfaces.
Hogwash	A packet scrubber to detect malicious packets.
Iptraf	A IP monitor that gives you statistics of IP traffic on your network.
mac-robber	Program that collects Modified, Access, and Change (MAC) times from files.
Nessus	A security scanner that identifies all ports and services running and tests them for vulnerabilities.
NAT	NetBIOS Auditing Tool scans Windows systems for NetBIOS shares.
Nmap	Port scanner and network device discovery checker. Identifies operating system versions and which firewalls are in use.
POf	Passive OS detection that maps foreign networks.
PsTools	A collection of response tools for Windows machines including 2000 and XP.
Snort	Intrusion detection tool for both Unix and Windows machines.
TASK	The @Stake Sleuth Kit is a collection of tools for forensics and investigations.
tcpdump	Dumps all the TCP traffic to a file.
tcpreplay	Can replay real background network traffic.
tcptraceroute	A traceroute utility that uses TCP SYN packets instead of UDP or ICMP.
TCT	The Coroner's Toolkit is a collection of tools for forensics.
TCTUTILS	Add-ins to the TCT.
user2sid	A Windows command line program to find the SID of a user and vice versa.

All the tools mentioned in Table 19-2 should be in their complete and compiled format so they are ready to install. Not all of these tools will be used in every case, but it's always better to have them all just in case. Check with the leader of your CERT to see if he or she has other tools that they consider "must-haves." Review the contents of the tool kit at least once a year to make sure that you have the latest version of these tools, too.

Heading into the Fray

This section deals with the actual nuts and bolts of looking for an intrusion and fixing the problem. If you're not an uber-geek, this section will probably be Greek to you and you needn't read it all. However, the CERT members should not only be able to understand the following, but be able to recite it by heart as well. This is their Bible.

Step one: The beginning

Before anyone touches a keyboard or anything else, the CERT needs to establish who is in charge of what. It's important that one person be the undisputed chief, one person be deputized to act as a liaison with management to give status reports, and one person be assigned as the recording secretary. The chief gives the orders, the liaison keeps the rest of the company informed and off the backs of the CERT members who are trying to do their jobs, and the recording secretary takes notes of anything and everything and is sure to time- and date-stamp everything.(Not only does dating everything help the CERT from duplicating efforts, but if they have to retrace their steps, they at least know where they've already been. In addition, these notes may become important evidence in a trial.)

When the roles have been established, get rid of all unnecessary personnel. You want to secure the area and get rid of visitors and gawkers. This includes upper management — no matter how important they are to the company, if they can't contribute anything to the team, they will only get in the way.

Under no circumstances are the CERT members to use electronic communications! The intruder may be listening and watching for signs that he has been discovered, and he may have the ability to ready all e-mails. If the CERT uses e-mail to communicate what they are doing, they may inadvertently tip their hand to him. Make good use of telephones, pen and paper, and fax machines.

The next step for the CERT is to sit down and interview the person who made the discovery and decided to call an emergency. In addition to knowing who discovered the problem, they need to find out what was discovered and how it was discovered. The more information they can get, the better as it saves them from second-guessing later on.

Step two: Making backups

Before any changes are made to the system and before any intrusion detection begins, they will make an *image* backup of all the affected systems. The CERT doesn't yet know what has been done or when it was done, so they can use the image backup as a snapshot in time to show the state of the network at the time of the discovery.

An image backup is the best choice because it includes all the existing, deleted, and changed files. If the CERT simply zips or tars the entire set of systems, these programs will copy only the data and not the actual blocks as they are located on the disk. (Zip and tar are file compression utilities.) The utility *dd,* which stands for Disk to Disk Dump, is ideal for this and should be on the CERT incident tool kit CD.

Before the CERT begins the backup, they should run the *ps* command and dump the results to a file. This gives them a list of all the processes that are running at that time. They should also run the *netstat* command with the option to report all open connections and dump the results to a file. When they do the backup, they should remember to include swap files and all files in all *temp* or *tmp* directories.

The imaged disks may be needed later for forensic analysis and should be protected as potential evidence. If the CERT need an image from which to compare changes to the system, then they should create two images: one for immediate secure storage to protect the chain of custody and the other to use for their comparisons and analysis.

It's important for them to protect the *chain of custody*. That is, who handled the evidence from the time it was found to the time it was presented to the authorities. If the team makes backups that many people have had access to, then their chain of custody is effectively destroyed because anyone could have made changes to it. The best thing to do is for the team to put the tapes or disks in a large envelope, seal it with tape around all seams, and two people sign their names with dates on the outside package. That package should then go in a locked safe. In doing this they have protected the integrity of their backups and the courts will be more likely to accept the tapes as evidence.

Step three: Rebooting

This is a controversial step because rebooting your system can destroy evidence that the forensic team could use to identify the intruder. However, the

CERT is not a forensic team and their job is to fix the problem and not necessarily to do "police" work. If you cannot get a forensic team in immediately, your CERT will probably have to reboot the system. In order to regain control of your machines, they will have to do this to boot the intruder off the network. This usually make the intruder run for the hills, but at least the CERT should have enough data now to find out what he has changed and how he got in. The easiest and most effective method is for them to reboot individual machines in *single user mode* or as the *local administrator*. Doing this prevents others from accessing or changing things on the target computer. If the CERT leaves the machine connected and running on the network, they could have the intruder walking right behind them and undoing their changes and no one would ever know. If the CERT decide not to reboot the computer, they should disconnect it from the network (if possible) and wait for the forensic team to take over.

Step four: Analyzing the intrusion

This is one of the most time-consuming and arduous tasks. At this point, the CERT has to run through all the files and directories in the operating system to see what, if anything, has been changed. If you had Tripwire installed ahead of time, their job will be a lot easier because they will have a baseline with which to compare the present files and programs. If Tripwire was not installed, you can check with the vendors to see if they keep *MD5 checksums* of their programs and the CERT can use those for comparison. If they can't determine whether or not changes have been made to a file or program, then they are going to have to reinstall it from scratch.

Once the intrusion has been fixed, now is the time for the CERT to install clean versions of the commands and tools that they will need to begin their analysis. If these items have been compromised with a rootkit, they can't trust their output. (A rootkit is a Trojan program that replaces normally used commands with Trojanized commands.) The CERT will copy these utilities from the original installation media or from clean copies on the tool kit CD. It's also important that these utilities be installed with *absolute links* as opposed to symbolic links.

You don't find much of this in Windows, but absolute and symbolic links are very common in Unix. Absolute links are directory or file listings that contain the complete directory path. A symbolic link is sort of like an aliased name or a short-cut and they don't contain the complete directory path. Absolute links take up more disk storage but it's safer to specify these links because symbolic links can be incorrect. If using a symbolic link can't be avoided, then the operating system can be forced to recognize the absolute link by adding a *load path* in the start up routines and libraries. A load path is very similar to the autoexec.bat file that DOS systems use to define paths to files and programs.

When the CERT has gotten these items in place, they will start nosing around the system. Some of the important things they will examine are

- Check that the SAM (Windows password file) or /etc/passwd file don't have entries that don't belong or look suspicious.
- Check to see if the /etc/inetd.conf file has been changed to turn services back on that had been disabled.
- Check to see what programs start at logon and look for suspicious or unknown programs.
- Check the /etc/host.equiv file for suspicious looking entries. These could identify other compromised systems.
- Check the .rhosts files for any entries not recognized. The .rhosts files can help identify other compromised systems or the system where the intruder launched his attack.
- Check for files with new SUIDs or new SGIDs.
- Check the users lists for odd users or group memberships.
- Check for changes in the registry (Windows only).
- Check for unauthorized and/or hidden shares.
- Check the integrity of files in Web pages, ftp archives, and users' home directories.
- Check for files or directories that begin with two or three dots (like ".." or "..."). Sometimes compromised files will begin with a space and then a series of dots.
- Look for files that begin with a space and then have recognizable, common names such as "(space)iexplore.exe".
- Check all processes running and see if there are any that look suspicious.

For all anomalies seen, the CERT will change them back to the original settings and will make note of everything else they do.

The CERT will also need to look for tools and data left behind by the intruder. Sometimes they may find these just by nosing around. Other times they may have to use some utilities from their tool kit. Some of the programs and files they will look for are

- Network sniffers that capture packets of network traffic
- Trojan horse programs
- Back doors
- Rootkits
- Log files

Frequently these things have been placed in hidden directories, or unusual places such as the devices directory. A good CERT will leave no stone unturned. If they don't look, they could be bypassing the one backdoor the intruder left behind.

The CERT will be getting close to the end of their search now and will review all the logs on the system. They will look for anything that strikes them as out of the ordinary. They will hard copy these logs, highlight the suspicious activity, and keep them with their written notes. Some log files appear in strange places, and they may have to check with the vendor to see where some of these unusual logs are kept. Windows systems generally dump all their logs in one place.

If, during the CERT's research and examination of the system, they may realize that other networks have been infiltrated. The correct course of action is to contact the administrators of those networks to let them know that their systems may have been compromised. If the other systems have been compromised, then the intruder may be able to walk back in to yours. I've seen this happen many times. Typically an attacker doesn't confine himself to just one system; he hops from network to network using compromised computers. Intruders hide their tracks and leave as many back doors as possible.

Let the designated liaison do the calling and of the other networks. The CERT's time is better spent at the keyboard right now. If, during the course of notifying other network owners that they may have been compromised, the liaison runs into an administrator who doesn't believe him, then he should not just give up. Just because that administrator doesn't cooperate doesn't mean that future security has to be sacrificed. In the past I have gone up the chain of command until I found someone who was willing to listen to me. The liaison should not scream and threaten people, but offer to help, and explain the consequences of a security breach to them. Sometimes all it takes is a soft voice and a lot of educating!

At this point the CERT should have a good idea where the attack originated. If it was from an external site, they will have to decide whether or not it's worth the risk to sever your network connections at the firewall. If the attack was internal, they can isolate the subnet where the attack originated. If it's feasible to take the entire network offline — at least overnight — the recovery will be that much quicker. Otherwise, the CERT have to slowly disable the network by taking individual computers offline until they are all fixed. They can't just fix a computer and throw it back on the network — it could be compromised again.

Step five: Rebuilding

Now that the CERT have identified and documented all the changes made to the offline system, they will have to restore it to its former, pristine state. The best source for clean operating systems are the original installation disks. Backups should not be used for restoration because the backups could contain compromises.

The CERT will have to reformat the disks and reinstall the operating systems and applications on all affected computers. They should harden the operating systems and applications by disabling all unnecessary services and installing the most recent security patches. They should change all default passwords, too. It's especially important that they close the holes that allowed the attack to happen in the first place. (See Chapters 12, 13, 14, and 15 for more on hardening your system and applying patches.)

The CERT will also have to restore the data files and some of the former configuration files. Before they restore the password files, they should make sure the permissions are correct and that there are no accounts with blank passwords. When they are restoring the data files, they should make sure they aren't overwriting files that you have already made changes to like the /etc/inetd.conf file.

The CERT will also enable the maximum monitoring and logging allowed by the system. They should make sure there is enough disk space for this as logs grow in size very quickly.

They should not put the machine back online until this process has been completed for all compromised computers. If you put computers back online too soon, the intruder may just come back and do what he did before.

Step six: Reviewing access devices

The CERT should review with you all of your ACLs on your firewalls, routers, and intrusion detection systems. Sometimes the compromise was initially made at the firewall or router because of a security holes or incorrect ACL on those mechanisms. The CERT should ensure that all devices have fresh copies of the ACLs and that all the rules are correct. Security patches should be applied to these devices as well.

Step seven: Back online

When they get ready to bring the network back up and online, they should do it slowly — one subnet at a time. If they try to do everything all at once, they may overload the system. It's like when the power goes out in your house during a storm. If you left the TV, the lights, the dishwasher, and everything else all on, when the power comes back, it creates a huge surge that can blow the circuits again. Trying to bring a network back online can create a similar surge to the routers that may cause them to overload.

Once the system is back online, the CERT should turn the system back over to its normal administrators. This is also a good time for all users to be forced to change their passwords. You can't be sure that the intruder didn't get all your password files, so don't give him an open invitation to come back in. There are numerous ways to force users to change their passwords the next time they log on — check the instructions for your particular OS to accomplish this.

Your administrators should begin monitoring all the logs again as soon as you are back online. They should watch for an increase in traffic, or for files that are growing quickly in size. They will be looking for signs that the intruder has come back.

Back to Normal

Whew! After all that you and your CERT deserve a two-week paid vacation in the Bahamas! There is still a little bit of work left to do yet, but it's not nearly as difficult. Keep the CERT involved in some of these steps. You may need them around to explain what happened and what was done to fix the problems.

1. **Report the incident to the CERT Coordination Center at Carnegie Mellon.**

   They have forms online for you to use and all data is kept confidential. Your report helps them determine if this is a new attack or if it matches a previous pattern. In any case, it helps everyone when you make a report. The online form can be pulled up and printed out from `www.cert.org/reporting/incident_form.txt`.

2. **Debrief all concerned parties within the company.**

   Have a "lessons learned" meeting and come up with appropriate changes. Not only can you learn what went wrong, you can also pat yourselves on the back for things you did correctly.

3. **Make changes to your security policies and procedures.**

   There will always be that one little thing you wish you had done differently. Document it and make it part of the overall plan.

4. **Calculate the cost of the incident.**

   This includes salary and wages, equipment, lost revenue, and damages. By calculating the cost of the emergency, you validate the money spent on the response. It also helps you to explain to upper management why money needs to be budgeted for security.

5. **Check with the legal department to see you have enough evidence to bring charges.**

   This step can actually occur at many different places during the response process and it depends on the severity of the attack. Local law enforcement and/or the local FBI field office may have been notified earlier, too. However, if none of was this done before now, this is the time to consider doing it. You may also want to report your incident to InfraGard, which is a joint government-private industry initiative to track and report incidents. All reports are kept confidential. You can find more information at `www.infragard.net/ireporting.htm`.

You've survived the attack and you're stronger for it. Get some rest and hope for a nice raise for all of your good work!

Chapter 20

Disaster Recovery

*N*o one wants it to happen to them. No one thinks it will happen to them. But, every year, it does happen to someone. Disaster. If you value your business, and you want to keep it going during and after a disaster, you have to plan as if it could happen every day. Statistics in a report done by Information Security News (www.infosecnews.com) in 1998 show that over half of the businesses that don't recover within ten days of a disaster eventually go out of business.

It's impossible to plan for every disaster type and situation, but what you can do is to plan for the service outages that are likely to occur — power, water, communications, and the like. You also have to consider that it may not be *your* disaster but one occurring somewhere else. A tornado that takes out a major network center could mean that you won't have communication capabilities until your provider gets up and running again. When the World Trade Center Towers collapsed on September 11, it took out Verizon's capability to send and receive cell phone signals for a large portion of the Northeast.

The key to all this is to actually have a *plan*. Even a rough outline is better than nothing. Developing a plan isn't fun, but it isn't that hard, either. It takes some time and, during the development, you may actually realize that your company can do things more effectively and efficiently.

In this chapter, I look at the different parts of a disaster recovery plan. Each part is separate but together they create a comprehensive plan to anticipating disasters, dealing with disasters of all types, and getting back to normal operations as quickly as possible. In researching for each portion of the plan, you will come to recognize situations and opportunities that you may have otherwise overlooked. A good plan is a complete walk-through from beginning to end.

Business Impact Analysis

Although it's difficult to imagine every possible disaster that could affect your business, it's important to try to imagine how these disasters may affect your company's ability to cope with the matter. This is done with a *business impact analysis* or *BIA*. It's roughly the same sort of analysis that went into the risk analysis for your network security plan. It's a part of your total disaster plan. You list the threats and vulnerabilities, assess the likelihood of them happening to you, how it would affect your operations, and try to come up with a dollar amount that would result from the incident. Like your security vulnerability assessment, you also take into consideration how many times a year each disaster is likely to happen so you can determine an *annual loss expectancy* (ALE). This shows you what disasters you can survive and what will destroy you. In each case you imagine the worst-case scenario. If you can survive the worst case, then you know you can easily survive minor- and medium-level crises.

Threats and vulnerabilities can come in three forms: natural, man-made, and technical. I've included Table 20-1) to help you to understand how to categorize various threats. A natural threat is like a tornado or flood while a man-made threat is like a bomb threat or arson. A technical threat is a power outage or loss of communications line. When you list all the threats, you also describe your company's vulnerabilities to that threat, which helps you to discover your company's critical resources. These are the resources required for your company's day-to-day operations, and they are more than just your computer network. After you've defined your critical resources, you begin to get an idea of how the loss of those resources will affect you. If your mail room was lost in a fire, would that be as important a loss as a fire in the server room?

Table 20-1	Types of Threats	
Natural Threats	*Man-Made Threats*	*Technical Threats*
Earthquake	Arson	Power outage
Flood	Embezzlement	Communications outage
Ice storm	Chemical spill	Data corruption
Hurricane	Bombs	Electronics failure
Avalanche	Vandalism	Hacking

You also need to quantify how each disaster would affect you. For example, if your area were hit by a tornado, would you lose the entire building or just a portion of it? You're probably not going to be totally accurate in estimating the damage, but your insurance company should be able to help you with these estimates. What is the building worth, and what would the loss be in dollars? The reason for quantifying a disaster is that it makes it seem more *real* to people. If I were to tell you that a flood would affect part of your house, what would your reaction be? If I were to tell you that a flood would cause $60,000 in damage to your house, your reaction would be quite different.

For your BIA, start with an extensive list of all of your resources. This includes the physical as well as the intangible. It's easy to put a dollar amount to a building, supplies, and equipment, but you also need to consider things like your customer service department. If you were unable to service your customers for three days, how much would that cost you in revenue? Prepare a standard questionnaire and give it to all your department heads and others within your company with special knowledge. They will be able to give you a much more in-depth understanding of how important the loss of capabilities in their areas would affect your company. Then conduct a brainstorming session to make sure that you've covered all your bases. You'd be surprised how easy it is to overlook the small things that are important in the overall scheme.

To help you decide the survivability of the loss of each resource, you can rate them using the following severity scale shown in Table 20-2:

Table 20-2	Severity of Loss
Rating	*Description*
1	Out of business
2	Major problems and significant financial impact
3	Great inconvenience and some financial impact
4	Minor inconvenience and very little financial impact
5	Nobody would notice

Don't forget to identify the critical functions of the various departments. Some you need to consider are

- Network support
- Communications

- ✔ Accounting
- ✔ Payroll
- ✔ Data processing
- ✔ Production
- ✔ Purchasing
- ✔ Customer support
- ✔ Transportation and shipping

You don't need to go into a great deal of granularity in describing these functions. If you do, it gets hard to decide on how to prioritize the needs and you get into a situation where you won't be able to "see the forest for the trees." You can use the departmental budgets to help you assess the importance of the department and how its loss would affect the company, too.

Business Continuity Plan

The *business continuity plan* or *BCP* is how you will continue operations in those first few critical days. You've already identified your critical operations and resources and what their loss would mean to your company and now you need to figure out how you'll continue so you can slowly get back to normal.

There are three phases to dealing with a disaster:

1. *Continuing* **operations.**

   This won't be business as usual, but a minimum level of services to keep you going.

2. *Resumption* **of operations.**

   This is pretty close to normal. You may still be without minor services, but the difference will be hard for your customers to tell.

3. *Restoration* **of operations.**

   This is when everything gets back to normal. Your property, services, and equipment are all back in order.

This section of your plan should be fairly straightforward. You need to assign a goal for each phase and describe what you need to meet that goal. The aim is to prepare for a gradual increase in capabilities so, every day, things get a little bit better. You don't set a goal, reach it, and then just stay there. You plan to go beyond each goal until you're fully recovered.

Some businesses have strict regulatory rules or laws by which they have to abide. These need to be taken into consideration as well as any fiduciary responsibilities owed to stockholders and owners. Confidential data still needs to be protected and the excuse of a disaster will not hold water in a court. The company executives have to be able to show that they performed due diligence in protecting the data as well as the structure.

In the following sections I've prepared information on the types of losses your business may suffer in a disaster. Each of these losses will affect you to a different degree and examining these losses will help you to decide the continuity measures that can be put into place prior to a disaster. In some cases the continuity measure will be to install additional equipment while in other cases you can decide which outside resources can be best used to your advantage.

Power

Obviously, your business needs electricity to run. You need lights, air conditioning, and power for your equipment. You can invest in *uninterruptible power supplies* or UPSs for the short-term outages. These are charged battery packs that hold from 15 minutes worth of power to several hours worth, depending on their size. These are good for keeping computer equipment up and running for a short time, but they can't run air conditioning systems. If you have high electricity needs, you may want to invest in back-up generators. These come in various sizes and capabilities and run gas or diesel fuel to create electricity. If you plan on using generators for power during outages, also make sure that you have enough fuel or have access to fuel during an outage. Because most gas pumps work on electricity, you won't be able to pump fuel held in storage tanks unless you have manual pumps for backup.

Telephone communications

What would a phone outage do to your company? Would you be able to stay in business for long without it? If not, you need to talk to your supplier to come up with contingency plans for outages. They are used to such questions and should be able to come up with an affordable plan. If they don't want to work with you on a continuity plan, then you ought to consider changing suppliers.

Remember that without phone lines you won't be able to call your back-up suppliers or your emergency staff! Mobile phone networks quickly become overloaded during emergencies, too. Your cell phone provider can help by providing you with pre-registered numbers that have priority calling status.

You can ensure that your emergency management team all have cell phones that work during a crisis. This capability will be limited, but it's much better than no communications at all.

You can also make sure that your key personnel don't all use the same cell phone provider. That way, if a supplier can't provide service, then at least some of the personnel will still be able to use their phones.

Electronic communications

As important as telephones are in an emergency, they can become unreliable when the phone network gets overloaded with calls. This is especially true during large, natural disasters that disable a community. You will need to stay in touch with your key personnel and there are some things you can do to communicate electronically during a crisis:

- ✔ Set up broadband Internet connections for your key personnel to use at home. DSL and cable are good examples. They allow for fast connections that don't rely upon telephone dial-ups and won't tie up important phone lines. Your personnel will be able to "talk" electronically and may also be able to conduct some business operations from home.

- ✔ Key personnel should have home e-mail accounts. If you can't call someone on the phone you may be able to contact them via e-mail. You can also transfer important data and files to home computers.

- ✔ Have your key personnel install Instant Messaging (IM) to be able to instantly chat when needed.

- ✔ Set up an emergency use Web site with a low cost provider. During a crisis you can update data to a Web site quickly and reach a large number of people. You can have special announcements for staff and press releases for the media. This is a good way to track the progress of your recovery efforts.

Your network communications are probably just as important as your phone communications, especially if you rely heavily upon the Internet to move data for you and your customers. Again, you will need to talk to your supplier about the possibility of installing duplicate or redundant networks. This solution is very expensive. One of my clients paid $50,000 a year for a duplicate network that had a guarantee to be up and running within four hours of an emergency being called. The figures from your BIA will help to justify these costs. For example, my client discovered that a five hour outage would cost more than $200,000 in lost business. For them, the $50K was good insurance.

You can also contract a "ready-to-go" computing center for use in an emergency. Ideally, this will be located some distance from your company. For example, if your area is flooded for miles around, it won't do you any good to have your fall-back systems located just blocks away. Chances are they will be suffering from the same set of circumstances.

Commercial recovery service providers are generally who companies that are affected by a disaster look to provide emergency centers and they typically offer three types of service, with small variations between the three. Your choices are

- **Hot site** — A self-contained facility ready to assume your network load in an instant (more or less). You have your own equipment, software, and data backups at this facility and it runs continuously. The facility has power, air conditioning, raised flooring, and telecommunication lines ready for your use.

- **Warm site** — A self-contained facility complete with equipment and network connections, but no software or data has been installed. This site may keep data backups for you in the eventuality of a disaster but you will still have to load software and configure the systems prior to their use. The facility will also have power, air conditioning, raised flooring, and telecommunications lines ready for use.

- **Cold site** — This is a reserved room or building that is ready to house your network equipment, but it does not have the equipment in it. It has power, air conditioning, raised flooring, and telecommunications capabilities, but none of the equipment needed for operations is included.

The advantage of a hot site is that you can get back to a low level of operations very quickly. Everything you need is there and you can test that everything works as needed beforehand. Cantor Fitzgerald, a company that suffered major losses in 9/11, had a hot site and was up to full operational levels within 47 hours of the attack. Their hot site was a complete mirror image of their own network and they had minimal loss of data during the aftermath of the attack.

The disadvantage of a hot site is the cost. Again, this is something you'll have to use your BIA to justify or not. As you can imagine, it's very expensive to pay the overhead costs such as rent, electricity, telecommunications, and equipment and not have the facility actually generate any income. You also have the costs of maintaining and updating the equipment as well as daily back-ups of data. For this reason, some companies go into a sharing agreement with business partners.

A warm site is less expensive than a hot site because everything is in place but nothing is running. You'll save on operational costs since the site is just sitting there waiting for its first use. However, those costs will rise tremendously during a disaster because all equipment will need to have its software installed and configured in the shortest possible time. You won't have the luxury of being able to test the system much before you have to put it online.

The big advantage of a cold site is that the cost, initially, is minimal. You only need to rent the space. However, there are distinct disadvantages, too. Since there will be no equipment, you will have to order the equipment and wait for its delivery. Then you have the installation of the network, operating systems, and applications and you won't be able to test the site to see if it actually meets your needs.

There is a mid-range solution that may be worth considering and that is a mobile computing center. These are offices on wheels that have small networks and other office systems installed and ready for deployment. They are relatively inexpensive but are limited in their capabilities. You'll also have to consider where you would locate the mobile unit and how you would get power, water, and telecommunications to it.

Personnel

During a natural disaster you have to consider that most of your employees will be concerned with themselves and their family's situation above that of the business. This is completely natural, but many companies forget that their most important people may be unavailable for a while. You need to have alternatives to key employees. For this reason, consider whether or not there are employees from outside your area that you can call in during an emergency. If you don't have remote staff, you can contact an outsourcing agency and identify the types of personnel you would need. There is no guarantee that they will be able to provide them, but it is worth considering.

All company employees and key personnel should have an emergency contact list that they keep at home. Make sure they have electronic copies as well as hard copies. Obviously, this list should be regularly updated.

Emergency suppliers

Always have a list of suppliers for goods and services needed in an emergency. If you need alternate office space, you will need to know the location of other facilities and who their leasing agents are. You could need office equipment, computer equipment, and phones. Don't forget the all important paper and pens, either!

It's a good idea to identify your suppliers ahead of time and establish a good relationship with them. During times of crisis, everyone will be trying to get the same things and if you are a favorite client, you will probably get favorite status in getting what you need. Obtain the Yellow Pages directories for your community and those outside your area. These will be important resource materials in an emergency.

There are companies who specialize in disaster recovery and you can usually find them listed in the telephone pages and on the Web. These companies offer a wide range of services and frequently will consult with you ahead of time to prepare your emergency plan. It's worth giving them a call just to get a feeling for how they operate. Some of the major companies who offer disaster recovery services are GE (www.gedisasterrecovery.com), SunGard (www.recovery.sungard.com), and IBM (www-1.ibm.com/services/continuity/recover1.nsf/documents/home).

Emergency funds

You should have an arrangement for key personnel to be able to obtain funds during an emergency. It's no good having to go through the arduous accounting procedures if you need money immediately. Your accounting department could be disabled by the emergency or the supplier could be demanding immediate payment. You can't expect your key personnel to have to pay out of pocket. You can have a special credit card account set up for this purpose, but make sure the key people have the cards in their possession. If the disaster has affected the community at large, you may need access to cash as credit card and ATM processing may be disabled.

Disaster Recovery Plan

This is the nuts and bolts package. What are you going to do? How are you going to do it? Who is the emergency team? You can't prepare a step-by-step guide on how to react to each type of disaster, but you can spell out the roles and responsibilities of people who will be key to getting you back to normal. Additionally, you'll set a series of goals towards recovery and prioritize the recovery efforts of your team.

First, however, pick your team. Also have alternatives to your team members in case the primary person is unavailable. The selection of your team members depends on what skills and abilities you will need and whether or not you will be able to depend on them in a crisis. This is no time to play favorites or to be political because you've done no one any good if that person can't or won't help when needed.

I know of a company that had the board of directors pick the emergency team. Unfortunately, the board members only knew people by their popularity and not necessarily by their abilities. When that company suffered a three-day network outage, only half of the team members ever bothered to show up. After the crisis was over, the board quickly reassessed their previous assignments. It was too bad that it took a big shake up for the company to see the error of their initial selection. Their recovery would have been less painful if they had a team they could depend on the first time around.

Disaster recovery team

Each member of the team needs to have their responsibilities detailed as well as their authorities and priorities. They need to know what they are expected to do, what their limits are, and who to contact if they reach impediments. When resources are slim, it helps if the roles and duties have been prioritized so some team members can be pulled from their own duties to help out in a pinch. I'm not saying these should all be hard and fast rules as some flexibility will always be required, but you do need to have guidelines.

Table 20-3 shows some examples of team members and what their responsibilities may entail.

Table 20-3	Recovery Team Members
Team Member	*Responsibility*
Recovery Coordinator	Initiates the emergency call and activates the recovery plan. Deals with company executives. Coordinates with emergency services such as fire and police. Coordinates efforts of all other team members. Liaison for the media if necessary.
Facility Manager	Assesses damages, plans repairs, and prepares move to temporary facility, if necessary. Obtains alternate power and water supplies, heating and cooling. Works with Operations Manager to ensure staff has a place to work.
Operations Manager	Defines staffing requirements and arranges support staff. Obtains business equipment (other than computing equipment) and works with Facilities Manager in making arrangements for a move.
Communications Manager	Responsible for restoration of voice and data communications. Works with suppliers for restoration of service or readies the hot/warm/cold site. Works with Operations Manager for phone supplies and with Systems Manager for data line requirements.

Team Member	Responsibility
Systems Manager	Obtains temporary hardware and manages team to reconfigure systems with appropriate software. Responsible for the safe back-up and restoration of all data. In the case of a move to a hot/cold site, manages the movement of data and the set up of the site.
Administration Manager	In charge of all personnel not required to work on recovery team. Assigns duties, assembles documentation needed to return to full operations. Makes alternate arrangements for payroll and accounting if necessary.
Administrative Assistant	Records all decisions made by disaster team. Notifies general populace of important announcements. Prepares press releases for media.

Of course this is just a very general list of roles and responsibilities. For example, you may also have a production plant and shipping department you have to consider. A sales team also needs to be able to continue selling and will need direction on what to tell customers and how to handle impending deliveries. There are hundreds of other jobs I could list, but you know your company's needs and can probably decide what other duties will need to be filled. When you are defining your team members and their individual responsibilities, be sure to take into consideration the interdependencies of team members. For example, if your building has been damaged and you need to move, the Communications Manager won't be able to start his job until the Facility Manager has obtained a new facility. In those situations they can work together towards a common goal.

Prioritize operations

Your business continuity plan will have helped you to decide which operations are absolutely essential to your business survival and it and your disaster recovery plan should list the operations in order of priority. What operations do you need to have up and running first, which come second, and which operations can come back much later on? Usually, one of the first operations given priority is Accounting. You will have immediate expenses and you can't operate out of a cash box for long. Employees need to be paid and suppliers will want their money, too. You may want to consider keeping a set of accounting records, back-up tapes, and checkbooks in a safe deposit box at a bank.

Not every emergency will have to be dealt with in the same way. Minor emergencies will have a different set of priorities than a major catastrophe. Therefore, it's important to list the priorities according to the type of emergency. You can segregate them into three different categories:

- ✔ **Interruption** — This is an emergency lasting less than 24 hours. No building damage will have occurred and the problem is probably technical in nature such as a network attack or power outage.

- ✔ **Minor Disaster** — This type of emergency lasts more than 24 hours but less than four days. Perhaps a fire has destroyed some parts of the building or a serious breach of security in the network has occurred. There will be major disruption in the day to day activities of personnel, but other than that, the situation is generally survivable.

- ✔ **Major Disaster** — This is closer to a catastrophe in nature and you can expect that it will be at least four days before you can get back to normal. An earthquake, a direct hurricane hit, a major flood, fire, or civil strike can cause this to happen. Personnel can be difficult to reach and operations are severely affected.

Your operational priorities will also dovetail with the recovery team's roles and responsibilities (mentioned previously). Be sure to update their duties as you work through the list of business operations that need to continue.

Inventories

Most companies have never taken a full inventory of their equipment, assets, software, and stored data. This is important to have in an emergency because you have to know what you have lost in order to replace it. This may seem like common sense, but usually the department heads carry a mental picture of such things and they are never written down. You cannot rely upon an accurate verbal assessment of your losses in an emergency. People get stressed, some people will not be available, and there will be huge duplications of efforts.

Your inventory should be more than just the make and model numbers of equipment. You should also include software versions, updates and patches, personnel records, and a list of suppliers and your contacts. The description and format of all stored data will be needed as well as copies of important documents and forms. Don't forget to include network diagrams and data flow diagrams, too. Keep your inventory stored safely off-site and take care to update the list at least annually.

Call-out list

Always have a contact list of personnel to be called in an event of an emergency. Again, the nature of the emergency will determine who gets called and how many are needed to respond. The easiest method is to set up a "calling tree" where each person is assigned to contact two other persons on the list (see Figure 20-1). You can contact a great number of people quite quickly in this manner. Be sure to include some overlap in who calls whom so that one "branch" of the tree doesn't die out from the lack of contact.

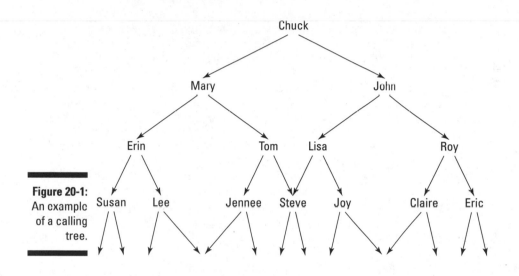

Figure 20-1:
An example
of a calling
tree.

Training and testing

Every plan should include some training and testing. The disaster team needs to know how to react and what is expected of them and the employees need to know how a plan is going to affect them. Just having a plan written and stored on a shelf is going to be worthless if it was filed and forgotten. Staff positions change, situations change, and procedures can quickly become outdated. While you are training your staff, inadequacies in your plan will quickly come to notice and you'll recognize redundancies as well. All disaster team members should be cross-trained as much as is feasible and alternates should be included in the training, too.

When your plan is in order, test the plan by having a fake disaster. This is similar to the disaster drills carried on by most community emergency response personnel. Your exercise should be coordinated with a few key persons and not announced publicly. You want people's reactions to be as close to natural as possible and the simulation should imitate a real-life situation.

During your drill you'll come across unexpected responses. Some single parents won't be able to attend for lack of child care. Other people may be outside of phone contact or may be on an impromptu getaway. Your drill will also be a test of your training and your plan in general. Inadequacies will become glaring omissions at this point. During one emergency drill I acted in, we realized we had not set up assembly points for the people evacuated from the building and there was no way to account for everyone. We didn't know if we had a full evacuation or if there were people still left inside. We also realized that we had not planned for easy access to the building for fire fighting equipment. The trucks had to run over the building's pretty landscaping in order to make the turns through the gates! A test drill can be pretty funny and it's better to find out your shortcomings ahead of time.

When testing your disaster plans for network recovery, resist the urge to undertake housekeeping, upgrades, or other changes in the system during the test. Since you are simulating network downtime, this would seem like an ideal opportunity to do some real work while you're at it. The problem is that mistakes could be made and then you could have a real emergency. I did that once with a team and we ended up in a real emergency that lasted four days! Major upgrades or changes in your network are risky enough as it is and they should be have their own plans and tests and not combine them with other exercises.

Call to Action

Although the step-by-step procedures may vary in implementation according to the nature of the disaster, you can rely on some basic structure. For example, a disaster has to be declared before the recovery team is called in. Your procedures should be defined in your plan and streamlined as you see fit. Everyone in the company should be aware of who to call to initiate a call to action. Disasters don't always happen during office hours!

1. **Ensure the welfare and safety of all personnel.**
2. **Call disaster team members.**
3. **Team members assemble at agreed upon "control center."**
4. **Determine the severity of the event and assess damage.**
5. **Establish communications methods and mechanisms.**

6. **Protect data or get ready to go to back-ups.**

7. **Protect mission-critical processes.**

8. **Contact clients prior to making media announcements.**

9. **Make initial recovery efforts.**

10. **Communicate status accurately and often.**

All members of the disaster team and other key personnel should have full copies of the disaster recovery plans at home. The plans won't do any good if they are all in a burning building!

Chapter 21

Who Did the Dirty: Computer Forensics

A key employee of a large corporation left to start a competing business. Before leaving, he formatted the hard drive of his company laptop in an attempt to destroy evidence of violating a confidentiality agreement. To his dismay, all his emails, letters, memorandums, and business plans were eventually recovered from the laptop. His previous employer sued him.

An employee left her job and shortly afterwards some irregularities were noted in the past billing of some clients. A forensic investigation was conducted on her old workstation and deleted invoices were found. She had been overbilling the clients, pocketing the difference, and then deleting the old invoices to cover her tracks. She was prosecuted.

An outside consultant was brought in to update some old software programs. He didn't think he was being paid enough, so he told the company he had planted a logic bomb in the software code. He told the company that if they didn't meet his demands, the entire system would be erased and destroyed at some date in the future. If they paid him, he would delete the offending code. The company called in some computer forensic experts and they found evidence of the logic bomb and the extortion letter. Not only was the consultant prosecuted, but he has to pay damages to the company he was trying to extort.

These examples are all scary but true. Prior to 1990 none of these cases would have been brought to justice. Not only were the forensic tools and techniques not widely available, but the computer crime laws were still being written. It's a far different world today as Fortune 500 companies employ in-house forensic experts and thousands of independent forensic labs have cropped up. Law enforcement offices try, with their restrictive budgets, to educate at least some of their officers and, of course, the FBI has their own computer crime division. Businesses have a much better chance at being able to find evidence of a crime and prosecuting the guilty.

That's not to say that computer forensics is easy. Far from it! This is definitely not something the inexperienced should try to do. You need well-trained, dedicated experts who can not only find the evidence but prepare it for the authorities and be prepared to act as an expert witness in a trial. You wouldn't want your builder to investigate a robbery of your house for the same reason you don't want a network administrator to investigate a break-in of your computer system. They can both probably figure out how the perpetrator got in, but that doesn't make them experts at gathering the evidence. Please leave that to the pros!

I can't teach you how to do a forensic investigation, but I can tell you some of the processes the experts go through. I'll explain how computers physically store data, how data is hidden, and how the experts find hidden information. In addition, I'll explain what you should and shouldn't do to help the investigators.

Data Storage

We should all know by now that data is stored on magnetic media — disks, tapes, CDs, and even different types of electronic chips. Anything that can hold a magnetic charge can be used to store data. The ones and zeroes that comprise the data are represented by either a magnetized or unmagnetized space on the media. This is roughly the same method used for storing bank account information on the black strip on the back of your ATM card. For that reason, you shouldn't keep your storage media on top of stereo speakers (which have large magnets in them) and you don't put your ATM card in a holder with a magnetic clasp. A magnet — even a magnetized paper clip — can alter the pattern of ones and zeroes and destroy sections of data.

To delete or overwrite the data on your media, the read/write mechanism in your computer alters the pattern of ones and zeroes to match the new data. This data starts out being stored in contiguous sections sort of like the grooves on a vinyl record. After time, however, the deletion of files leaves gaps on the storage media. Because of this, the data gets shuffled around and ends up scattered all over the media. This is known as *fragmentation*. A heavily fragmented disk is slower to read than one with contiguous segments of data and there are hundreds of utilities available that will *defrag* the data so it is more efficient for your computer to read.

Whether your media is fragmented or not, there are still small areas of the disk that contain data you don't see or know about. This data is generally hidden from casual viewing, but can be seen and reassembled with special software utilities or tools. These tools are the basis for a forensic evaluation of any media.

Unallocated space

A file is not really deleted when you issue the delete command on your computer. The data still resides on a physical section of the disk, it's just that the operating system has been told that the space can be physically occupied by another file as soon as it is needed. In that way, new data is actually overlaid on top of older data. Because of this, it's possible to resurrect old, deleted files. We've all made the mistake of deleting the wrong file at one time or another, so vendors have made available many commercial utilities that help you to find and recover a file you deleted by mistake. As long as the file hasn't already been overwritten by another file, you can usually restore the entire file. Thank goodness for these utilities!

When a file is deleted or removed, its "address" is removed from the file directory. That address is just a pointer to where the data had resided on the physical media. Just because the address has been taken away, though, doesn't mean the data isn't still there. It's like a renter who has to move by the first of the month, but hasn't quite finished getting all of his stuff out of the apartment. The landlord shows the property as empty and available to rent, but there's still some debris laying about. This non-rented but available space on magnetic storage media is called *unallocated* space. It's not really empty but can be occupied by another file. As long as the space hasn't been occupied by another file, the old data is still there. As soon as the new file is written in that space, the old data is gone forever.

The software tools that the forensic experts use can examine the physical arrangement of the ones and zeroes on the media without regard to the file format, address pointer, or data type (such as binary or ASCII). The software has the ability to display the data on the screen or it can be stored as a text file. What the forensic expert sees is lots of words, letters, and special characters that are all run together. It's kind of like reading a book with few spaces and no punctuation between words. The software also lists the physical location on the disk that the data was found. What's really amazing is that some applications store the keystrokes used to create the data inside the file. This means that corrections, deletions, changes, etc. can be seen with these tools. For example, if you typed, "my boss is a jerk" and then changed it to "my boss is the best", what you may find on the disk is "my%boss%is%a%jerk ^C^C^C^C%the%best".

When a disk or other media has been used for a long time, the amount of data left in the unallocated space really adds up. I've seen disks that had as much as 75MB of data left over in the unallocated space. The actual amount of unallocated space is only limited by the size of the disk. This can be a real boon for forensic examiners who are looking for a pattern of behavior or abuse. This can also work against them if more than one person has been using the computer as it becomes very hard to attribute the original owner of data found on a disk.

You may think that overwriting or reformatting a disk a number of times would get rid of all the residual data. Reformatting a disk means that the ones and zeroes are realigned and the address pointers are all removed. However, this isn't necessarily true. While reformatting or overwriting multiple times, the data can still be left over. There is anecdotal evidence of data being recovered from disks that have been reformatted up to nine times. For this reason, government agencies are required to physically destroy media that has been used to store Secret and Top Secret information. You simply cannot trust that the data is gone unless the media has been turned into dust.

Slack space

Did you know that files often contain data that has no relation to the data you saved? Strange, but true! In Windows machines especially, the operating system tries to make the data fit into predetermined sized "boxes" — sort of like pigeon holes. If the data doesn't fit exactly into the box, the operating system needs to pad out the extra space sort of like a putting a shim in a door frame or bubble-wrapping in a package.

Windows stores data in "boxes" or chunks that are a minimum of 512 bytes in size. So, if your file is only 500 bytes long, there are 12 bytes to be padded out. This extra space is called *slack space* and it's located everywhere on a drive or a disk.

The Windows operating system takes superfluous data from wherever it can find it in memory, and stuffs it into the slack space. Often, the extra data comes from the keyboard buffer and other stuff temporarily stored in RAM. Things like passwords, user names, and parts of email messages can actually be stored in the same file space that you thought was just your resume! That's scary! Usually, the data stored in the slack space when the file was created will stay as is unless or until the original file is changed or moved. Imagine all the "secret" stuff stored in your files!

Again, the forensic software tools can find the data stored in the slack space on a disk. I've found URLs of Web sites, email addresses, parts of personal correspondence, printer names, passwords, and file directories all stored in slack space. It's a potential gold mine for forensic examiners because this data was not intentionally stored. It captures just a small snapshot of what was being done with the computer at a given time. However, because the data stored there is not an actual file, there are no time stamps or dates associated with it. It can be hard to determine when exactly that data was stored.

Swap space

When your computer is multi-tasking, it is swapping portions of data from random access memory (RAM) to your hard drive and back to RAM. This data can be temporarily stored in either slack space or unallocated space. It doesn't matter to the operating system just as long as it can find it when it needs it. It's like the Post-It Notes commercial where the squirrel uses the notes to remember where he buried his nuts. The operating system is storing little notes to itself all over your drives. This space is constantly being over-written until the system finally dumps everything that is in memory. The system always has data being held in memory until it is shut down. When a Windows system is shut down (with the Shut Down command), some data is sent to a permanent swap file.

Whether or not to shut down a Windows machine is an important consideration for forensics because the shutdown processes are written to the swap file during this time. This could potentially overwrite other information in the swap file that is needed for evidence. And, when Windows is restarted, more swap files are created and others are deleted. I'll discuss what you should do with Windows machines later in this chapter.

Caches

Caches are a bit like swap files except they tend to be associated with specific applications — like your Web browser, for example. These files store temporary data in order to maximize performance. It's easier for the program to temporarily store the data on your disk drive than to hold it in memory. These caches can sometimes be really huge. I've seen browser caches as large as 100MB in size. This is what the browser uses to store the history of all the URLs you typed and all the links you clicked on and the associated files that have been downloaded. All of this can be a wealth of information. Typically, when porn rings are discovered, it's usually via the browser cache files that this data was found.

Temp files

All systems contain temporary (temp) files. Some of them are temporary temp files and others are sort of permanent temp files. These are not usually hidden from view and you won't need special software to see them, but they are very useful to forensic examiners. Often a temp file will hold information about when and where a program was installed and by whom.

Preparing the Evidence for Collection

It goes without saying that you have to collect the evidence before anyone can examine it. But, what exactly is the evidence? Basically it is everything! The log files contain information about what has been accessed, what processes have been run, and what connections have been made. The keyboard will have data in its buffers containing the last things typed on the keyboard. Of course there are the permanent files and the temporary bits of data I've just discussed. There's also the active connections and processes and the users who are currently logged on.

There are two problems with trying to collect evidence:

- ✔ If you are in the middle of an emergency response situation, the things you need to do to save your system can be contrary to what is needed to collect forensic evidence. As you work from the keyboard and running programs, you are inadvertently overwriting data that may have been important.

- ✔ How you disconnect or shut down the computer can inadvertently cause important data to become overwritten or dumped from memory.

There's little you can do to mitigate these problems, however. Your first order of business is probably going to be to protect your systems in whatever manner you can. However, forensic investigators are used to having to deal with these circumstances and they will do their best to reconstruct the evidence you will need. The fact is that emergencies never happen to plan and you have to do the best you can.

There is a method to the madness and there are some things you can do to help.

1. **Do not turn the computer off.**

2. **Clear everyone out of the room who is not needed.**

3. **Take a picture (if you can) of what is on the screen, the computer setup, all the peripherals, and the connections to the network.**

   A regular film camera is better because the photos cannot be digitally altered. Try to have this all witnessed by at least one other person, but not more than two or three people. Too many witnesses tend to confuse things.

4. **Make a drawing of the computer, all the peripherals, and all the connections as you found it.**

   Make a couple of copies of the drawing. Have the original drawing witnessed, put it in an envelope, seal it with tape, sign your name over the tape, and store the envelope securely. Make sure that there is limited access to that envelope.

5. **Label all of the cables connected to the computer.**

6. **If the computer is connected to a modem, unplug the modem from the wall.**

   Do not disconnect the session. Do not turn the computer off. Do not use the phone line that was used for the modem connection. It will retain the last number called which may be important.

7. **If the computer is connected to the network, unplug the cable from the wall.**

   Do not logoff and do not turn the computer off.

8. **If you feel you must document the connections and the running processes, be aware of the fact that you may be destroying evidence.**

   If you must run the commands to discover these things, be sure to direct the results to a fresh, new floppy disk straight out from the box. If you type the commands and store the data to the hard drive, you will be destroying slack and unallocated space and changing the memory buffers. The floppy needs to be completely new and previously unused or it will contain residual data and will not be good for evidence.

9. **Document everything, have it witnessed, and lock it up.**

   What were the circumstances that made you suspect a problem? Who was involved? At what time and date did you begin to take action? What did you do and what order did you do it in? Even if you haven't followed all the steps or the order the steps should be executed, document them as they happened. Every little bit of trivia should be noted. You can't have too much information at this point.

10. **Call in the experts.**

   Do this quietly and without fanfare. Don't add grist to the rumor mill by announcing their arrival. The experts will probably want to interview people, too, and the experts will have an easier time of it if employees have not been sharing their stories amongst one another.

11. **Secure access to the computer and wait for the experts to arrive.**

   Lock the door, put a cover over the computer, put a guard on duty, or whatever you have to do to make sure that nothing is done to the computer! Do not turn it off.

You must protect the chain of evidence from now on. Everyone who comes even close to the computer can be suspected of changing the evidence and will be challenged by a good defense attorney. It's like the scene of a crime. It IS the scene of a crime. You never know what will be important to the investigation, so keep everything as it. Any files, notes, books, equipment, etc. that is in the vicinity should also stay there. If you don't know of any computer forensic experts in your area, try calling your local police force. Failing that, your local FBI office may be able to give you some advice. There are also listings of experts on the Web. You won't have much time to check references, so be careful and don't just choose the first name on the list.

What the Experts Will Do

Once you have secured the scene of the crime and the experts have arrived, they will need your help for a little while before they can begin. They will thoroughly interview you and everyone involved with the discovery. They will ask you what you did and how you did it. You can show them the documentation you made and stored in envelopes if they ask for it. They can re-secure the evidence in a manner that will be acceptable in a court of law. After they are done with you, leave them alone to do their work. It could take them a long, long time to put all the pieces together for you as computer forensic examinations are tedious and time-consuming.

Shutdown

The experts will decide whether or not to shut down the computer. Chances are that, if it is a Windows machine, they will just pull the power plug from the wall. This will keep the system from overwriting the temp files and the slack space. Windows systems are usually harmed by a sudden loss of power. However, if it is a Unix system, they will probably have to run the shut down routine because a power loss to a Unix system can be catastrophic. In either case there are pros and cons to each procedure and your expert is fully aware of them and will do what s/he thinks best for the given situation.

Reboot

Next the expert will reboot the machine from a floppy disk. The reboot will be to DOS or the command line. Booting to Windows or a windows-like environment will destroy evidence. There are special ways of doing this to ensure that nothing is written to the hard drive during this process. You don't want any changes to your evidence! Your expert will make sure that the drives are all locked against changes. There are special programs they can use to do this.

Mirror imaging drives

Once the system has been rebooted, the next step is to create a couple of physical backups of the hard drives. This is not a simple backup like you do to save changes in data but an absolute mirror image of the physical attributes of the disks. A normal back-up will only store the viewable data and not the hidden data. The hidden data is most important and can only be captured by a sector by sector exact copy. This collects and stores the exact patterns of ones and zeroes from the suspect or target machine.

Setting up the imaged disks is very tricky and is done with special software tools. It's easy to confuse the copies with the original and the last thing you want to do is to change the original. Multiple copies are made of the drives so the expert has copies to play with and doesn't have to fiddle with the original. The original drive will be packaged up, sealed, signed, and locked away and not touched again. From now on, all the work will be on the imaged drives.

Initial inspections

Before an all-out thorough investigation can proceed, there's still some initial discovery and cataloging to take place. This is like the evidence gathering you see on TV or in the movies. The team of investigators will slowly look for some obvious signs of evidence before they can start beating the bushes for less obvious evidence. Chances are there will be no "smoking gun" sitting in clear view.

The investigators will pull out their tool kits and start doing key word searches of the raw data on the disks. The log files will be viewed for recent activity and the contents of the disks is catalogued. If the computer in question is a Unix based machine, the contents of memory can be stored in a file called a *core dump*. If a file was made of the running processes, connections, and logged on users was created, they will be examined, too. All of the results of their searching will be output to text files on some sort of external media like a Jaz drive or an external hard drive. All the media used to store the findings must be pristine, previously unused media. This is the only way to ensure that no residual data resides on the external media that can corrupt the findings.

Once the findings have all been stored on the external drive, a "fingerprint" of that data is created to ensure that the data is not altered in any way. This is done using a program to create an *MD5 hash*. MD5 is a one-way hash algorithm that takes any length of data and produces a 128 bit *fingerprint* or *message digest*. The fingerprint is a series of numbers and letters that will look something like this:

```
1eabd3dbc0746c8a4b5467f99a4f8823
```

The fingerprints are always unique and are used to make sure that a file has not been altered. If you check the file and the fingerprint does not match, then you know something has changed in the file and its authenticity cannot be trusted. MD5 is often used to preserve and certify any data that you want to keep for future evidence.

After the fingerprints for the output have been created, the files are encrypted using public/private key encryption. The encryption doesn't actually change the file, so the fingerprint will remain the same. However, the file cannot be easily read without the decryption software and the keys used to create it.

Continue or stop?

After the collection of evidence and the initial examination of the evidence at hand, the investigator will probably be able to determine a "go" or a "no-go" point. Either he has enough evidence to prove a crime has taken place or he hasn't. If he hasn't, does the company have the resources to continue? Will the cost of the investigation cost more than the damage? It's not uncommon for simple investigations to cost tens of thousands of dollars. Sometimes company politics get in the way and an investigation just stalls in its tracks.

There are many reasons why an investigation might stop short of a prosecution and you may want to decide when and where to halt an investigation before it gets started. Discuss your guidelines with your forensic team, and they'll let you know when they've reached their limits.

Has a Crime Taken Place?

Statistically, there is only a 50/50 chance that a crime has taken place. Many times what looks like an attack has been caused by the failure of network mechanisms — hard drives, routers, network cards, or the like. If you have controlled the situation and few people know about the investigation, you will save yourself a lot of embarrassment if the "crime" ends up being a false alarm.

What the investigators end up searching for will depend upon what you think was happening at the time of the event. If there was a suspected breach of the firewall, the firewall logs will be examined for anomalies and clues. If the computer was being used to access other machines or other networks, the presence of Trojan horses, rootkits, and other hacking tools will be checked. The system being examined will also be checked to see if large numbers of files were being deleted or changed during a relatively short period. It's possible that the email "out box" will be checked as well as any recent FTP connections or Web sites visited. Additionally, the logs of other computers may be checked to see if the suspect computer had been involved in any recent activity on those machines.

There are basically three types of tools that will be employed during the investigation:

- **Log Parsers** — Because logs are hard to read line-by-line, a parser can help sort and assemble similarities and anomalies found in the logs. You can search for specific events, too.

- **Forensic Software** — These are the tools used to examine the confiscated drives for evidence. They can look for patterns, key words, and/or anomalies.

- **Tracers** — Things like network sniffers and port monitors can look at the activity happening on the lines and are particularly useful if the intruder is still active.

At times, the investigation of a possible crime will reach beyond your local network. There may be evidence that the intruder came through another network. At that time the forensic investigator may need to call in the local law authorities. Only the legal authorities can get search warrants to examine other computers and court orders for ISPs to release logs and user data. If the intruder is still active, the authorities may be possible to get a court order to be able to tap and trace the intruder's activity.

It will be up to the forensic investigators to decide whether or not a crime has actually taken place. The investigator's previous experiences in the field, the data found on the computer(s), and the results of interviews will all lead him to his conclusion. Sometimes a large amount of "gut instinct" will also be involved in making the decision. If the investigator has found evidence of a crime, he will do what is necessary to ensure that the evidence can be used in a trial and may have to act as an expert witness on the stand. His reputation is at stake, too. If he doesn't think a crime has been committed, or if he doesn't think the evidence will support the claim of a crime, you'll have to listen to him. Ultimately you are paying him for his skill and advice.

Involving the Authorities

Deciding when or if to call in your local, state, or federal law enforcement officers is a difficult call. If yours is a high-profile case and the press has already gotten whiff of a scandal, the call may not even be yours to make — the law will be knocking at your door soon enough. On the other hand, if no damage was done or if the cost of prosecution would be more than the amount of damage you suffered, you may decide just to let sleeping dogs lie. If you do have to call in the authorities, your case may also take a low priority with them as they are more concerned with murders and robberies than trying to track a ghostly, seemingly intangible "intruder."

When should you call in the cops, though? Here are some thoughts for you to consider:

- Have you suffered big losses or lots of damage?
- Do indications point to an organized fraud scheme?
- Is child pornography involved?
- Is public safety at risk?
- Have banks or financial institutions been involved?
- Have you discussed the problems with your attorneys?

If the computer crime ends up being no big deal to you, chances are the law won't be interested. However, if your network was used to attack other networks or has been used to transfer pirated or stolen information, you could be charged as an accessory after the fact. By all means, discuss this with your attorney. Remember — if you decide not to call in the authorities it could be very hard to explain why you didn't if the crime ends up being a big deal later on.

So, who do you call? The local police? The Sheriff's Department? The State Attorney's Office? Or, do you call in your local FBI branch? It all depends on the jurisdiction of the crime. The jurisdiction depends on the geographical extent of the network used to commit the crime. For example, if one of your employees used your local network to embezzle funds held in your local office, the geographic location of the crime is limited to your office. In that case, it sounds as if only the local authorities should be called in. On the other hand, if your employee used a network that connects branches of your company across state lines, then an interstate crime has been committed and the FBI will need to called in. The location of the computer doesn't necessarily determine the jurisdiction of the crime. The jurisdiction is determined by the type of crime committed and the geographic extent of the crime. When in doubt, however, please contact your local FBI office as the experts there should be able to point you in the right direction.

Generally, you can choose one of three avenues to pursue:

  ✔ Handle the crime internally.
  ✔ Prepare a civil case against the perpetrator.
  ✔ Involve legal authorities and let them take over.

If you choose to handle the situation internally, you can keep the amount of gossip and public discussion to a minimum. This is the course usually taken if the crime is minor and the company wishes to avoid adverse publicity. If the person responsible was one of your employees, you can always terminate that person, but be aware of the fact that you cannot tell that person's future employers exactly what happened. It's not fair, but there have been many companies successfully sued when they gave unfavorable information to potential employers.

If you choose the civil suit route, you are exposing yourself to possibly some adverse publicity. You may not receive much in the way of damages, but you can help to keep from letting this person commit the same acts because it will be part of the public record. Civil suits are expensive but it may be worth it to you. The only cases I've heard of that seem to be worthwhile are those involving corporate espionage. However, the choice is up to you.

Criminal legal cases have a life of their own and there's not much you can do to control it. In these cases you should have a public relations expert involved so the publicity doesn't end up hurting your business more than the original crime did.

The Aftermath

It's important to learn from our mistakes and the aftermath of a crime is not the time to sweep things under the carpet and play ostrich. A big problem happened. It disrupted operations and probably cost you a lot of money. You need to find out what the circumstances were that led to this problem and how you can correct the situation so it doesn't happen again in the future.

Obviously, you are going to have to look at your rules and procedures. Were they ignored or did they just not work? You may need to change them to meet new requirements. This is a fact-finding mission and not a witch hunt. There's time enough later on for punishment — now you have to make corrections. Did your security mechanisms fail? How did they fail and can it be corrected? Were the security mechanisms adequate to begin with? Do you need to install more security?

Your forensic investigators will be able to help you in making these determinations and may be able to suggest some fixes. Chances are they've seen similar situations before.

Part VI
The Part of Tens

The 5th Wave

By Rich Tennant

"A centralized security management system sounds fine, but then what would we do with the dogs?"

In this part . . .

The chapters in this section will become part of your networking security Bible, so keep the book in a prominent place on your bookshelf. In this part, you get rules, guides, tips, and all that other neat security stuff you need to know. I've searched through my bookmarks high and low for the best just so you could find them the easy way — enjoy!

Chapter 22

Ten Best Security Practices

*O*oops. I guess I can't count because there are more than ten security practices listed in this section. Oh well, I was never that good at math, but you get more good advice in return.

These security practices apply to networks of any size, shape, or form. If everyone followed these practices — even if they didn't install all the various security mechanisms — there would be fewer systems for hackers to hack because all systems would be that much stronger. I'm not advocating that you don't use additional security mechanisms; I'm just saying that, by following these simple rules, you make your systems much harder to crack for very little expenditure on your part.

Here then, without further ado, are the eight commandments of secure computing (plus four more).

If everyone would apply the best security practices to their network, we'd all experience fewer attacks and problems with our systems. Studies have shown that a majority of intrusions and attacks could have been prevented if some simple things had been fixed or changed, so take this advice to heart. Who knows — it could save you a lot of money in the long run!

Use Strong Passwords

Too many hacks can be traced back to the use of either default passwords or passwords like *password, letmein,* or *guest.* Some of the common passwords are part of the default installation of a software application and are not only well known, but are documented on hacking Web sites as well. Even worse than a bad password is no password at all. Because passwords are the main security mechanism used for anything and everything on networks, they are the skeleton key for all the locks. Even firewalls have passwords that have been guessed.

The good password rule of thumb is

- At least eight characters in length
- A mixture of UPPER and lower case letters
- Include numbers and/or special characters such as !@#$%^&+?
- Not easily guessable or be found in a dictionary

We all are guilty of using the same password to access several accounts, which means that hackers can get into more than one account if they guess or crack your password. Hackers count on us doing this. Therefore, change the passwords you use frequently. Changing them every six months is good, but changing them every three months is even better.

Use Anti-Virus Software

One of the easiest ways for a hacker to gain access to your system is via a Trojan horse program. A Trojan looks like something common — like a screen saver — but it works secretly in the background. It's easy to get a fun looking attachment from a well-meaning friend, double-click it, and install a Trojan instead. You won't even know it has happened, either.

Some viruses can do serious damage to your computers as well as disrupt network traffic. E-mail viruses can quickly overload your e-mail servers and bombard friends, family, and clients with copies of the virus. Some viruses are difficult to remove, too.

Anti-virus software can stop Trojan horses as well as those pesky, irritating e-mail viruses that are going around like crazy. They use a search engine combined with a database of known viruses to search your computer. Anti-virus programs are relatively inexpensive, are tested by independent labs, and are easy to install. Just remember to update the software at least weekly in order to keep it operating correctly. It's just plain silly not to protect yourself this way.

Never Accept Default Installations

Many software programs have no security features, and those that do are installed by default and use only the weakest settings. On top of that, most default installations include the running of services that you may not need — such as telnet and FTP. These additional services are not securely configured, either. Not only do hackers know about these weak configurations, they also know how to search for them — and they will find them!

Whenever you install an operating system or application, be aware of the security settings available for that software and make the appropriate changes. For example, the default installation of Microsoft SQL Server leaves a blank password, which you need to change. The default installation of Windows installs Web server and FTP capabilities, which you usually don't need. Another thing you don't need are operating systems that include a Guest account with a blank password.

Finding suggestions on the security settings from the vendor's Web site or from any one of the numerous security Web sites on the Internet is easy enough. Just be sure to make the changes to all the machines on your network that are affected; otherwise, you are defeating the purpose of the security changes. You'd be surprised how much stronger your system becomes when it's securely installed and configured.

Don't Run Unnecessary Services

This is a bit of a corollary to the recommendations on default installations mentioned previously. If you don't need a Web server, don't let it run. If you don't need FTP or telnet, don't let them run. If you don't send mail on your system, then there is no reason to use a sendmail program or SMTP. Why not? Because these services all have exploitable security holes. In any case, why have something running on your system that's not going to give you any benefit? All they do in the end is use up computing resources and expose you to security breaches.

Install Security Patches Immediately

All software, even security software, occasionally contains bugs or holes that can be exploited. Typically, the vendor has the appropriate fixes located on their product Web site along with any instructions you may need to apply the fix.

Why apply these patches immediately? Because agencies send out alert notices when major security problems arise. The hackers monitor these alerts regularly and when they see one of interest, they start looking for systems on the Internet that are vulnerable to the problem. They count on the fact that most network administrators are too busy with their regular duties to stop everything to apply fixes and patches. This is one of the most common ways that hackers get into a system, and it falls into the category of "it could have been prevented if . . . ."

Make sure you're on the mailing list for your software vendors' updates as well as the security alerts sent out by various agencies and Web sites. When you download a patch, don't let it just sit there — install it immediately.

Back Up Your Data

The most complete security in the world won't protect you if all your data is lost in a fire or other disaster. Make sure that complete backups are done once a month and incremental backups are made daily. That way, if all your data is lost, you can usually recover everything up to the day before the disaster struck.

Test your backups once every three months to make sure they can be read. It's very easy to issue the wrong backup command and save files in a format that is not easily recoverable and data can become corrupted. Testing ensures that you are saved from the horror of finding you cannot recover from your backups.

Protect Against Surges and Losses

All electronic equipment should be connected to surge suppressors to prevent destruction in the event of power surges. Even if you don't live in an area prone to heavy weather with lightning, you should have surge protectors installed on every piece of equipment because all electricity sources can suffer from peaks and spikes. All it takes is one fried component to unsettle even the most stable computer.

In addition to surge protectors you should also install Uninterruptible Power Supplies (UPSs) on all your most important computers. Most UPSs have a battery pack that will keep your computer running long enough for you to safely power it down. Most Unix systems suffer horribly when they are not powered off in the correct manner — resulting in corrupted data or operating system. You can get UPSs with varying levels of battery storage. Some will only keep equipment powered for fifteen minutes while others have the capability to keep equipment running for several hours.

Know Who You Trust

This goes for users, clients, and other networks you trust to connect with yours. Give each user or connection only the level of access they need to accomplish their tasks and no more than that.

Knowing your users is important because you don't want to give too much trust to someone who has had problems with authority and has a checkered employment history. You can always start out with a low level of trust on the network and increase it as the employee shows that he deserves your trust.

Many Business to Business (B2B) networks have interconnectivity with a number of other corporate networks to increase efficiency. For example, one company may regularly need parts from another company and the interconnectivity means that they can quickly access inventory levels of the product. In any case, you need to know that your business partners in these connections are trustworthy and that they have done their best to secure their networks against attacks. If you are connected to a network that has little or no security installed, an attacker can gain entry to that system and, because it has a trusted relationship with your network, the attacker can use that trust to access your network, too.

Enable Logging and Review Logs

It's important for your systems to keep logs of what is happening on your network. This includes who is logging on and off, what applications are being run and by whom, and what connections are being made and by whom. Your operating system has logs available, but only if you enable them. Firewalls and intrusion detection systems create very large logs with enormous amounts of data.

Your logs aren't going to do you any good if you don't actually read them regularly. They can be tough to read, but there are log parsing utilities that can group and sort them for you to make it easier to review. You need to know what looks normal on your logs or you'll never know what an abnormal situation looks like.

You can find many log parsers or analyzers for Windows and Unix systems at `http://online.securityfocus.com/tools/category/71`.

Expect Protection to Fail

Almost every security mechanism you can think of has an electronic element to it, and electronics can and do fail. Therefore, you shouldn't rely too heavily upon the protection being there — don't put all your eggs in one basket. Firewalls, routers, intrusion detection systems, and access control mechanisms often fail without warning, and you likely won't recognize that something bad has happened for some time. Your best defense is to have prepared a plan of action ahead of time, and the best plan of action is to have a layered approach to security. Establish your perimeter with filtering routers, firewalls, and intrusion detection, but protect your interior with access controls and hardened software. If one layer of your protection fails, at least you'll have some other forms of security to fall back on.

Manage User Accounts Well

As soon as a person terminates employment, disable his or her account. Don't wait a week or a month or a year. While you're at it, look at all the other accounts on your network. Are there old accounts that should be deleted? Are there inactive accounts that should be disabled or removed? Are there any accounts that look strange to you? When was the last time anyone changed their passwords on their accounts? Hackers often look for accounts that have been inactive for long periods and attempt to crack their passwords. A hacker needs only one account to get in. After the hacker has a legitimate account, he can possibly create administrative level accounts that would give him full control of the system.

Managing accounts can be a real pain, especially if you have thousands of users on your network. However, these are the people you have given open-door access to your system. Review user records on a regular basis to make sure that the accounts are accurate and have secure passwords.

Educate Your Users

Security doesn't happen in a vacuum. If people don't know the rules, how can they adhere to them? If people don't know what suspicious activity to look for, how can they know when to call security? Many companies have made the mistake of spending lots of time and money to set up security rules and safeguards and then forget to tell the rest of the world what they've done. Don't make this same mistake, or you could lose an important security resource — the many eyes and ears of your users!

Your staff needs to know what dangers can appear, from viruses and Trojans to unidentified personnel snooping around the server rooms. They also need to know how to use the security tools you place at their disposal like anti-virus software and encryption software. Your staff needs to know all this stuff, and they will be knowledgeable only if you make the effort to educate them. It doesn't have to be a fancy class with lots of bells and whistles, but it does have to inform and educate.

Whatever you do, don't educate via e-mail — we all know that people don't read their e-mail messages.

Chapter 23

Ten Best Security Web Sites

*T*hank goodness for the Internet! Not only did the Internet make it easy to research information for this book, but it is a real life saver for people who need the answer to their question NOW.

Without further ado, here are what I consider to be the best Web sites for network security information (in no particular order of significance). Enjoy!

www.cert.org

The Computer Emergency Response Team (CERT) at Carnegie Mellon University get my thumbs-up for one of the best security Web sites. Not only do they give you up-to-date information on current vulnerabilities and threats, but there is excellent information in the form of articles, white papers, and reports at `www.cert.org/nav/allpubs.html`.

http://online.securityfocus.com

SecurityFocus Online is like a huge library. When you first pull up the page, it looks like a newsletter and you have to look hard to see the text in the gold navigation buttons below the banner at the top of the page. The navigation buttons say The Basics, Microsoft, Unix, IDS, Incidents, and Virus. In these buttons, you'll find a goldmine of articles and information. This information is always current and topical. There is also a large library of papers available at `http://online.securityfocus.com/library`.

http://rr.sans.org

The Sans Organization is a large computer security training and conference company, and they have an excellent resource available in their Reading Room. You have to sign up and get a password, but membership to the Reading Room is free. After you gain access, there are so many choices you won't know where to begin but you may want to start with either "Security Basics" or on the operating systems section. You can choose articles on your particular operating system.

All the papers and articles in the Reading Room have been vetted for accuracy and are dated as to when they were written. The most recent papers and articles are listed first. If you find problems with any of the papers, you are encouraged to report what you've found. The list of available topics is practically endless. I have spent hours there and sometimes just nose around for fun. Of course, their parent Web site, `www.sans.org`, is great, too!

www.antionline.com

The tag line to Antionline is "Hackers Know The Weaknesses In Your System. Shouldn't You?" It's a bit of an iconoclast, but that's what I like about it. There are tons of security-related downloads, message boards and chat rooms, and a good career center. Their articles are good, if a bit biased against MS products. If you're curious about hackers, there's a fair bit of basic information about them, too.

www.ciac.org

This is the Computer Incident Advisory Capability put together by the U.S. Department of Energy. Imagine that — a government agency that actually got its act together and put some useful stuff on the Web! I'm always a bit surprised that it's owned by the DOE and not some agency that is obviously into computer security. Look here for in-depth information about vulnerabilities and alerts, papers on various aspects of security, and security tool downloads. They also have a wonderful section called "Hoaxbusters" that's fun to read in addition to being informative.

www.datafellows.com/virus-info

This is a company called F-Secure that makes anti-virus software. If you've ever wondered whether a virus alert is real or a hoax, this is a good place to find out. You'll also find lots of good technical detail on current viruses in the wild, a virus test file, and tons more information.

www.theregister.co.uk

This is another iconoclast and I love it! Its tag line is "Biting the hand that feeds IT," and its mascot is a vulture. Appropriately, its online merchandise is sold through the "Cash n Carrion" section. This is a great site for getting the other side of news stories and other interesting tidbits.

www.cerias.purdue.edu/hotlist

This is the Center for Education Research in Information Assurance and Security (CERIAS) from Purdue University. The hotlist is a portal to tons of other security-related sites and information.

www.cnet.com

This is a great online technology magazine to go to when you're in the market for hardware or software. They have good reviews and price comparisons and also have a great list of downloads for utilities and specialty software.

www.secinf.net

This is the Network Security Library. Lots of in-depth papers and booklets for free. And this is the only site I've found that has the actual Department of Defense Rainbow Series of books online. So if you've ever wondered what that infamous Orange Book for Trusted Computing is about, you can find out here!

Chapter 24

Ten Security Tools Every Network Security Geek Should Have

*T*here must be literally thousands of free and low-cost network security software tools available on the Internet. I try to bookmark the page every time I find one that looks interesting, and my bookmark file goes on for miles.

These tools are not necessarily easy to use, and some can do some serious damage to your network if you're not careful. The best way to find out what these tools can really do is to use them and play with them, but be sure to try them on a small test network before you run them against your entire system.

Nessus

Available at www.nessus.org. Runs on Unix.

This is a security scanner to audit a network and determine whether bad guys may break into it or misuse it in some way. Nessus tells you what's wrong on your network by testing its vulnerabilities, and will, most of the time, tell you how to prevent hackers from exploiting the security holes found. There is a security risk level associated with each problem found.

Netcat

Available at www.atstake.com/research/tools/index.html. Runs on Unix and Windows systems.

Netcat is a well known TCP/IP scanning tool that lets you check for open ports, which is great to find out what data will be allowed in or out of your system. This is also a good way to find out if you've got your firewall rules set up correctly.

Tcpdump

Available at www.tcpdump.org. Available for Unix systems only.

Tcpdump has been around for a long time and is used to dump captured tcp traffic on a network to a file. The dump includes packet headers. This is a good tool to try to troubleshoot problems on your network. There is also a Windows version called WinDUMP, which is available at the same Web site.

Snort

Available at www.snort.org. Runs on Unix platforms and Windows.

Snort can be configured to be a packet sniffer, packet logger, or a simple network intrusion detection system. Because it's free and relatively easy to set up and use, many people just use it for the intrusion detection capabilities. Snort can save you a lot of money if you just want something small, or you can use it to see if you need something bigger and stronger.

Whisker

Available at www.wiretrip.net/rfp/p/doc.asp/d21.htm. Runs on Unix or Windows (but Windows must have Perl installed).

This is a nice little utility written by Rain Forest Puppy to check your CGI scripts for vulnerabilities. A must have whether you write your own code or borrow it from the Net to put on your Web servers.

Tripwire

Available at `www.tripwire.com`. Commercial version runs on Unix or Windows. The free source code is available, but that only runs on Unix systems.

This is free for academic uses but fees apply for commercial use. Tripwire is a file and directory integrity checker. It creates a "fingerprint" of files or programs and can notify system administrators when a file is being or has been tampered with.

L0pht Crack (LC4)

Available at `www.atstake.com/research/lc/download.html`. Available for Windows systems only.

Originally released by L0pht Heavy Industries and now known as @Stake, L0phtcrack's name has been changed to LC4. It is the best password cracker around for Windows-based systems. An absolute must-have to check the strength of your users' passwords. The source code for an older version is still free but the new version is available for purchase.

SAINT

Available at `www.wwdsi.com/products/saint_engine.html`. Available for Unix systems only.

SAINT stands for *Security Administrator's Integrated Network Tool* and was based on an earlier tool called SATAN. This is a commercial version and is a bit pricey for those on a budget, but if you want an easy way to check your network's vulnerabilities, this is the tool. It scans through firewalls and includes updated security checks from CERT & CIAC bulletins. Nice interface and reports, too.

PortSentry

Available at `www.psionic.com/products/portsentry.html`. Available for Unix systems only.

This used to be known as Abacus Portsentry and is a tool that alerts administrators of port scanning happening on their network. It can even detect stealth scans, which can indicate malicious intent. PortSentry attempts to block the scans when it sees it happening.

Cheops

Available at `www.marko.net/cheops/index.shtml`. Runs on Unix only.

This is a neat tool to discover and map the extent of your network as well as all the operating systems on the various hosts and desktops. It can scan ports to detect running services and gives great graphical maps and reports. It can help to troubleshoot problems on the network, too.

Chapter 25

Ten Questions to Ask a Security Consultant

*T*here may come a day that you decide to try a security consultant, which is not a bad thing. There are so many aspects of network security that it's nearly impossible to do it all yourself. Sometimes it helps to bring in an expert to help you through some rough patches or to get you moving in the right direction. If you can't find security consultants listed in your phone book, the Internet is always a good place to look.

But after you've made the calls and decided to bring a few people in for consideration, what do you ask? Here I give you the top ten questions and the acceptable responses to those questions. After you've gone through the interview, though, don't just rely upon the answers to your questions. Remember that you are going to have to trust this person with a lot of sensitive data. Your gut reaction can be a guide as to whether or not you two can actually work together.

Question 1: Is This Your Day Job?

You may laugh at this one, but I'm serious. There are a lot of people out there who work as network administrators who want to go out on their own and start a consulting company. However, they don't have the clientele built up enough to be able to quit their day jobs.

If your consultant is in this category, play it safely. This may be the perfect person for the job, but will he/she be able to give you the support you really need? The rest of the questions may help you decide.

Question 2: How Long Have You Been Doing This?

Again, don't laugh because this is a completely reasonable question. If you were going to hire the person for a full-time position, you'd certainly ask this.

Hopefully, you're not the first client for this consultant. A good answer would be at least three years. Security consultation is not something that can be totally taught in school, and a person needs to have a number of years in real-life situations to be able to make good recommendations.

Question 3: Are You Bonded or Insured?

They should be. A bond helps to verify the veracity of the person and can give you some comfort that he or she won't run off with your secrets. Insurance is important in case things go wrong. The bonding or insuring agency will do a check to make sure the consultant is who he says he is. It's acceptable for a consultant not to be bonded, but he should at least have insurance to cover errors and omissions.

Question 4: What Certifications or Training Do You Have?

Security training and certifications are a fairly recent development. Ten years ago it would have been difficult to find anyone who held certifications, but computer security wasn't a big deal then, either. Nowadays most good security personnel have at least one certification or another. Here are some of the widely acceptable certifications:

- **CISSP — Certified Information Systems Security Professional.** Testing is based on a general level of knowledge in all areas of security. Certification issued by ISC² www.isc2.org.

- **SSCP — Systems Security Certified Practitioner.** Given by the same folks who issue the CISSP certifications. This is a slightly less stringent certification than the CISSP, but is more technically focused.

- **CISA — Certified Information Systems Auditor.** This is also a general certification. Certification issued by www.isaca.org.

- **CPP — Certified Protection Professional.** Issued by ASIS International at www.asisonline.org, this certification indicates a general level of proficiency in security management.

- **GIAC — Global Information Assurance Certification.** There are actual multiple levels to this certification, and each level indicates proficiency in a particular area of security. This is a relatively new program developed by SANS and governed by www.giac.org.

- **Security Certified Program.** This is another good certification program with certification for both a Network Architect and a Network Professional. More information can be obtained at www.securitycertified.net/certifications.htm.

- **Cisco certifications.** Cisco Systems is a hardware vendor that offers network engineering certifications based on proficiency with their products. These are not security certifications, per se, but indicate a good level of understanding of networking technology. You can view the various certifications and training requirements at www.cisco.com/warp/public/10/wwtraining/certprog.

- **Microsoft certifications.** MS certifications come in all shapes and sizes and, because they are vendor-specific, indicate a level of knowledge with those products only. These are not security certifications, but some security knowledge is implied. You can obtain more information from Microsoft at www.microsoft.com/traincert/mcp/default.asp.

There are probably other certifications available that I am not aware of, but the ones I've listed are the most common. Just having a certification does not mean the person is an expert. You also have to take into consideration the number of years of experience the consultant has in the field and what her specialties are. None of the tests for the previously named certifications are easy, but you shouldn't rely upon certifications only.

Question 5: Have You or Any of Your Staff Been Arrested or Charged with Illegal Computer Activities?

This does not ask if the consultant or his staff has been *convicted* of any computer-related wrong-doing, just if they have ever been suspected of it. This is important because it may indicate whether or not the consultant is a reformed hacker or if the company employs former hackers. This is the consultant's opportunity to make an important disclosure, and it should be answered honestly. As a potential employer, you can check with your local law enforcement to see if the person has a record.

If the consultant answers yes, you need to take into consideration at what age this occurred. Many former or reformed hackers got into trouble in their teens and have truly changed their ways while others still dabble in the "dark arts." There are many arguments pro and con about hiring former hackers. They may have the skills for the job, but is their sense of honesty and dependability intact? You can get their permission to run a background check, but the doing the check may be a bit pricey for you.

Question 6: Do You Have Any Ties or Associations with a Particular Vendor?

This may indicate bias toward one set of security solutions as opposed to others. Ideally, you want someone who is able to look at all possible solutions without prejudice. On the other hand, if the consultant is a reseller for a particular vendor, he or she may be able to get better prices for the products. Again, there are pros and cons to this, and the vendor should be honest in his answer.

Question 7: Do You Offer Any Guarantees?

Believe it or not, but the answer to this should be no. The reason is that no network can be made completely secure. New methods of breaching the security of networks are discovered every day. Additionally, the consultant may install a security mechanism that works, but he can't guarantee that you won't make changes to the system that alter the security level. I'd be wary of anyone who offers guarantees because it's nearly impossible to guarantee any security work.

Question 8: Do You Offer Support for Emergency Situations?

What will the consultant do if the firewall he installed stops working? Will he help you track down an intruder if one penetrates the security mechanisms the consultant set up? Will the consultant be willing to be on call to you 24 hours a day?

The consultant should be able to at least offer this service at additional cost. If he cannot offer it himself, then he ought to be able to offer some sort of support solution. If security consulting is not his day job (see Question 1), then he probably won't be able to commit to 24-hour support.

Question 9: What Would You Do If You Discovered One of My Employees Doing Something Questionable or Illegal with My Computers?

This is an ethics question. There is no law or rule that says the consultant *must* do anything, but he should feel duty bound to tell you what he discovered.

This can be a very touchy area because things are not always as they seem. For example, finding hacker tools on your network does not necessarily mean that your employees are hacking into your system. Those same tools are used to check for vulnerabilities in a system. Someone may have taken it upon himself to check the security of your system without your knowledge.

In any case, your consultant should be prepared to share with you any irregularities found in or on your network.

Question 10: Do You Have References or a Client List?

Remarkably, the consultant may well answer, "I have many clients, but I'm not at liberty to tell you who they are." This is due to the confidentiality agreements between the consultant and his clients. Many companies don't want to advertise the fact that they've hired outside help. They also don't want others to know what the consultant did for them.

If your consultant can't give you a list of clients or references, he should be able to give you an idea of the types of work he has done and the sort of companies he has worked with. For example, he may be able to say "I've installed firewalls and designed extranets for the automobile industry." That sort of information is hard to confirm, but you should be able to get enough information out of the consultant that gives you some feeling of comfort.

Index

• *D* •

• *I* •

Notes

Notes

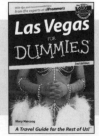

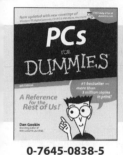

FOR DUMMIES®

Helping you expand your horizons and realize your potential

INTERNET

0-7645-0894-6

0-7645-1659-0

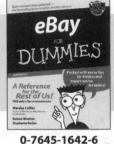

0-7645-1642-6

DIGITAL MEDIA

0-7645-1664-7

0-7645-1675-2

0-7645-0806-7

GRAPHICS

0-7645-0817-2

0-7645-1651-5

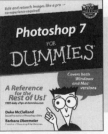

0-7645-0895-4

Available wherever books are sold. Go to www.dummies.com or call 1-877-762-2974 to order direct.

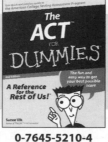